Environmental Ethics

ENVIRONMENTAL ETHICS

An Overview for the Twenty-First Century

Robin Attfield

polity

First published in 2003 by Polity Press in association with Blackwell Publishing Ltd.

Editorial office:
Polity Press
65 Bridge Street
Cambridge CB2 1UR, UK

Marketing and production:
Blackwell Publishing Ltd
108 Cowley Road
Oxford OX4 1JF, UK

Distributed in the USA by
Blackwell Publishing Inc.
350 Main Street
Malden, MA 02148, USA

A catalogue record for this book is available from the British Library.

Library of Congress Cataloging-in-Publication Data
Attfield, Robin.
Environmental ethics : an overview for the twenty-first century / Robin Attfield.
p. cm.
Includes bibliographical references and index.
ISBN 0–7456–2737–4 (hb : alk. paper) — ISBN 0–7456–2738–2 (pbk. : alk. paper)
1. Environmental ethics. I. Title.
GE42 .A78 2003
179′.1—dc21

2003001594

Typeset in 10.5/12pt Palatino
by Graphicraft Ltd., Hong Kong
Printed and bound in Great Britain by MPG Books Ltd, Bodmin, Cornwall

For further information on Polity, visit our website: www.polity.co.uk

Contents

Acknowledgements

I am glad and grateful to acknowledge the permission of Edinburgh University Press to use short passages previously published in Robin Attfield, *The Ethics of the Global Environment* (Edinburgh University Press, Edinburgh, and Purdue University Press, West Lafayette, IN, 1999), and that of *Inquiry* to use three paragraphs from Robin Attfield, 'Environmental Ethics and Intergenerational Equity', *Inquiry*, 41, 1998, 207–22. Gratitude should also be expressed to the Association of Commonwealth Universities for funding a two-year joint project on sustainable development, the theme of one of the chapters of this book. Thanks are also due to Cardiff University for granting me a semester of study leave to complete this book, and to my colleagues of the Cardiff Philosophy Section for undertaking my normal duties and thus making this possible. Thanks belong also to anonymous publishers' reviewers for their comments, and to my family and friends (not excluding colleagues) for their encouragement and support. Above all, however, special thanks go to my wife, Leela Dutt, but for whom this book would not have been begun, let alone completed.

Abbreviations

CFCs	chloro-fluoro-carbons
DDT	dichlorodiphenyl-trichloroethane
IMF	International Monetary Fund
NGOs	non-governmental organizations
NIMBY	Not In My Back Yard
UNCED	United Nations Conference on Environment and Development
UNED forum	United Nations Environment and Development forum
UNESCO	United Nations Economic, Scientific and Cultural Organization
UNO	United Nations Organization
USS	Universities' Superannuation Scheme

Preface

A new century and a new millennium call for new reflection on the environmental issues that beset our planet and our societies, and on the ethical principles and policies needed to tackle them. Ethical principles are not treated here in isolation from economics, technology or politics, but turn out to have far-flung implications, with extensive consequences both in space and in time. At the same time, these principles and the values implicit in them hold out new opportunities as well as new challenges to make possible the flourishing of life (both human and non-human) and of society.

This book has been written both for students and for researchers and scholars of environmental ethics. As such, it is intended both to explain the relevant concepts and issues, and to contribute to their discussion and development (the latter particularly in the later chapters). A wide range of leading writers and schools of thought are discussed, in the course of an argument in defence of a particular normative theory (biocentric consequentialism) and related local and global policies. For the sake of students, opportunities are offered to pause and review issues that have recently been raised, summaries of each chapter are provided, a glossary of key terms has been supplied, and further reading and useful websites are suggested. (The lists of titles for further reading are not in alphabetical order, the main criterion employed being the order of subject matter within the preceding chapter and a subordinate criterion being relative importance.) Terms explained in the Glossary appear in bold in the text (some more than once), whether at their first main appearance or in a more central passage (or, where this could help readers, in two or more significant passages). The

Bibliography and the Notes appended to the text have been devised to assist researchers and those wishing to take the subject further.

Chapter 1 introduces environmental problems and environmental ethics, and some of the potentially conflicting values arising. It surveys theories of the sources of the problems, and introduces the stewardship approach as tenable either in a religious or in a secular form. Chapter 2 discusses central debates surrounding the stewardship tradition, which it defends, surrounding normative ethics, where it advocates biocentric consequentialism, and surrounding meta-ethics, in which it defends objectivism. Recent contributions to all these debates are reviewed.

In chapter 3, enlightened versions of human-centred ethics are found to deepen our grasp of human good without being equal to the full range of ethics or of human motivation. Environmental ethics itself is shown to be capable of making a significant difference, and biocentric consequentialism to be capable of coping with criticisms in matters of population and of preservation. Chapter 4 considers issues relating to the nature, grounds and limits of future-related responsibilities, which include resisting environmental injustice in the present and call for representation of future interests in present decision-making.

Chapter 5 explores the internationally endorsed concept of sustainable development, and argues that it is capable of coherent exposition and of a radical interpretation suited to tackling, through integrated policies, a wide range of problems including poverty, population and biodiversity preservation. The Precautionary Principle supports such an interpretation, and these policies are also shown to cohere with a liberal democratic framework. Chapter 6 explains the kind of global ethic and global citizenship required by global problems, presents the global commons as the common heritage of humanity and at the same time as held on trust for the sake of life on earth, discusses making global governance more equal to the problems, and illustrates the problems with a discussion of global warming, to which certain principles prove relevant. The final section brings the book's conclusions together.

While the main purpose of this book is to enhance the study and critical understanding of environmental ethics, a further purpose is to foster the kind of campaigning which the study of this subject often encourages, and, for some, makes possible. It will thus have served a good deal of its purpose if readers are enticed to explore the websites mentioned and come to participate in one or other of the kinds of activism they commend. If readers also come to enjoy and appreciate the 'music for environmental ethicists' mentioned at the end of chapter 1, so much the better.

1 Environmental Problems and Humanity

What are **environmental problems**? How are they to be identified, and what generates them? While the answers may seem obvious, these questions turn out to repay reflection, not least because problems are identified differently by different perspectives, and different problems are identified as problems. In this chapter, issues considered include how environmental problems are identified, the range of values that people bring to them, theories about their causes, and whether humanity can have a constructive role in curing or alleviating them. The nature and role of **environmental ethics** itself are also considered.

Introduction: environmental problems and the global environment

Environmental problems are those problems that arise from human dealings with the natural world and its systems. Human beings cannot help using and modifying tracts of the natural world, since we depend on nature for food, clothing and shelter, for our water supply, and for the air we breathe. But the unintended impacts of human actions are now creating problems like global warming and the extinction of multitudes of species, problems which raise profound issues about how we should live our lives and organize our societies, and which present challenges never encountered by previous generations.

Not everyone means the same thing when they speak of '**environment**' or 'environmental problems'. They often (and this is a first meaning) mean 'the surroundings', natural or otherwise, either of an individual for the duration of her life, or of a society for the duration of its existence, but they sometimes mean (secondly) the objective system of nature that encompasses either local society or human society in general, and that precedes and succeeds it. Alternatively (and thirdly) they sometimes have in mind the perceived surroundings or familiar *milieu* of an individual person or animal, the territory or pathways that give that individual a sense of belonging and comprise her home. However, while everyone has an environment, the mobility of modern life means that not everyone has such an environment in this third, home-territory, sense, as many people have little sense of being at home in the place where they currently find themselves living.[1] Fortunately many individuals prove able to 'put down roots' and form attachments in unfamiliar places and to develop a sense of belonging in more than one setting. In any case, people also prove capable of caring not only for their native territory but for the various shared surroundings and natural systems that we also refer to when we use 'the environment' in the other senses.

Besides, there could not be perceived environments, environments formed by the thoughts and activities of individuals (environments in the third sense), nor physical environments surrounding individuals either (environments in the first sense), if there were no environments in the sense of objective systems of nature, such as mountains, valleys and islands, forests, seas and rivers, and the natural cycles and processes that make them what they are (environments in the second sense). These objective systems both precede and outlive individuals, and, while they are far from immune from human action and its impacts, they supply the shared settings of our lives, and thus the very possibility of perceived environments and of familiar surroundings. I am not suggesting that all environments are benign, particularly as many have been ravaged by human industrial activity, or turned into deserts through human neglect. Indeed we have to be prepared to distinguish between social environments, whose defects stem from human action, and the underlying natural systems, inhospitable as these sometimes are. While these systems do not always suit human interests or comfort either, they nevertheless comprise public goods, making possible much of what is valuable in our lives; hence the high importance of our capacity to care for shared surroundings and natural systems.

So, unless the context specifies otherwise, 'environment' in this book normally means 'objective encompassing system of nature'. This usage of 'environment', besides cohering with concern for local natural systems and settings, also makes sense of talk of 'the global environment', a newly crucial topic granted the discovery that humanity has been disrupting the natural systems and cycles of our entire planet in recent decades. Such disruption has taken place, for example, through global warming, through emissions resulting in acid rain, through radioactive discharges, and through the release of chemicals such as **CFCs** that have damaged the ozone layer, which protects terrestrial species from skin-cancer. Like weather systems, environments refuse to observe international frontiers. Thus emissions of radioactivity, of greenhouse gases and of CFCs from anywhere on Earth are all liable to impact worldwide on the shared natural system of the planet (the system of systems). Hence the importance of reflection, not least in environmental ethics, on the global environment. The meaning of this phrase should here be clarified. By 'the global environment' I mean not the environs or surroundings of our planet, much less the planet as a field of significance, but rather the actual natural systems of planet Earth. This shared environment will assume a prominent place in this text.

Brief excursus on the Gaia hypothesis

The global environment remains important whether or not we accept **the Gaia hypothesis** of James Lovelock, namely that the Earth is a self-regulating system, maintaining the conditions that support life. To take two examples of apparent regulation, the proportion of oxygen in the atmosphere and the salinity of the oceans have remained constant for billions of years; the constancy of the protective ozone layer seemed, at least until recently, to supply another example. Lovelock suggests that the explanation of such phenomena is that the complex system of life on our planet ensures its own continuation.[2] He does not claim that Gaia acts knowingly or purposively, but does regard it as a superorganism with pervasive capacities for self-repair.[3] These claims, however, may exceed the evidence,[4] even though some ethicists have endorsed them and concluded that what is needed is loyalty to Gaia.[5] Thus the presence of oxygen in the atmosphere is more favourable to some kinds of life than to others; and, as Andrew Brennan remarks, the natural systems that regulate the content of the oceans and the atmosphere may be simpler than Lovelock suggests, without it being any the less important not to disrupt them through our practices of production, consumption and waste-disposal.[6] This, however, serves to underline the importance of reflection on planetary problems as well as on local ones.

Local and global environmental problems

Besides the different senses of 'environment' (as discussed in the previous section), much variation is also found in people's understanding of **environmental problems**. This diversity arises because people diverge enormously in their assumptions about what constitutes a problem, or about what makes problems problematic.

While some people consider as important nothing but impacts on local people for the near future, others may take into account impacts on the whole of humanity,[7] and/or the entire foreseeable future, and/or other species too; and all kinds of intermediate stances are also taken. So from some perspectives water shortages in the Middle East or the loss of species in Amazonia or the Asian Brown Cloud, a three-kilometre-high blanket of **pollution** discovered in 2002 to stretch from Pakistan to Indonesia, are not problems at all, since they affect distant rather than local people and environments; and the same might be thought to apply to greenhouse gas emissions if regarded as more likely to affect future decades than the present. But at least one perspective, the perspective of what Arne Naess has called 'the Deep, Long-Range Ecology Movement',[8] considers that environmental problems include developments that adversely affect the natural systems of the Third World, of the further future and of non-human species, as well as issues affecting just Western countries and the human interests of the present. (**Deep Ecology** is a movement which aims at the flourishing or self-realization of all Earth's species, and urges us to identify with the totality of life on Earth, the planetary biosphere.) If we adopt anything like this perspective, then we shall count all developments of the kinds just mentioned as environmental problems, as well as ones impinging mainly on affluent people in developed countries for the next two or three decades. We can do this whether or not we subscribe to the specific tenets of Deep Ecology (in Naess's sense). I shall be arguing in this book that we need a broad enough value-theory to allow us to take all these impacts seriously, and to recognize the full range of environmental problems for what they are.

Such a broad value-theory does not make local environmental problems any the less important. The loss of many species of flowering plants, butterflies and songbirds from the British countryside, or the pollution from a local, inner-city factory, blighting the lives of already disadvantaged people, call for action at local, regional or national level. Indeed, such issues often open people's eyes to wider, worldwide problems arising from the human treatment of nature.

But the longstanding environmentalist slogan 'Think globally, act locally'[9] has become outmoded, granted that the global environment is itself now at risk, and that many environmental problems have become global, either in the sense of being repeated all over the world, like traffic congestion, deforestation and chemical pollution, or in the distinct sense of problems of interconnected global systems, such as the droughts, wildfires and floods that are generated by the impact of global warming on global weather patterns.[10] Nowadays, even people mainly concerned for their local territory need to be alert to the global environmental change that often threatens it, and self-interest is added to love of others and love of nature as a motive for environmental concern at the global level.

While local problems (such as litter or smog) often generate environmental awareness among communities, some go unremarked for many years, as did the toxic effects of lead pipes on drinking water for many centuries from Roman times, and of asbestos on healthy air for many decades. Problems, then, can exist unnoticed; greenhouse gas emissions supply a global example. Nor does consciousness of situations as problems invariably make them authentic problems; the NIMBY (Not In My Back Yard) syndrome often betokens concern over the impact of a new development on local property values as much as genuine environmental disruption. Besides cases of community concern, local problems include issues principally related to particular localities but paralleled elsewhere, from the loss of topsoil in parts of the United States to overfishing in particular seas such as the North Sea or the Grand Banks off Newfoundland. Localized problems merge into regional problems in cases like the evaporation and shrinking of the Aral Sea, due to misguided irrigation schemes and agricultural projects in the former Soviet Union; this ongoing problem is now affecting several of the new Central Asian republics and thus has an international dimension.

Global problems of the repetitive or cumulative kind include, in addition to those already mentioned, the oil slicks that now besmirch all the principal sea-lanes of our seas and oceans, losses of species and habitats across most of Earth's ecosystems, and loss of wetlands (often due to agricultural expansion) and of forests (through profiteering companies and the need of afforested countries to service their international debt). While these problems may not reflect interconnected global ecological problems, they do seem to be worldwide side-effects of the global economic and financial system.[11] Meanwhile other global environmental problems are systemic, having become embedded in the ecological systems of the planet, including the worldwide effects of the insecticide DDT (that has long since been affecting even the penguins of the Antarctic), and of radioactive strontium (circulating in the stratosphere since nuclear tests of the 1950s, and still polluting our rainfall). Similarly the worldwide growth of deserts probably reflects global **climate change**, and comprises a further consequence of global warming.

The very scope and range of these problems (both local and global) present a challenge to environmental ethics. For those who work in this field need to sustain principles of right action and of value adequate not only to concerns such as resource conservation, wildlife protection and species preservation, but also to the full range and extent of the problems depicted in this section.

Animal-welfarism and environmentalism

Ethics, however, has a yet broader scope, for it is concerned with inter-human dealings as well as with human dealings with nature. Its concerns include both relations between individuals and the rules of society; with how individuals ought to treat one another, and with how societies ought fairly to be organized. And relations between individuals might reasonably be held to include relations between human agents and individual non-human animals. In any case, the ethics of the treatment of animals is an important area of contemporary ethical debate.

For some readers, the ethics of the treatment of animals will appear simply a part (even possibly the central part) of environmental ethics, while for others these two areas may seem separate and even potentially in conflict. The different groundings of these stances warrant discussion here, although debates about fundamental values and priorities, and how to study them, will be reserved for later chapters.

The case for regarding the treatment of animals as continuous with (and possibly central to) environmental ethics goes like this. The key factor that qualifies anything for moral consideration is either its capacity to suffer, or alternatively its having a perspective or point of view of its own. Most non-human animals have this capacity, albeit to different degrees, and, to the extent that they are conscious, have points of view, from which things can go better or worse for them. Because like cases should be treated alike, non-human animals should be given consideration comparable to human beings with respect to these shared capacities, though this would not apply where human beings (or most human beings) have capacities that non-humans lack. Creatures that lack both sentience (the capacity to feel and to suffer) and consciousness, and thus have no point of view, lack the kind of interests that warrant such consideration. (Let us call the adherents of this position 'sentientists', a term that is more closely defined in the coming section.) These principles are just as relevant to environmental issues as they are to (say) agricultural issues, or to issues of research ethics.

Positions of this kind are held by philosophers and ethicists with a great variety of outlooks. (We return to the particular theories in greater detail in chapter 2, and the point here is to note the range of positions held and some of the leading thinkers who hold them, rather than to study their details or differences in depth at this stage.) These philosophers and ethicists, then, sometimes include **consequentialists** (theorists for whom the morality of actions and policies depends on foreseeable outcomes). More precisely, they include the kind of consequentialists who, like Peter Singer, regard the interests of conscious (as opposed to self-conscious) creatures as turning on pleasure and absence of suffering.[12] There again, they also include **rights-theorists** such as Tom Regan,[13] who hold that having a point of view betokens having fundamental rights (rights that are not derivative from anything else), including the rights not to be made to suffer, not to be confined, and not to be killed by human agents. And there are further approaches again. Despite their differences, all these ethical systems have emphasized either sentience or consciousness, and the related interests, whether these interests figure as consequences, as rights, or (to mention yet a further possible approach) as themes in an imaginary contract.[14]

Accordingly environmental problems will consist in problems either for human interests or for the interests of non-human animals, and an acceptable environmental ethic would have these individual interests as its grounds. Indeed those who believe that only sentient or conscious creatures have interests and that having interests is necessary for warranting moral consideration will hold that nothing else has interests on which environmental problems could turn. Problems for ecosystems are thus held to turn invariably on the interests of sentient or conscious individuals. And within such an ethic, priority is liable to be placed on averting suffering or premature death for vulnerable individuals, whether this is best done by the introduction of humane methods of farming, by abstaining from eating meat (or at least meat from factory-farms), by curtailing human interventions in the natural order, or even possibly by intervening to reduce the suffering inflicted (for example) by predators on prey. Millions of people are influenced by such an ethic, and their approach to environmental problems would often follow the general pattern just mentioned (or some elements of it).

Others, however, suggest that environmental ethics must start somewhere quite different. Thinking about the environment involves taking much greater account of ecological systems than such an individualist approach can do, and if we fail to understand the natural systems of our planet we are likely to generate ecological catastrophes, either by neglect or through seeking to rescue individuals while the systems on which they depend are crumbling. By the time we have understood such systems, our focus will no longer be on individual suffering or survival, since far more is at stake, such as the survival of whole species, and the viability and health of whole **ecosystems**. For example, if grasslands are at risk of becoming deserts, measures to protect the grassland system (for example, by planting trees) take priority over efforts to care for ailing individual animals there.

Thus many environmentalists prioritize the **preservation** (or in some cases the rehabilitation) of species and of ecosystems. While all of them would recognize that the survival of species and systems is functionally necessary for the existence and well-being of individuals, some go further and maintain that it is ultimately the species and ecosystems that should be valued, and that the importance of individuals is dependent on their contribution to the good of the species or the ecosystem, or to the good of the biosphere (the system of living and non-living systems) as a whole. At the level of theory, this is a **holistic value-theory**, which locates independent value in wholes (such as species and ecosystems); in some ways it resembles (and sometimes consciously imitates) social and ethical theories that locate value in society as a whole, rather than in its individual members.[15] However, without invariably adhering to such a holistic value-theory (or **axiology**), many people (once again in their millions) take the view that in practice environmental policies must focus on preserving systems or species or their diversity, rather than on enhancing the lives of individual wild creatures. They would often add the goal of conserving resources, with a view to the well-being of future human generations; but this does not suggest that human well-being is their only goal, unless their concerns for preservation are made entirely subordinate to the goal of conserving resources; and this is far from always the case.

So there is a potential clash of values, as well as of policies, between the animal-welfare approach (let us call this **animal-welfarism**) and many kinds of environmentalism. The value-theory that animal-welfarists tend to adopt, which prioritizes the well-being of individual animals, is potentially in conflict with the holistic axiology of some environmentalists, which ultimately locates value in the health of ecosystems, or in the continuing existence of species, or in biological diversity, and measures the value of individuals by their contribution to this. This latter position often appeals to the famous passage of Aldo Leopold: 'a thing is right when it tends to promote the integrity, stability and beauty of the biotic community. It is wrong when it tends otherwise',[16] far removed as Leopold's ethic is both from animal-welfarism and from the ethic of traditional humanism alike. The divergences of these three positions explain the title of an early paper about their clash, J. Baird Callicott's 'Animal Liberation: A Triangular Affair'.[17] This clash became apparent earlier in the 1970s, when the two newer positions, animal-welfarism and ecological holism, were each put forward, by Peter Singer and by Arne Naess respectively, as the new ethic necessary to make good the shortcomings of traditional humanism.

While the merits of these diverse positions cannot be sifted at this stage, readers are entitled to know how I react to them. Unlike Singer and Regan, I do not accept that creatures (such as trees) that lack both sentience and consciousness lack the kind of interests that warrant consideration. Unlike ecological holists, I do not grant that independent value lies in the good of systems or wholes (such as forests) and not in that of individuals. But unlike human-centred ethicists, I shall argue that moral standing cannot be restricted to humanity alone. (For example, the reported European Commission plan to test chemicals for toxicity on as many as 50 million animals, all of which would be killed after the tests, cannot, I suggest, be appraised simply in terms of human interests.)[18] I shall also be suggesting that ethicists can take both the good of non-human individuals and the systems of nature fully into account without becoming either sentientists or holists.

> Issues raised so far on which you are invited to form views of your own include the core meaning of 'environment', what makes global environmental problems global, and whether animal-welfarism and environmentalism have values in common. The issue of why environmental problems are problems has also come into view, but possible answers remain to be developed in coming sections.

Theories of value

The view just mentioned, that moral standing can be restricted to humanity alone, is called **'anthropocentrism'**, a term that is also used of the related value-theory that none but human interests or concerns matter, in the sense of having independent value. As we have already seen, this position is rejected by (among others) **sentientists**, who hold that all sentient creatures (or all conscious creatures) have moral standing, and that their interests have **independent value**, value that is not dependent on human interests or on any other kind of value. Some anthropocentrists believe that understanding of and compassion towards animals is grounded in human interests, of which they give a very broad interpretation; compassion, for example, is desirable ultimately because it is good for us. But sentientists stoutly maintain that animal interests are important irrespective of human needs and sensitivities, and that an animal's suffering would matter (and ought to be prevented) even if no human being would be adversely affected in any way whatever by awareness of this suffering. Many people, however, consider both anthropocentrism and sentientism too narrow to supply convincing theories either of moral standing or of value.

Broader theories take the forms of **biocentrism** and of **ecocentrism**. Biocentrists maintain that all living creatures have a good of their own, and have moral standing as such, and further that their flourishing or attaining their good is **intrinsically valuable**, valuable, that is, because of its very nature. Having a good of one's own does not turn on sentience or the capacity for feeling; even a human being in a coma has interests, and the common interest of humans and of other animals in health seems not to depend on the feelings of the individual concerned. Similarly, creatures that lack feelings, such as plants, still have a good of their own, consisting in their developing such capacities as those for growth, photosynthesis, respiration, reproduction and self-repair. Given that the health of sentient creatures has independent value, it is difficult to deny that the health of insentient creatures has value on the same basis. (This is even true of genetically engineered creatures, inclined as we may be to regard them, as Keekok Lee does, as 'biotic artefacts'.)[19] Intrinsic value, then, is carried by individual living creatures or their states. Biocentrists do not deny that ecosystems have great value; but this value arises (according to biocentrism) from the way that ecosystems facilitate the lives and the flourishing of the numerous individual creatures that comprise them or depend on them. The same holds for the entire systems of nature and of evolution; such systems too have high value not in themselves but because of the lives that they generate or make possible. (Sentientists can make parallel claims about ecosystems and the system of nature, except that they have to hold that what gives these systems their value is nothing but the sentient creatures that the systems facilitate.)

Ecocentrists, however, maintain that ecosystems have a good independent of that of their component individuals, and as such have their own moral standing; their attaining their good has intrinsic value on much the same basis as biocentrists claim for individual organisms. (Parallel claims are sometimes made by ecocentrists about species.) While some ecocentrists suggest that systems (and possibly species) alone have intrinsic value (an unqualified holist position), others hold that the intrinsic value of systems and of species coexists with that of individual creatures. Ecocentrism is held to take systemic factors more seriously than rival views. However, biocentrists and others can recognize that systems shape the development of life and of evolution in a causal manner, without recognizing either that these systems have an identifiable good of their own or that they should be given consideration over and above their living members. Clearly the lives of many individual members turn on the continuation in existence of a relevant ecosystem; hence the systems need to be preserved if the members and thus their species are also to be preserved. If so, biocentrists maintain, it is unnecessary to reason as if the health of the relevant systems mattered independently.

The debate between anthropocentrism, sentientism, biocentrism and ecocentrism is considered further in chapter 2, and cannot be resolved here. Besides, there are some questions that need to be considered first about these theories: what kind of theories are they, and what kind of difference would adopting one of these theories make?

To consider the first question first, these theories are (among other things) theories of the scope and extent of moral standing. To adopt the definition of Kenneth Goodpaster (who coined the phrase 'moral considerability' to express the same idea), **moral standing** belongs to things that ought to be taken into consideration when action is in prospect, and that thus warrant respect. Goodpaster's own theory is that moral standing attaches to everything that has a good of its own (independently of the good of its owners, producers or users), and that this includes all living creatures (at least). Goodpaster also raises (without settling) the question of whether ecosystems have a good of their own and are also to be included. If so, his theory is ecocentric, and if not, it is biocentric.[20] However, he is clear that inanimate entities lack moral standing, as they have no good of their own, and thus cannot be benefited.[21] This does not mean that followers of Goodpaster would have to regard (say) works of art as unimportant. Efforts to display and conserve them, however, would be grounded not in consideration or respect for the works of art themselves, but for the human beings who are capable of appreciating them.

Besides being theories of the scope and extent of moral standing, these theories (anthropocentrism, sentientism, biocentrism and ecocentrism) are also theories of the location of intrinsic value. As the above passage about things that are intrinsically valuable suggests, something has **intrinsic value** if it is valuable because of its nature, or because of what it is in itself. Intrinsic value contrasts with **extrinsic** (or derivative) **value**, for example the **instrumental value** that things (such as tools and machines) have because of their actual or potential usefulness, or the value that (say) works of art have because people are benefited through appreciating them (a kind of value for which philosophers have devised the term '**inherent value**'),[22] and it is important to avoid the widespread confusions that misrepresent aesthetic value or even all non-instrumental value as intrinsic value. The theories just listed claim to disclose that intrinsic value is located either solely in human good (or human interests), or in the good or flourishing of all sentient beings, or of all living creatures (future ones included), or (either additionally or instead) of ecosystems; in other words, the good of these entities comprise fundamental (non-derivative) grounds or reasons for action (e.g. to benefit or foster or preserve the things in question).

Some clarification is here in place, because writers sometimes misleadingly suggest that the various kinds of value are simply and invariably functions of what people value. Thus instrumental value is suggested to be nothing but what people value as a means, and intrinsic value to be nothing but what people value as an end, or for its own sake. Granted that these terms are occasionally used in these senses, it is important to observe that 'valuable' standardly means 'what there is reason to value' or 'what is worthy of being valued', and not merely 'what is valued'. Thus things centrally and characteristically have instrumental value when there is reason to value them instrumentally (for example, when they really do serve agreed purposes, as opposed to just being regarded as serving them), and, more importantly, things have intrinsic value when there is reason to value them for what they are in themselves, rather than when they are simply valued as ends. (Many people value money as an end in itself, but this does not mean that money really has intrinsic value.) All this underlines the significance of theories of intrinsic value. Rather than conveying anything about valuings or praise or esteem, such theories convey that certain things (such as the good of living creatures) are fit to be valued, and thus supply reasons for action (as facts about valuings or praise or esteem could never do).

Accordingly, the theories that we are considering, besides being theories of the scope and extent of moral standing, and of the location of intrinsic value, comprise fundamental theories of **normative ethics**. For any general theory of normative ethics (that is, theories of what ought to be done by agents of one kind or another, and of the related principles and criteria) will need an account of which things have moral standing and which things have intrinsic value. (Thus, to take the example of utilitarianism, moral standing is usually ascribed by holders of this theory to sentient beings, and intrinsic value is located in pleasure or in happiness.) Since theorists are prone to make assumptions in such matters, it is a merit in all the theories currently under consideration that their stance in these matters is explicit. Just because they purport to say which things have moral standing and where intrinsic value is to be found, they potentially supply at least some of the foundations that a general theory of normative ethics requires.

All this helps with our second question, the one concerning what kind of difference the adoption of one of these theories can make. A key part of the answer here is that, just because these theories have the fundamental role just mentioned, the adoption of one or another of them importantly affects what we recognize as a problem, as well as what we accept as a proper way of confronting such situations. (The fundamental role of these theories also helps explain the relation between perspectives and recognition of problems, already mentioned in the second section (p. 4). It is not only what we recognize as right action that is affected by our value-theory, but also what we are able to recognize as a practical problem in the first place. It goes without saying that practical problems are bad states of affairs that are in principle capable either of solution or of alleviation.[23] However, anthropocentric theorists are prone not to recognize as bad or as problematic states of affairs that biocentrists and ecocentrists readily recognize as such.

Thus John Passmore, whose value-theory is largely anthropocentrist, is reluctant to recognize loss of wilderness as an ecological problem.[24] (I say 'largely anthropocentrist' because Passmore, who is basically a traditionalist, also gives a welcome to animal-welfarism; but this welcome seems not to extend to sentientism, or therefore to concern for the future of wild creatures dependent on the continued existence of wildernesses.)[25] Passmore's reluctance to count the shrinking or disappearance of wildernesses as a problem has led to criticism from Val Routley (now Val Plumwood), because of his restricted view of what amounts to a problem. In her judgement, Passmore's conclusion that his ethic is adequate to the various problems is no more than a hollow victory, because his anthropocentric approach recognizes nothing but threats to *human* interests as problems in the first place. Hence it is not surprising that the related anthropocentric ethic is capable of solving or mitigating the particular range of problems that he actually recognizes as such.[26] By contrast, a value-theory concerned directly for the good of wild creatures or their habitats will identify **ecological problems** against its broader perspective, and will recognize wilderness loss among them. It would not follow that all failures to preserve wilderness are wicked, for the interests of wild creatures might sometimes have to be overridden. But the good of these creatures ought at any rate to be taken into consideration, as is done by biocentrists and by most kinds of ecocentrists. (Incidentally some versions of anthropocentrism would also claim to recognize the importance of preserving wilderness and wild species, albeit ultimately on the basis of human interests;[27] hence the debate about anthropocentrism should not yet be regarded as resolved.)

Yet a key part of the answer to the second question is by now clear: the adoption of one or another value-theory can actually affect and mould our recognition of problems as well as our understanding about what individuals or other agencies such as governments ought to do about them. Some people might treat this finding as a cue for relativism; what we regard as problems and as solutions is (at least in part) perspective-dependent, and perspectives (it might be suggested) are themselves just a matter of preference. However, I shall be arguing to contrary effect; there can be good grounds for choices between value-theories (see chapter 2). If so, then the finding just mentioned supplements and underlines the importance of endorsing one value-theory or another.

Some people suggest, however, that sentientism, biocentrism and ecocentrism are not really alternatives to anthropocentrism after all, because all valuing is ultimately human valuing, all valuations human valuations, and hence all values are anthropocentric in the sense of being generated by human beings, however biocentric (etc.) they may seem. But this reasoning (however it is to be assessed itself) is beside the point where the above debate between value-theories is concerned. This is because the meaning of 'anthropocentric' has shifted from 'deriving from human interests', to 'generated by human judgements'. This is a different concept, for which philosophers use the term **'anthropogenic'** (meaning 'generated by humanity'). Besides, anthropogenic theories of value concern the status of judgements about value, rather than their normative content, and even if they were true it would still be possible to defend any of the normative value-theories discussed above. Thus even those who endorse the anthropogenic argument need not be anthopocentrists (in the normal sense). In any case, this argument itself is highly suspect, implying as it does that if human valuers had never evolved there would have been nothing bad about the pain of sentient animals, because there would have been no human valuers to confer on pain its badness or disvalue. (I have argued this point in greater detail elsewhere.)[28] Indeed if, as was argued above, 'having value' does not mean 'being valued by someone or other', then the theory that it is human valuations that confer value on things that would otherwise lack such value can in any case be seen to be difficult to defend. Rather than our making things valuable by judging them so, their value is typically something that we recognize or discover.

Environmental ethics and its neighbours

Granted that '**environment**' standardly (both here and standardly elsewhere) means 'objective encompassing system of nature', **environmental ethics** is the study of the ethics of human interactions with and impacts on such systems. It includes both normative ethics (the study of relevant principles of value and of obligation, and their bearing on action and policy) and meta-ethics, the study of the basis and status of all such discourse. For example, the questions of the grounds for pursuing sustainability and the forms that it should take are normative questions, while the issue of whether there are true answers to questions such as these, or whether the answers are all relative to perspectives, are meta-ethical questions.[29] Some key normative questions and meta-ethical questions are discussed in chapter 2.

   Accordingly, environmental ethics is defined by its sphere. There are several adjacent or overlapping spheres, to which its findings will often be relevant, though they cannot all be studied here. They include forestry ethics (the sphere from which environmental ethics historically emerged), agricultural ethics, the ethics of animal welfare (links with which have already been noted), **development** ethics (the ethics of social and economic development), business ethics, biomedical ethics, the ethics of genetic engineering and population ethics. Other adjacent fields are transport policy, planning policy and policies concerning recreation and tourism. In order to have a bearing on adjacent fields, as well as strictly environmental questions, it is important that the full range of value-theories (including anthropocentrism) is included in this field of study.

Different understandings of 'environmental ethics' are exhibited by different writers, some of whom define the discipline not by its sphere but by its values. Thus 'environmental ethics' is sometimes defined not as above, but as the kind of approach to environmental issues which finds independent value to be situated not only in the interests of humanity or of sentient creatures, but also in the good of natural living creatures or their ecosystems.[30] While many environmental philosophers in fact adhere to this kind of approach, many are instead anthropocentrists or sentientists. This being so, it would be unwise to treat the work of the latter as lying outside environmental ethics. Accordingly commitment to either biocentrism or ecocentrism should not be regarded as essential to environmental ethics (a verdict that Christopher Belshaw has recently underlined).[31] The debate concerning the location of intrinsic value can then continue to take place within environmental ethics. Equally, we can avoid making the precise location of the boundaries of environmental ethics a battleground about values; wherever the boundaries lie, there should be plentiful traffic across them, with exchanges of visits between those concerned with related or overlapping study or reflection.

On this basis, environmental ethics can remain a neighbour of population ethics, biomedical ethics and the rest, rather than a rival approach with essentially different values of its own. The alternative might even incline neighbouring disciplines (biomedical ethics, for example, which has to reflect on the ethics of experiments on animals) to become exclusively anthropocentric, confident that non-human interests would be stressed by environmental ethicists. In any case it is greatly preferable if environmental ethics can contribute to interdisciplinary discussions, for example, of planning strategies, on an equal footing with other branches of ethics and with other disciplines such as (in this case) economics and sociology; there is no need for it to be regarded as essentially a school or a movement, although there is plenty of scope for schools of thought (such as Deep Ecology) within it (or within the broader field of environmental philosophy).

Accordingly environmental ethics may be regarded as concerned with a variety of practical issues arising from human interactions with the natural world. For all value-theories, these include: pollution and its prevention or mitigation, the availability of natural resources (both for use and for energy generation), human impacts on the local or the planetary climate, and the preservation of biological diversity (or **biodiversity**), in terms of diversity both within

and among species, subspecies and habitats. Biodiversity preservation, however, is likely to be stressed particularly by biocentrism
and ecocentrism, which also emphasize issues of loss of habitat
and of wilderness (topics that sometimes trouble anthropocentrist
and sentientist theorists as well, but from one or another narrower
basis). The issues already mentioned involve the related issues of
deforestation, the loss of wetlands and of coral reefs, and the growth
of deserts, and also bring in aspects of transport, of planning, and
of the growth of the human population. Additionally, they raise
aesthetic issues such as provision for spaces for refuge and recreation and the preservation and appreciation of landscape,[32] and issues of environmental health such as the importance of clean water
and uncontaminated fresh air. Environmental concern can also
embody issues of identity, of community and of belonging. Yet it
also transcends such human-related issues in favour of concern for
the living systems, the evolutionary processes and the entire biosphere of the planet; and the scope of environmental ethics is equally
extensive.

By this stage, you should be forming views about what has moral
standing and intrinsic value, and about the scope and limits of environmental ethics. You should also have grasped how different
environmental problems are recognized by different perspectives
(such as anthropocentrism, biocentrism and ecocentrism).

Theories of the genesis of the problems

While ecological problems are too diverse to admit of any single
cause, it will prove useful to survey some of the proposed explanations for such problems at this stage. The theories surveyed here
variously attribute these problems to: population, affluence, technology, capitalism, absence of markets, patriarchy, growth and religion. But conclusions about both causes and solutions must await
consideration in later chapters of the potential role and significance
of environmental ethics itself (see chapters 3 and 6).

Many people think that ecological problems, whether local, regional or global, are due to the growth of the human population
(which has now reached just over six billion). For the problems are
caused by human actions, and the more humans there are (they
say) the worse the problems are bound to become. However, many
human communities, far from making the problems worse, live

harmoniously with the land, and much of the worst environmental degradation bears more relation to technological production than to population density or growth. Problems are likely to emerge later this century in supplying the growing population with food and fresh water, and with the electricity that future people are likely to need to satisfy their basic needs; hence population levels need to stabilize, if possible at levels compatible with sustainable resource use and with preservation of biodiversity. But such stabilization is possible, at least in principle, at a higher level of population than that of the present. Besides, even if population levels were somehow to decline, that would be no guarantee that ecological problems such as global warming, deforestation, desertification or nuclear pollution would disappear, or even diminish in proportion. Accordingly, population growth, important as it is, does not seem pivotal to the problems. (Its relation to environmental problems and to poverty will be further discussed in chapter 5.)

Others focus on affluence and overconsumption as the key factor. Through increases in the Gross National Product of most countries of the rich North, modern consumers often command many times the horse power (or the slave power) of even the richest of their predecessors, and in combination with this power their expectations and often wasteful lifestyles either initiate or at least exacerbate the erosion of the natural world.[33] Yet many environmental problems (such as those to be witnessed in the slums of the great cities of the South) are due not to affluence but to poverty – and the same is probably true of rapid population growth. In any case, increases in consumption are insufficient to account for increases in levels of pollution; to explain these increases, as Barry Commoner has argued,[34] new technologies of production have to be taken into account. As with population, the consequences of untrammelled growth of affluence could be dire, and sustainable lifestyles are likely to be needed in place of throwaway consumption. Yet no amount of changes of lifestyle are capable of curing ecological problems in isolation, granted the powerful structures that exist at the levels of corporations and governments. Affluence does not lie at the heart of the problems. (The relation of ethics to lifestyle choices and to economic structures is further discussed in chapter 3.)

A similar picture emerges when high technology is suggested as the root of our problems. While modern technology helps explain levels of pollution and, in some cases, resource depletion, it cannot explain those problems that result from poverty; nor are its consequences uniformly harmful; nor can it be regarded as an autonomous force, and thus the source of ecological problems, as if no further explanation were needed. Indeed, modern technology will often be needed if the problems are to be tackled, whether in matters of agriculture, or of electricity generation, or of replacing ozone-depleting propellants such as chloro-fluoro-carbons (CFCs). The attitude of managerialism, displayed by some technologists, could still generate problems, and will be discussed in the coming section. But to distinguish between beneficent and other applications of technology, we need to look further.

Not even global **capitalism** seems sufficient to explain the generality of the problems, despite the considerable contribution of market forces and of self-seeking corporations to problems such as deforestation, pollution and global warming. Capitalism may well be unsustainable, as Martin O'Connor suggests,[35] and certainly in a wide range of cases it well explains the aggressive impacts of technology; yet other even more intense instances of technological-induced pollution came to light just after the Cold War at the end of Communist rule in the countries of Eastern Europe such as (the then) Czechoslovakia and East Germany.[36] It should also be recognized that capitalist corporations have been discovering new opportunities for investment in energy-efficient, low-pollution green technology capable of contributing to sustainable solutions. While corporations and the governments that support them need to exercise their power far more responsibly before sustainable global solutions can even be in prospect, capitalism cannot be considered the unique source of all our discontents.

Nor, come to that, can the absence of markets. Some theorists suggest that environmental problems derive from inefficient use of resources, itself explained by the lack of markets to ensure their efficient distribution and deployment.[37] For example, carbon dioxide emissions currently overuse the absorptive capacities of the atmosphere supposedly because there is (as yet) no international emissions market to assign them their proper cost. But this theory implies that where markets and private enterprise prevail, environmental problems are absent. Yet this implication conflicts with widespread experience of toxic emissions, whether around chemical plants as at Bhopal (India), or in polluted rivers such as the Rhine, or at nuclear energy generators like the one at Three Mile Island, where nuclear meltdown was only narrowly avoided. It also implies that where land is held communally on an inalienable basis, and there is thus no market in land, degradation is inevitable, again contrary to experience.[38]

Patriarchy, or the oppression of women by men, has also been suggested (not least by some **ecofeminists**) as underpinning the oppression of nature,[39] whether because belief in the superiority of male rationality devalues females, emotions, the body and the natural, or because all the various kinds of oppression (whether on the basis of gender, class, race, or species) reinforce one another, and must be combated together. Granted that each kind of oppression tends to beget other kinds, however, the conclusion to be drawn (as other ecofeminists have recognized) is that all oppression, exploitation, and unjustified discrimination are to be contested,[40] and not that any one kind, such as patriarchy, underlies all the others. Whether patriarchy invariably generates or even accompanies exploitation of nature can in fact be questioned;[41] for example, in Ethiopia traditional Oromo culture is deeply patriarchal but enlightened with regard to the preservation of species.[42] Nor could the overthrow of patriarchy be expected of itself to overcome alienation from nature or to deliver the disappearance of ecological problems, any more than the overthrow of racism or of class-division could, although the demise of all these forms of oppression would make an important contribution. (Some more constructive **feminist** insights are introduced in the final section of this chapter and in the first section of chapter 2.)

The view has, however, been proposed that the pursuit of economic growth, whether through capitalism, communism, national socialism, or any other such system, lies at the root of the problems. As the authors of Limits to Growth would maintain,[43] the unlimited drive for growth in production as well as of population is likely to prove fatal not only locally but globally too. Yet not all ecological problems are due to growth, for some are due either to poverty or to passivity, and draconian ceilings to growth could even prevent the phased introduction of sustainable solutions (which would in some cases involve investment in forms of development to overcome poverty). Thus particular kinds of growth need to be considered case by case; some kinds, such as growth in global warming, need to be halted and if possible reversed, while others (such as investment in agriculture, water supply and energy generation from renewable sources) may actually be necessary in the cause of sustainable solutions.

The possibility remains that human beliefs and attitudes may partially explain the problems. To suggest, as some have,[44] that Christian and Jewish beliefs (about creation and the roles of humanity and nature) comprise the root of the problems involves unduly disregarding economic factors and forces, as well as (arguably) doing violence to history.[45] My own past suggestion that the problems have partly been caused by belief in perpetual material progress, its rightness and its inevitability was already explicitly qualified by awareness of possible interplay between the influence of material factors and of ideas,[46] and was qualified later in the same text by recognition of 'the crucial role of the world system of economic relations and power relations'.[47] Despite this, I have recently been berated for neglecting the socio-economic context in which beliefs and attitudes might exercise an influence.[48] But economic factors and human beliefs can both be significant. For example, ethical and metaphysical beliefs should not be disregarded, such as the teaching of Descartes that non-human animals are machine-like entities, entirely lacking in consciousness, and may be treated accordingly,[49] or the contrasting belief in stewardship, which is discussed below. Such beliefs might still contribute, through a variety of social mechanisms, either to the problems or to possible solutions, alongside some of the other factors discussed in this section. Whether this suggestion assigns too much influence to ideas and attitudes will be discussed further in chapter 3, while the debate about the impact of Christianity and Judaism will be further considered in the coming section and in chapter 2.

Human stewardship of nature

Since at least the seventeenth century, it has been explicitly maintained that human beings hold the Earth as a trust, and are not only responsible for its care, but also answerable for the delivery of their role as stewards or trustees. Not surprisingly, these beliefs have religious origins, particularly among Christians and, to a lesser extent, among Jews and Muslims; and their origin is widely held to derive from much earlier centuries, granted that the Old Testament is often interpreted as embodying a message of stewardship (and in the views of many scholars, rightly so interpreted).[50] But many non-religious people adhere to much the same beliefs, and secular versions of stewardship are coming to be accepted without any religious overtones whatever, for example by the World Wide Fund for Nature, Scotland.[51]

According to both the religious and the secular belief in **stewardship**, human beings do not own the Earth, but hold it as a trust, not least for the sake of future generations. In the Bible, the Earth is understood as belonging not to humanity but to God (Psalm 24), and the land is understood to be held as a leasehold (Leviticus 25:23), and subject to ethical conditions, including taking care of the poor (Leviticus 25; Deuteronomy 15). Correspondingly, secular writers (including Karl Marx) deny that the current generation of human beings can own the globe, and stress that it is a patrimony for our descendants.[52] Both kinds of believers in stewardship recognize widespread responsibilities to care for the Earth and preserve it intact for our successors. While stewardship does not offer any comprehensive ethical theory, these particular ethical implications, at any rate, are clear.

But believers in stewardship characteristically believe that humans are answerable for their performance as trustees; can this belief be sustained? The religious version of stewardship, whether Christian, Jewish or Islamic, holds that it is to God that humans are answerable. This is not the place for a discussion of grounds for belief in God, particularly as I have discussed these matters elsewhere.[53] Rather the problem is how the secular version can accommodate such belief in answerability. Current human beings cannot strictly be answerable to future generations who do not yet exist (even though environmentalists sometimes talk as if they could be); but they can be answerable to the present generation of humanity as a whole, or perhaps to the community of moral agents (present and future) which shares these responsibilities. A large part of this community is currently alive and competent in the present (which makes answerability a serious possibility), and could reasonably hold to account individuals or peoples who fail to play their part, despite their having been able to do so. This community does not need to be organized into some kind of world government to make such answerability a reality; morally, current agents could be answerable however ill-organized the world community may be, although this answerability is more likely to make a practical difference if international civil society or institutions organize themselves enough to make their presence felt.

Belief in stewardship, then, is a coherent possibility. It has also been criticized, on historical as well as on ethical grounds. Not all the criticisms can be considered here.[54] But one criticism should be tackled directly, the criticism that belief in human stewardship does not cohere with the biblical belief in human **dominion** 'over all the Earth' and its non-human creatures (Genesis 1; Psalm 8). Talk of 'dominion' is prone to conjure up images either of **domination** (an objectionable relationship) or of domineering (an objectionable form of behaviour). However, the concept of dominion conveys no more than the ability to rule or govern that makes responsibility possible. And dominion in the Bible was always conditional, and subject to ethical requirements. Hence the kind of dominion ascribed there to human beings actually clashes with domineering over the Earth and with domination (whether local or global). By the same token this dominion was compatible with notions of (what later came to be called) stewardship. So it is mistaken to contrast dominion with stewardship; belief in stewardship, as previously mentioned, is becoming regarded as a reasonable interpretation of what the Old Testament (Genesis included) has to say about the relation of humanity to the Earth.

Belief in stewardship also has its dangers. While stewardship is usually regarded as aimed at 'preserving the face of the earth in beauty, usefulness and fruitfulness' and therewith Earth's species,[55] attempts to take control of the entire surface of the planet, or of the entire evolutionary process, have been suggested in its name by (among others) the social ecologist Murray Bookchin, as realizing the creativity implicit in nature.[56] This, however, is a domineering approach, out of keeping with stewardship (which involves respecting what is held in trust), and also focuses excessively on human interests as if there were no other interests or as if they were of no importance. Yet even anthropocentric ethicists such as Bryan G. Norton hold that Earth's species and ecosystems should be preserved for the sake of human well-being,[57] while most adherents of stewardship reject anthropocentrism, and at the same time any approach such as Bookchin's that adopts an exclusively instrumental view of non-human creatures and treats them as dispensable raw material. Stewardship, then, is actually incompatible with the instrumental approach of managerialism. It can take the form of leaving creatures and their habitats alone ('letting-be'), and should not be confused with instrumental attitudes to nature or with the perpetual pursuit of interference or even of change. (Likewise, Martin Heidegger rejects the view that nature comprises a 'standing-reserve', insisting instead that humanity is, in the full sense of the word, its 'care-taker'.)[58]

Besides, a renunciation of the human stewardship of nature could be disastrous. Human beings cannot help drawing their food, clothing and shelter from the natural world, and if in doing so they attempt to throw off all ethical constraints (and thus concern for contemporary and future humans and for fellow creatures), the outcome is likely to be the exercise of power without any pretence at responsibility. This remains the case even if people tell themselves that what they are doing is ignoring moral inhibitions or conventional values, fulfilling their instincts and/or identifying with nature. If the world of nature is full of value, then agents are needed who recognize and respect that value, developing a sense of responsibility and, if possible, of answerability at the same time. However, many related issues need to be considered if stances such as this one are to be defended. Some of the relevant debates are discussed in chapter 2.

But is caring about the environment really possible?

Sometimes it is suggested that our sympathies are too confined and narrow to allow us to care either about the human future or about the natural environment. Some, who believe that we are all basically self-interested, infer that we are incapable of caring about the distant future, and conclude that therefore we can have no obligation to care.[59] Others, such as David Hume, have rejected such **psychological egoism**, but have held that our sentiments (of which Hume considered moral discourse an expression, not itself subject to reason) are so restricted as to support recognizably useful systems of property and justice, and (where obligations are concerned) little more.[60] Yet others have regarded human society as a contract between self-interested individuals, allowing of only those motivations and responsibilities derivable from an ultimately egoistic basis. However, with the possible exception of Hume, who at least recognized sympathy as a natural sentiment, these thinkers adopt implausibly atomistic assumptions about human nature,[61] as if human beings did not begin life as dependent infants, and, as adults, had little or no inclination to tend and nurture such vulnerable beings.[62] In trying to understand both ethics and society on this basis, such thinkers disregard significant aspects of common human experience which may well underlie and make possible empathy, altruism and a sense of social solidarity.[63]

This **feminist** critique of atomism and of egoism crucially modifies the setting to which theories of motivation and of normative ethics are applied. Once the model of agents being imprisoned in self-interest is questioned, it becomes possible to take into account the plentiful empirical evidence that 'people are often motivated to act out of concern for the interests of people of the future'[64] and of members of other species. Psychological egoism attempts implausibly to reduce the wide range of human motivation to a single pattern, and perforce either ignores or misrepresents acts of which the main outcomes are intended and expected to fall after the agent's death, plus self-sacrificial acts of compassion or mercy, and (there again) acts intended to foster causes such as protection of species or habitats. Ernest Partridge has even argued that people have a need to undertake causes of this general type, ones in which we transcend our narrow self-interest (see chapter 4).[65] Whether or not there is a universal need for such self-transcendence, the capacity to care for another not on the basis of self-interest, but in the sense of taking the other's point of view and doing what seems best from that perspective,[66] is undeniably widespread; and this rightly suggests that acting for others' good, or for the sake of the common good, is equally a widespread motivation (and for that matter one that makes stewardship, as discussed above, a significant possibility).

As we have seen, things are intrinsically valuable when there is reason to promote, cherish or protect them for no reason other than their own nature. Such value is manifestly to be found in states of affairs such as the health and flourishing of (at least) human beings and (perhaps also) of members of other species. Granted all this, there will often be ample reason to promote, cherish or protect such states of affairs, and the various goods on which they depend. Since environmental concern is a form of concern to promote, cherish and protect such goods (whether for human beings or for all species), it need not evoke surprise, and stands in no special need of explanation; in fact it is a phenomenon as unsurprising as ethical concern of any (other) sort.

> You are invited to ask yourself your preliminary view on the genesis of environmental problems, the aptness of regarding humanity as stewards of the natural world, and the possibility, given human nature, of human beings sufficiently caring about it.

Summary

Environmental problems arise from human dealings with the natural world, and can be either local or global, and either cumulative or systemic. Animal-welfarism, environmentalism and humanism seemingly embody contrasting values, and we need to distinguish between positions that are anthropocentric, sentientist, biocentric and ecocentric. These contrasting positions concern the scope of moral standing and the location of intrinsic value, and choosing between them affects not only what we recognize as right action but also what we count as a problem. Environmental ethics studies all such issues, and is defined and contrasted with neighbouring disciplines by its sphere and not by its values. Environmental problems are not explained by any single factor, neither population, nor affluence, nor technology, nor capitalism, nor lack of markets, nor patriarchy, nor growth, nor religion. However, beliefs may be influential as well as structures, and belief in the human stewardship of nature could form part of their cure. Feminist critiques of individualism show that human beings are not incapable of the kind of caring that this belief presupposes.

Notes

1   David E. Cooper, 'Other Species and Moral Reason', p. 145.
2   James Lovelock, *Gaia: A New Look at the Earth*; *Gaia: The Practical Science of Planetary Medicine*.
3   See the discussion of Lovelock's Gaia hypothesis in Andrew Brennan, *Thinking About Nature: An Investigation of Nature, Value and Ecology*, at pp. 129–31.
4   James W. Kirchner, 'The Gaia Hypotheses: Are They Testable? Are They Useful?'; Christopher Belshaw, *Environmental Philosophy: Reason, Nature and Human Concern*, pp. 285–8; Michael Allaby, *Basics of Environmental Science*, p. 7.
5   Stephen R. L. Clark, 'Gaia and the Forms of Life'; Mary Midgley, *Science and Poetry*, pp. 171–86.
6   Brennan, *Thinking About Nature*, p. 131.
7   This, combined with technological optimism, is the perspective of Björn Lomborg, *The Skeptical Environmentalist: Measuring the Real State of the World*.
8   Arne Naess, 'The Shallow and the Deep, Long-Range Ecology Movement: A Summary'. Some of the implications of Deep Ecology, such as its advocacy of the goal of a reduced human population, are highly problematic.
9   A slogan of René Dubos. See Gerard Piel (ed.), *The World of René Dubos*, Part 8, 'Think Globally, Act Locally: Local Solutions to Global Problems'.
10   These senses of 'global' are distinguished in B. L. Turner II, Roger E. Kasperson and William B. Meyer, 'Two Types of Global Environmental Change'.
11   See Lester R. Brown, 'Challenges of the New Century'.
12   See Peter Singer, *Animal Liberation: A New Ethic for Our Treatment of Animals*, and *Practical Ethics*.
13   Thus Tom Regan, *The Case for Animal Rights*.
14   Thus animal-welfarism also encompasses certain contract-theorists such as Mark Rowlands. Contract-theorists hold that ethical practices are ones that individuals who were ignorant of their own future would freely choose if they were bargaining on an utterly equal basis. Rowlands contrives to bring animal interests into such a contract: see Mark Rowlands, *Animal Rights: A Philosophical Defence*.
15   J. Baird Callicott, 'Animal Liberation: A Triangular Affair'.
16   Aldo Leopold, *A Sand County Almanac and Sketches Here and There*, pp. 224–5.
17   Callicott, 'Animal Liberation: A Triangular Affair'. A reconciliation of these tendencies is attempted in James Sterba, *Justice for Here and Now*, p. 132, and in *Three Challenges to Ethics: Environmentalism, Feminism*

and Multiculturalism, p. 43; but his prioritizing of the basic needs of all humans over those of all non-humans seems discriminatory (as is argued in chapter 2).

18   Andrew Osborn, '50 Million Animals in Mass Test Plan'.
19   Keekok Lee, *The Natural and the Artefactual: The Implications of Deep Science and Deep Technology for Environmental Philosophy*, pp. 51–4.
20   Kenneth E. Goodpaster, 'On Being Morally Considerable'.
21   Goodpaster, 'On Stopping at Everything: A Reply to W. M. Hunt'.
22   Robin Attfield, 'Postmodernism, Value and Objectivity'.
23   John Passmore, *Man's Responsibility for Nature*, pp. 43–5.
24   Passmore, ibid., pp. 110–11.
25   Passmore, ibid., pp. 111–21.
26   Val Routley (now Plumwood), Critical Notice of John Passmore, *Man's Responsibility for Nature*.
27   See Bryan G. Norton, *Toward Unity Among Environmentalists*.
28   Attfield, 'Evolution, Theodicy and Value', and 'Rehabilitating Nature and Making Nature Habitable'.
29   For a recent discussion of meta-ethical issues in environmental ethics, see Attfield, 'Postmodernism, Value and Objectivity'.
30   Thus Janna Thompson, 'A Refutation of Environmental Ethics'.
31   See Christopher Belshaw, *Environmental Philosophy*, p. 216.
32   See Allen Carlson, 'Nature and Positive Aesthetics', p. 24.
33   For recent philosophical discussions of the ethics of consumption, see David A. Crocker and Toby Linden (eds), *Ethics of Consumption: The Good Life, Justice, and Global Stewardship*.
34   Barry Commoner, *The Closing Circle: Confronting the Environmental Crisis*, pp. 140–77.
35   Martin O'Connor (ed.), *Is Capitalism Sustainable? Political Economy and the Politics of Ecology*.
36   On environmental destruction in the former Soviet Union, see also Murray Feshbach and Alfred Friendly, *Ecocide in the USSR*.
37   See Terry L. Anderson and Donald R. Leal, *Free Market Environmentalism* and Terry L. Anderson 'Free Market Environmentalism'.
38   See Martin Adams, *Breaking Ground: Development Aid for Land Reform*, pp. 9–12.
39   As Val Plumwood explains, this position is held by some ecofeminists, but is not the mainstream position of ecofeminist writers. See Plumwood, 'Nature, Self and Gender: Feminism, Environmental Philosophy, and the Critique of Rationalism', pp. 22–3, and nn. 22 and 23, pp. 24–5.
40   See Attfield, 'Development and Environmentalism'; also Warwick Fox, 'The Deep Ecology/Ecofeminism Debate and its Parallels'.
41   That there is an essential connection between patriarchy and the oppression of nature has been maintained in Karen Warren, 'The Power and Promise of Ecological Feminism', and disputed in Margarita Garcia Levin, 'A Critique of Ecofeminism'. The various kinds of oppression would seem capable of independent existence, but often systemically related. For representative ecofeminist writings, see

Michael E. Zimmerman (ed.), *Environmental Philosophy: From Animal Rights to Radical Ecology*, pp. 253–341. For a survey of ecofeminism, see Des Jardins, *Environmental Ethics: An Introduction to Environmental Philosophy*, 3rd edn, pp. 249–57.

42   Workineh Kelbessa, *Indigenous and Modern Environmental Ethics: A Study of the Oromo Environmental Ethic and Oromo Environmental Ethics in the Light of Modern Issues of Environment and Development.*

43   Donella Meadows et al., *The Limits to Growth*, a report for the Club of Rome's Project on the Predicament of Mankind (1972); see also Donella Meadows, Dennis L. Meadows and Jørgen Randers, *Beyond the Limits: Global Collapse or a Sustainable Future.*

44   Thus Lynn White Jr, 'The Historical Roots of Our Ecological Crisis'.

45   See chapter 2; also Attfield, 'Christian Attitudes to Nature' and 'Western Traditions and Environmental Ethics', both reprinted in Attfield, *Environmental Philosophy: Principles and Prospects.*

46   Attfield, *The Ethics of Environmental Concern*, pp. 8–17; for the interplay of the influence of material forces and ideas, see pp. 8–9.

47   Attfield, *The Ethics of Environmental Concern*, 2nd edn, pp. 197–8.

48   See Barnabas Dickson, 'The Ethicist Conception of Environmental Problems', pp. 132, 137 and 148. I have written further about power relations and structures of injustice in *Environmental Philosophy: Principles and Prospects*, pp. 221–35.

49   The relevant passages of Descartes are gathered together in Regan and Singer (eds), *Animal Rights and Human Obligations*, pp. 60–6.

50   Clarence Glacken, *Traces on the Rhodian Shore: Nature and Culture in Western Thought from Ancient Times to the End of the Eighteenth Century*; Eric Katz, 'Judaism and the Ecological Crisis'.

51   World Wide Fund for Nature, Scotland, *Stewardship of Natural Resources.*

52   Karl Marx, *Capital*, vol. 3, p. 776.

53   Attfield, *God and the Secular*, chs 5 and 6.

54   For discussion of the various criticisms, see Attfield, *The Ethics of the Global Environment*, ch. 3.

55   Sir Matthew Hale, *The Primitive Origination of Mankind*, sect. 4, ch. 8, p. 370.

56   Murray Bookchin, 'Thinking Ecologically: A Dialectical Approach'.

57   See Norton, *Toward Unity among Environmentalists*. Norton's position is made more explicit in 'Epistemology and Environmental Values'.

58   Martin Heidegger, 'The Question Concerning Technology', pp. 298 and 305; Bruce V. Foltz, 'On Heidegger and the Interpretation of Environmental Crisis', pp. 336–7. For a comparable, more recent approach, see Jeremy Rifkin, *The Biotech Century: Harnessing the Gene and Remaking the World* (Tarcher-Putnam, New York, 1998).

59   Thomas H. Thompson, 'Are We Obligated to Future Others?'.

60   David Hume, *A Treatise of Human Nature*, Books II and III, and *An Enquiry Concerning the Principles of Morals*. J. Baird Callicott and Alan Carter have each attempted to ground an environmental ethic on Humean foundations (Callicott in 'Hume's *Is/Ought* Dichotomy and

the Relation of Ecology to Leopold's Land Ethic', and 'Animal Liberation and Environmental Ethics: Back Together Again'; Carter in
'Humean Nature'). However, these attempts miscarry, Callicott's for
the reasons given by Carter in 'Humean Nature' and by Y. S. Lo in 'A
Humean Argument for the Land Ethic?', and Carter's partly because
of the exaggerated roles for reason and objectivity that he ascribes to
Hume, and partly because Carter's view that the intrinsic value of
natural creatures is projected onto them by humans, however Humean
itself, is subject to the difficulties encountered by the anthropogenic
theory of value, discussed in this chapter and in chapter 2.

61 Mary Midgley, 'Duties Concerning Islands'.
62 See Doris Schroeder, 'Homo Economicus on Trial: Plato, Schopenhauer
    and the Virtual Jury', pp. 69–70.
63 Paula England, 'The Separative Self: Androcentric Bias in Neoclassi-
    cal Assumptions', p. 45.
64 Joseph R. Des Jardins, *Environmental Ethics*, 3rd edn, p. 84.
65 Ernest Partridge, 'Why Care About the Future?'.
66 Des Jardins, *Environmental Ethics*, p. 85. Discussion of the possibility
    of caring for the environment as a common human heritage is to be
    found in chapter 6.

Further Reading

Brown, Lester R., 'Challenges of the New Century', in Lester R. Brown,
    Christopher Flavin and Hilary French, *State of the World 2000*, Linda
    Starke (ed.), (Earthscan, London, 2000), pp. 3–21. On tackling global
    problems in the twenty-first century.
Wenz, Peter S., *Environmental Ethics Today* (Oxford University Press, New
    York and Oxford, 2001). Benign, wide-ranging survey in popular for-
    mat, but without bibliography.
Commoner, Barry, *The Closing Circle: Confronting the Environmental Crisis*
    (Jonathan Cape, London, 1972). Excellent interdisciplinary survey of
    the problems (as then understood) and their causes.
Goodpaster, Kenneth E., 'On Being Morally Considerable', *Journal of Phi-
    losophy*, 75 (1978), 308–25. The definitive paper on moral standing.
Mary Midgley, *Animals and Why They Matter* (Penguin, Harmondsworth,
    Middlesex, 1983). Ably conveys animal-welfarist concerns. The book
    that persuaded Callicott to discard his initial holism.
World Wide Fund for Nature, Scotland, *Stewardship of Natural Resources*
    (WWF, Scotland, Aberfeldy, 2001). Secular endorsement of stewardship.

Some Useful Websites

www.cep.unt.edu/theo.html Website of University of North Texas; lists
    systematic works in Environmental Ethics.
www.wwf-uk.org Website of WWF-UK. The World Wide Fund for
    Nature describes itself as 'the global environmental network'.

www.gechs.uci.edu/envethics.htm Website of Global Environmental Change and Human Security, University of California, Irvine, section on environmental ethics; includes useful bibliographies.
www.unedforum.org Website of UNED UK. Includes preparatory papers for United Nations World Summit on Sustainable Development of 2002.

Music for Environmental Ethicists

Rautavaara, Einojuhani, 'Cantus Arcticus, Op. 61: Concerto for Birds and Orchestra'; CD (HNH International, 1999) available from Naxos.

2 Some Central Debates

In this chapter, some central debates in environmental ethics are discussed in greater detail. Many of these debates concern **normative ethics** theories, theories about which states of affairs are valuable and which conduct is right or obligatory, and also their environmental implications; readers whose main interest lies with these issues could proceed directly to the third and subsequent sections of this chapter. Later, **meta-ethical** debates are reviewed, debates, that is, on issues such as whether judgements of value can be objective, and whether or not values always depend on human judgements. First, however, the debate about **stewardship** and the role of humanity is further discussed, as was promised in chapter 1, for it is best to reflect first on such metaphysical issues so as to set the stage for the others.

Dominion and stewardship

The theory that Jewish and Christian beliefs about creation and the role of humanity *vis-à-vis* nature underlie ecological problems was presented by Lynn White Jr, and has generated considerable controversy.[1] According to White, these beliefs about creation involve humanity being given dominance ('rightful mastery') over all fellow creatures,[2] which were themselves created simply to serve human purposes.[3] This extreme kind of anthropocentrism goes beyond the **normative anthropocentrism** which limits moral standing to human beings and confines the scope of morality to human interests (see chapter 1). The belief that the whole of creation exists for the sake of humanity is known as **'teleological anthropocentrism'** (literally, anthropocentrism of goals or purposes). Teleological anthropocentrism is sometimes thought to supply a basis for normative anthropocentrism.

However, teleological anthropocentrism is itself rightly berated by ecofeminists such as Val Plumwood, on several counts. One of these is its **instrumentalist view of nature** (nature being treated exclusively as a means to human ends). Another comprises its related **dualistic** representation of nature and of human rationality (as if nature and humanity were two sharply discontinuous entities). A third consists in the self-divided conception of human nature which it is sometimes prone to instil in its adherents (a conception in which people locate the essence of humanity in rationality, and contrast this with their physical and emotional nature).[4] Plumwood's criticisms are well taken; but White's ascription of all this to Judaism and Christianity could still be inaccurate.

White proceeds to ascribe to Christianity the beliefs that humanity is superior to nature and transcends it,[5] and that living creatures lack feelings and have instrumental value only.[6] However, since White is seeking to explain the scientific and technological superiority of Western Europe over other civilizations including 'the Greek East',[7] he exempts Greek Christianity from his charges of arrogant and aggressive activism, and applies them just to the medieval Latin West and its modern successors, whose science and technology now extend worldwide. Hence his charge that Christianity preaches human despotism, according to which (as John Passmore puts it) humans have the right to use nature as they please,[8] is not aimed at Christianity in general, but only at Western Christianity and its sphere of cultural influence.

White's account of Christian attitudes to nature is a far cry from the stewardship interpretation presented in chapter 1, and his interpretations, despite their widespread influence, have not generally been found convincing. For example, John Passmore has argued that the Old Testament is neither anthropocentric, nor dualistic, nor despotic. Its teaching about the dominion of humanity (in Genesis 1 and Psalm 8) has sometimes, he suggests, been interpreted in a despotic sense, but sometimes as stewardship.[9] Here I would go further. For any serious study of the Old Testament makes it difficult to understand how either despotic or anthropocentric interpretations (in any sense of 'anthropocentric') could be credited at all.

Thus Psalms like Psalm 104 convey the belief that God is just as concerned for wild species and their habitats as for human beings, as do chapters 38 and 39 of the book of Job, while passages like Proverbs 12:10 urge care for domestic animals. As for charges of arrogance and superiority, one passage even declares that 'man has no advantage over the beasts . . . all are from the dust, and all turn to dust again' (Ecclesiastes 3: 19–20). Besides, the passages mentioned above in chapter 1, applying ethical conditions to the use of the land (Leviticus 25 and Deuteronomy 15), conflict with interpretations upholding human despotism or 'rightful mastery', and lend support rather to the stewardship interpretation, as does the story of the Garden of Eden in Genesis 2.[10] Further, the teaching of the Old Testament, where not explicitly superseded in the New Testament, is also assumed to be authoritative by the writers of that Testament, where passages like those about the birds of the air and the lilies of the field (Matthew 5: 26–30; Luke 12: 24–8) appear to subscribe to the intrinsic value of non-human creatures.[11]

None of this shows that Christians have never adopted despotic or anthropocentric attitudes. Biblical teachings in Genesis 1 about humanity being created in the image of God and about human dominion over nature, as René Dubos remarks, have sometimes provided an excuse for policies of exploitation.[12] Yet most pre-Christian and non-Christian civilizations, as Dubos further observes,[13] have also generated ecological problems and damaged their own environments. Besides, it was not only the saints (much venerated in the medieval period) whose dealings with animals expressed a respectful, non-anthropocentric attitude to nature;[14] it was also influential church leaders such as Basil the Great, who prayed for 'the humble beasts that share with us the heat and burden of the day',[15] as later did the Western Christians who participated in the medieval Roman liturgy,[16] and Hildegard of Bingen, with her celebration of the natural world.[17] In the Orthodox Church, Maximus the Confessor taught that humanity is a mediator between God and the cosmos (the created order), a stance incompatible both with domination and with teleological anthropocentrism.[18] On the other hand, in the twelfth century in the West, Thomas Aquinas (who many centuries later became the official philosopher of the Catholic Church) adopted both teleological and normative anthropocentrism, and an instrumentalist attitude to animals, although he did not represent the human essence as confined to rationality.[19]

White suggests that St Francis of Assisi be adopted as a patron saint of ecologists, with his humble teaching of the democracy (or equality) of all God's creatures as our brothers and sisters.[20] But Dubos is reluctant to endorse such passively reverential egalitarianism, and instead adopts Benedict of Nursia (sixth century) 'as a patron saint of all those who believe that true conservation means not only protecting nature against human misbehavior but also developing human activities which favor a creative and harmonious relationship between man and nature'.[21] For Benedict (who was influenced by Basil) inaugurated the Benedictine rule, which fostered manual as well as intellectual work and prayer, and, through its widespread application in Western monasteries, served to enhance the beauty and fertility of the land.

Benedict's follower St Bernard of Clairvaux (twelfth century) combined an appreciation of natural beauty with a belief that it was a duty 'to work as partners of God in improving his creation'.[22] (Indeed attitudes such as these led to technological developments such as the use of water power,[23] which are among the examples of medieval Western technological superiority presented by White.) Reverence for nature, suggests Dubos, is not enough, as humanity inevitably has impacts on nature, and constructive impacts are likeliest when such reverence is combined with 'willingness to accept responsibility for a creative stewardship of the earth'.[24] While it might be doubted whether such reverence was universal among adherents of the Benedictine rule, they cannot fairly be accused of the despotic arrogance or the instrumental attitudes to nature that White ascribes to the generality of Western Christians.[25] Indeed they can probably be credited, as Dubos suggests, with being 'the first to develop on a large scale a pervasive concern for land management and an ethic of nature'.[26]

A recent critique

New light has been shed on the debate about **dominion** and **stewardship** in a recent essay by Peter Harrison.[27] Harrison points out that whether Christian attitudes to nature have been exploitative turns not so much on what the biblical writings meant originally or how they should best be interpreted as on how they were received historically. For 1500 years, passages about dominion over nature were mainly interpreted allegorically, as meaning dominion over our own rebellious animal nature. Likewise, the natural world was typically interpreted as supplying moral lessons (ants signifying industriousness, and foxes deceit). Since the lessons were for humanity, this was an anthropocentric approach, but entirely non-exploitative. It coincided with 'the transformation of woods and swamps into fields and pastures' on the part of monasteries, and with improvements in technology too, but without any sentiments of indifference or hostility towards nature, for the motive of all this activity was simply the universal one of meeting basic human needs.[28] It should be added that the evidence supplied above (about prayers for animals, etc.) indicates that it would be a mistake to ascribe to the Christians of this period an anthropocentric ethic (even if this would be Harrison's understanding).

With the sixteenth-century Reformation, as Harrison explains, allegorical interpretations were widely replaced by more literal ones, natural objects ceased to be regarded as signs or lessons, and dominion over nature (as in Genesis 1) came to be taken (as seldom if ever previously) to refer to human power.[29] It was this dominion that Francis Bacon (1561–1626) and his followers of the Royal Society (given its Charter in 1662) aimed to restore through scientific investigation, while the story of the Garden of Eden in Genesis 2 came to be understood as a mandate to work the earth to make it fruitful. Thus White was correct to find the creation story as crucial to the development of science and technology, but mistaken in locating this relevance earlier than the seventeenth century.[30] However, early modern science was not, as White had claimed, anthropocentric, for a succession of seventeenth-century scientists and theologians explicitly rejected anthropocentrism; indeed, the perceived indifference of nature to human ends is what made experimentation necessary. Besides, far from the new science being motivated by arrogance, disdain or exploitation, the aim was a restoration of the order and perfection of the time before the Fall.[31] So the new science (surprisingly enough) shared with much modern environmentalism the goal of the restoration of 'the natural condition of the Earth', albeit with a different conception of what constitutes that natural condition.[32]

More controversially, Harrison suggests that the long-standing distinction between attitudes of despotism and stewardship has outlived its usefulness. Explicit adherents of stewardship, like Matthew Hale, were expressing one aspect of seventeenth-century ideology, of which subjecting the Earth to human control was another, the overall aim being to restore its lost perfection.[33] But this interpretation may well underestimate Hale's originality, and the contrast between his stance and that of despotism. Harrison's view is far more plausible when he writes that 'during this period of history at least, the impulses of dominion and stewardship were directed toward a common goal'; for stewardship has long been regarded as a central interpretation of biblical passages about dominion. (The problem with Harrison's remark here concerns whether there is sufficient evidence that Hale's contemporaries, as opposed to his successors such as John Ray and Alexander Pope, shared his specific understanding of the role of humanity as trustees or stewards.)

Despotism, however, is another matter, as it conveys not just human control in general (ethical or unethical), but also human domineering or **domination**, as when humans treat the non-human world as they please, with little or no respect, and often other humans as well (as ecofeminists and social ecologists rightly point out).[34] Hence despotism and stewardship are incompatible approaches, and those (like Hale) who understand themselves as stewards perforce disown the role of despot. More constructively, Harrison proceeds to emphasize that belief in stewardship is entirely compatible with a theology for which the creator is not an absentee deity, relating only to humanity,[35] but is also concerned for, and possibly present in, the entirety of nature or creation.[36] Since one criticism sometimes made of stewardship is that it supposedly implies an absentee deity for whom nature comprises nothing but resources,[37] Harrison's recognition that stewardship has no such implication is a constructive and salutary development.[38]

Stewardship, then, is the most coherent available interpretation of the central beliefs of the Bible and of most of the subsequent centuries of Christianity and of Judaism (and arguably also of Islam)[39] about the relations of humanity and nature. As such, it contrasts both with the posture of despotism and, in typical forms, with the metaphysic of teleological anthropocentrism as well. The stewardship interpretation does not exhaust religious attitudes to nature. But its implications of human responsibility and answerability, and of the high value of the natural world with the care of which humanity is seen as entrusted, turn out to be coherent and defensible.

These implications have proved (and continue to prove) capable of inspiring environmental concern both among believers and, with suitable adjustments, among non-believers too. Recent related secular statements include one made in 2000 by the former President of Iceland, Vigdis Finnbogadottir, which extends stewardship to outer space: 'The Earth and Space are not ours; they are treasures, both literal and metaphorical, that we must preserve for our descendants',[40] and another made in 2001 by Alain Pompidou on behalf of the UNESCO Commission on the Ethics of Space: 'There is no reason justifying the appropriation of extra-atmospheric space by humanity'.[41]

Even if it is not the role of humanity to restore the natural condition of the Earth (let alone of space), the role of humanity as trustee, answerable to the community of moral agents, natural or supernatural, remains a significant metaphysical belief, capable of inspiring more specific principles of environmental ethics (see below), and capable also of motivating people to live responsibly. This is why the metaphysical backdrop of environmental ethics has been discussed first in this chapter. The time has arrived, however, to return to environmental values and ethical principles.

Issues to consider include the acceptability of regarding humanity as trustees of the Earth (this time on a less preliminary and more informed basis), the possibility of adhering to traditional versions of this belief, the credibility of its secular versions, and the spatial limits (if any) to which human stewardship of nature may be subject. A more refined understanding of stewardship becomes possible for those who reflect on belief in the Earth as the common heritage of humankind, discussed in a context of global citizenship in chapter 6.

The emergence of environmental ethics in the early 1970s

Environmental ethics was founded as a philosophical discipline in the early 1970s, with essays advocating a new approach to ethics from the Australian Richard Routley,[42] the Norwegian Arne Naess[43] and the American Holmes Rolston III,[44] and the publication in 1974 of John Passmore's *Man's Responsibility for Nature*,[45] defending the adequacy of Western ethical traditions. True, philosophers had been commenting on environmental issues (such as the loss of the top-soil of Attica) since the days of Plato's 'Critias',[46] and the metaphysical systems of philosophers such as Aquinas and Descartes had exercised a significant (and arguably undesirable)[47] impact on attitudes to nature. But, despite the works of philosophers such as Plato, Thomas Robert Malthus, Ralph Waldo Emerson, John Stuart Mill and Friedrich Engels,[48] it was not philosophers that alerted humanity to environmental problems. This was the role of the ecologist George Perkins Marsh, author of *Man and Nature* (1864),[49] who stressed the unintended impacts on nature of humanity. It was later (and much more influentially) the role of the forester and wildlife manager Aldo Leopold, author of *A Sand County Almanac* (1949),[50] one of the earliest advocates of a new ethic of conservation.

What brought ecological problems newly to consciousness in the 1970s was the nuclear arms race (and nuclear weapons tests) of the fifties and sixties, the awareness of unintended harms produced by the use of herbicides, fungicides and pesticides, as brought to light by Rachel Carson in *Silent Spring* (1962),[51] and the ethical issues (including defoliation) raised by the Vietnam War. The first professional conference on environmental ethics seems to have been that organized at Athens, Georgia, by William T. Blackstone in 1971,[52] at which a celebrated but essentially conservative paper by Joel Feinberg was first presented.[53] However, the growing awareness that human agency was destroying ecosystems on which both humanity and other species depended incited Richard Routley (consciously appealing to Leopold) to urge (as in the title of his 1973 presentation) 'the need for a new, an environmental ethic', which would be 'an ethic dealing with man's relation to land and to the animals and plants that grow upon it'.[54] A survey of Routley's and others' early contributions to environmental ethics will also facilitate here a discussion of the various broad kinds of **normative ethical theory**.

Routley argues that traditional Western ethical systems, being based on freedom to do whatever harms neither the agent nor other people, fail to account for certain increasingly widespread judgements of cases where human interests are not central or not at stake at all. Just such a judgement is evoked by Routley's thought-experiment of the **Last Man** (the last human survivor of a global catastrophe) who needlessly and aimlessly destroys the living animals and plants around him (out of frustration, perhaps). Most people who consider this scenario condemn what the Last Man does.[55] To account for such judgements, Routley suggests, an environmental ethic is required, for which human obligations are generated by the good of animals and plants (whether or not these creatures are ascribed rights).[56] While Routley's view can be challenged that all mainstream Western ethical systems (including the stewardship approach) marginalize non-humans,[57] his crucial claim is that no anthropocentric normative ethic is compatible with widespread judgements like the one just mentioned concerning the Last Man. Instead, he held, a new ethic is needed that can cope with such judgements. John Passmore was shortly to argue that traditions like stewardship already embodied the 'seeds' of an ethic capable of coping with ecological problems,[58] and more recently Routley's claim has been directly disputed by avowed anthropocentrists (see pp. 42–3, 67–73). Yet this claim has served as a challenge to theories both anthropocentric and otherwise to explain how they can deal with judgements such as that about the Last Man.

Meanwhile, Arne Naess was favourably comparing the Deep, Long-Range Ecology Movement with its Shallow counterpart. Positions in **ecophilosophy** are deep rather than shallow if and only if they are concerned with future generations rather than just the next few decades, with the Third World rather than just the developed world, with non-human species as well as human interests, and with cultural diversity and resistance to economic and cultural domination rather than uncritical endorsement of the status quo. Thus rather than just campaigning against the short-term problems of the inhabitants of the affluent North, such as pollution and resource-depletion, philosophers and ethicists should take seriously relations between generations, cultures, countries and species. The supreme value advocated by Naess (later included in the **Deep Ecology** platform, jointly devised by Naess and George Sessions)[59] was the flourishing or self-realization of all creatures. Relatedly, and as an explicit rejection of anthropocentrism, Naess presented as a key tenet 'the equal right' of all species 'to live and blossom' (described by Naess as 'biospheric' or 'ecological egalitarianism'), a right that was clearly ascribed not only to living creatures such as wolves, but to rivers and mountains too.[60] This tenet is discussed below.

For his part, Rolston too argued for an obligation to preserve the **integrity of ecosystems** transcending obligations based on human interests.[61] Here he was seeking to interpret Leopold's conclusion that the criterion of rightness is conduciveness to the integrity, stability and beauty of the biotic community. But where Rolston regarded this as one obligation among others, J. Baird Callicott (the pioneer of environmental ethics teaching in the USA) proceeded to claim that all value and all obligations turn on the integrity, stability and beauty of the biosphere, which alone have intrinsic value. Such holistic views are compared with rival approaches in the coming section.

Holism, anthropocentrism and biocentrism compared

According to Callicott, the value of individual humans and other creatures is instrumental, and consists in their contribution, positive or negative, to ecosystemic integrity.[62] While this is what Leopold, taken literally, seems to have been saying, this form of ecocentrism can easily be shown to be unacceptable. Thus the keeping and breaking of promises, having little or no impact normally on ecosystems, would each become morally neutral, rather than right and wrong respectively; and much the same applies to killing human beings. Callicott also maintained (on ecological grounds) that the human population should ideally become roughly twice that of the population of bears, disclosing the extreme implications of ecological holism for the value of individuals.[63] Clearly no recognizable version of normative ethics could have such a basis or content. (Callicott was later to retract the views mentioned here.)[64] We can conclude that no value-theory focusing entirely on the collective good rather than on that of individuals can even begin to be plausible.

At the other end of the spectrum of possible theories, Joel Feinberg's paper 'The Rights of Animals and Unborn Generations' made environmental obligations turn on rights, and ascribed rights to animals and (despite various misgivings) to future generations, although not to plants or to species.[65] But there is no need to make everything in ethics turn on rights, as Routley had perceptively remarked;[66] thus there could be obligations not to neglect the animals in one's care, even if no corresponding right belonged to the animals in question. We need to distinguish, as Kenneth Goodpaster later did, between holding moral rights (with its overtones of eligibility to make claims) and having moral standing or considerability (that is, warranting being respected and having interests taken into account: see chapter 1).[67] Whatever has moral standing clearly falls within the scope of morality, and this, as both Goodpaster and I later argued against Feinberg, can be held to include non-sentient living creatures such as trees and other plants,[68] partly on the basis that they have inbuilt, inherited natural tendencies and a related good of their own, with respect to which they can be benefited, and partly on the basis of thought-experiments like Routley's Last Man scenario, which appear to suggest that the plants as well as the animals destroyed ought to be taken into account.

These criteria for having moral standing do not reintroduce holism, since species and ecosystems are not living organisms and lack a good of their own in the sense just specified. (The sense in which species and ecosystems have a good of their own resembles the sense in which weather systems and traffic systems have a good of their own; but we are not inclined to suggest that weather systems or traffic systems have moral standing.) Thus Feinberg's conclusion that we have no direct obligations to species (by contrast with obligations to their members)[69] could still be accepted, particularly if modified so as to endorse obligations with regard to future members as well as present members. If all these actual and possible future beings have moral standing, there is no need to ascribe moral standing independently to the species that they comprise; and there is good reason to avoid ascribing it twice over, once to species as populations of members and a second time to species independently of their members. These obligations would then be an important part of the basis of duties to preserve species; besides human interests, duties to preserve a species are grounded in the moral standing of current and future members of the species, and involve allowing current members to flourish and make the continuing existence of members of the species possible.

Yet the holisms of Naess and of Rolston remain to be considered. Naess's belief in 'the equal right to live and blossom' might be re-expressed as simply affirming the moral standing of members of all living species, if it were not for his stress on their 'equal right'.

This, however, suggests that the members of each species have equal moral significance (Goodpaster's phrase) or importance, irrespective of their differing capacities, and would conflict with Singer's plausible view that equal interests (and their holders) should be given equal consideration,[70] relevant differences thus justifying different consideration.

Test cases include cases of conflict between the continued existence of a creature that has autonomy and wishes to stay alive and one lacking such capacities and wishes. In such cases, there is good reason to prioritize the survival of the first creature (whether it is a human being, an ape or a cetacean) over the second; indeed priorities of this general kind are universally embedded in ethical codes to the extent that autonomy is respected. Further, the readiness of Naess and many other ecocentrists to ascribe rights to rivers and mountains would be hard to justify. Thus Naess's principle should not be accepted. However, his concern that the fulfilment of the members of all the different life forms should be fostered (clashes permitting) can and should still be accepted, together with his concern for the continued existence of biological diversity. We do not need to regard the survival of every species as equally valuable as that of every other (another possible interpretation of Naess, but still an implausible view) to seek the survival of as many as possible, plus that of the ecosystems in which they participate. None of this requires an ecocentric theory, either of moral standing or of the location of intrinsic value.

Could there still be obligations to ecosystems, as Rolston suggests? His view that there are obligations that transcend human interests would clearly be true as long as either cruelty to animals or the destruction caused by the Last Man is wrong irrespective of human interests. Besides, to recognize what seems like a crucial premise, care for ecosystems is also of great importance, since life as we know it, with all its fulfilments, would be impossible without many such systems. But this importance could still be due to the value of the creatures these systems support, or of the flourishing of such creatures. Rather than ecosystems embodying all value (as Callicott used to hold) or at any rate somehow embodying independent value (as Rolston sometimes seems to suggest),[71] our obligations in their regard could relate primarily to living creatures, present and future, without the importance of ecosystems being in any way downgraded or diminished. If the phrase 'instrumental value' (when used of such systems, or of the biosphere) inappropriately conveys that such systems are dispensable, then it may be preferable, as Rolston suggests, to use the phrase **'systemic value'** instead,[72] partly in recognition of the vital facilitating roles of ecosystems, of the biosphere and of the evolutionary process. But recognition of holism of this kind (or, come to that, of James Lovelock's Gaia hypothesis)[73] is compatible with moral standing still belonging to individual creatures (plus the organizations that they consciously constitute),[74] and is not recognition of duties to ecosystems as such.

But was the rejection of anthropocentrism on the part of the pioneers of environmental ethics (such as Routley, Naess and Rolston) premature? While there are nowadays few explicit defenders of teleological anthropocentrism, normative anthropocentrism has several vigorous champions.[75] Their work cannot be discussed in detail here, but several strands of argument should be remarked, and will receive further discussion in the next two chapters. One argument, from Bryan Norton, concerns the shared evolutionary context of humanity and other species. 'Policies serving the interests of the human species as a whole, and in the long run, will serve also the "interests" of nature, and vice versa', because 'no long-term human values can be protected without protecting the context in which they evolved.'[76] (But these policies could fail to protect inaccessible tracts of nature, or distant tracts of the future.) Another argument has been advanced by John O'Neill. 'The flourishing of many other living things ought to be promoted because they are constitutive of our own flourishing.'[77] (But, granted the need for a broad understanding of human flourishing, does it really require the flourishing of all or even most non-human species? Arguably not. This debate is revisited in chapter 3.) A third argument, from Norton, contends that our obligations to future humans generate and support the same policies as those advocated in approaches that recognize intrinsic value in non-human nature and direct obligations towards it, since 'our culture's distant future' is at stake.[78] (But plausibly much more is at stake. We return to Norton's claims in chapter 4.)

For non-human creatures could outlive humanity for millions of years, if not extinguished by humans before the demise of humanity. So the non-human interests of this (hopefully remote) post-human period are at stake when extinctions are in prospect. But it is implausible that human cultural interests require the continued flourishing of non-humans across this period, or that human well-being in the present is constituted by *this* flourishing, or that policies devised to protect the human future will perforce protect this further future. Besides, large numbers of the planet's estimated 30 million species are currently being extinguished, many before they have even been identified; and it is again implausible that all or most of them (particularly the undiscovered ones) are constitutive of human well-being. Thus if, as most people believe, there are obligations to preserve as many species as possible and, in so far as it is up to us, ensure or at least facilitate their future flourishing, then these obligations must have some basis independent of human interests. Thus not even the combined arguments of sophisticated anthropocentrism show it to comprise an adequate or acceptable normative ethic. Some kind of non-holistic biocentric theory turns out to be needed, recognizing loyalties that transcend human interests without subordinating individuals to the valuable systems that make their lives possible. Such theories are discussed in the next section.

Biocentric consequentialism

The rejection of anthropocentrism involves taking non-human interests seriously enough for them sometimes to outweigh human interests. For example, baiting bears for the sake of human entertainment cannot be justified. Yet no credible system of ethics treats equally in all regards a creature that has autonomy (and wishes or preferences about its future) and one lacking such capacities (and thus such preferences or wishes). Interests in the exercise of sophisticated capacities such as self-determination require that these interests be recognized as more significant than those of creatures that lack such interests.[79] These interests also help explain why creatures conscious of their future should be consulted about it, instead of (for example) their wishes (and their votes) being aggregated with the preferences of all other creatures and being weighed no more highly than those of the rest.

Some writers suggest that if interests such as those in self-determination are distinctively recognized like this, then human interests are being prioritized as such after all. Even if this position, they suggest, is not anthropocentrism, it is humanism in disguise, since the prioritized interests turn out to be human interests.[80] Yet it is likely that many non-humans share in these interests, and many human beings certainly lack them, even though these are characteristic human interests. So theorists like Peter Singer who prioritize such interests are not open to charges of discriminating on the basis of species (speciesism),[81] or of making humans more significant one for one than non-humans ('Greater Value Theories' in the terminology of the late Richard Sylvan).[82] On the contrary, they make it possible to combine rejection of anthropocentrism (with important implications for inter-species ethics) with respect for rationality and autonomy as well as for vulnerability, and thus with a recognizable version of inter-human ethics. A wider range of capacities than the ones Singer takes into account (effectively just those for sentience and for self-determination) needs to be recognized,[83] and a wider range of bearers of moral standing than just sentient creatures too, but he is right to acknowledge these capacities and their distinctive roles in ethics.

He is also right (I suggest) to hold that nothing but the difference agents can make to the balance of good over bad (foreseeable) states of the world supplies the criterion of rightness and of obligation. This view comprises the core of **consequentialism**. One strong ground for accepting this view is as follows. If reasons for action are ultimately grounded in intrinsic value and disvalue, and it is states of the world that have such value and disvalue, then the reasons that make actions, policies and practices right and/or obligatory must be grounded in foreseeable differences that can be made to the value and disvalue of states of the world. Hence it must be differences such as these that make actions, policies and practices right or obligatory, as consequentialists maintain.

One important implication of an acknowledgement of the role of sophisticated capacities like autonomy is that ethical theories that recognize equal moral significance in all living organisms are seriously adrift.[84] The level at which living organisms are equal (I have suggested) is that of all having moral standing (biocentrism). But moral standing, as Kenneth Goodpaster has argued,[85] is compatible with different degrees of moral significance. It would be wrong to share the last available water equally between a plant and a person both dying of thirst, and yet biocentric egalitarianism, strictly interpreted, suggests that this is just what we should do. Only when the different capacities and interests of different creatures are recognized to uphold differences of moral significance can a defensible and viable ethic be held.[86] Although egalitarian writers such as Paul Taylor (who rejects such differences of moral significance) advance defensible principles for practical life, and even principles of priority to resolve conflicts between these principles as well,[87] no such principles can be derived from his egalitarianism.

Nor does the non-egalitarian biocentrism of James Sterba fare much better. Sterba takes pains to recognize the importance of inter-species justice and the general desirability of non-interference, and presents one of the more cogent deontological versions of normative environmental theory yet devised. But in giving an overriding priority to the basic needs of all human beings as such over those of all non-humans, it pays insufficient regard in inter-species issues to complex and sophisticated capacities such as autonomy and the related interests of their bearers, which are in many cases non-human creatures.[88]

So we need to combine a biocentric understanding of moral standing with a form of consequentialism that recognizes the full range of capacities whose development or fulfilment comprises the good of various creatures including human beings, and which also recognizes the greater value of the interests that relate to complex and sophisticated capacities such as autonomy. Actions will then be right either when they optimize the foreseeable balance of good over bad (value over disvalue) thus understood (from among the interestingly different options[89] available to the agent, including inaction), or when they comply with practices that overall optimize the foreseeable balance of good over bad at least as well as alternative practices (or states of society lacking such practices). The inclusion of practices makes room for the rightness of complying with practices like promise-keeping and like just procedures, and makes this theory a form of **practice-consequentialism**. A theory that makes no room for practices such as these cannot plausibly be considered a defensible or a viable theory. The inclusion of non-human (and non-sentient) interests explains why it is called 'biocentric consequentialism', and allows it to supersede both anthropocentrism and Greater Value theories too.

Besides, without claiming that human beings have greater value as such, biocentric consequentialism can justify (as Taylor's egalitarianism cannot) giving water to a dying person rather than to a dying plant on the basis of the value of interests such as autonomy likely to be involved. Yet, unlike Sterba's variety of biocentrism, biocentric consequentialism would reject removing vital organs from autonomous creatures such as apes even if this were the only source of transplants needed to save the life of a severely mentally defective human being, or in most circumstances to save the life of any human being. There again, in cases of conflict between the continued existence of a creature that has autonomy and wishes to stay alive and one lacking such capacities and wishes, it supports preserving the former, parting company both with the neutrality of Taylor's egalitarianism and with Sterba's prioritizing of human needs over all others. While this is not the place for a detailed defence of this normative theory, it is appropriate to consider here some recurrent objections, and then to compare it with some rival theories, and thus to discover whether or not it copes with a range of challenges as well as or better than they do.

Recurrent objections include the problem of weighing the various goods of different creatures, and doing so from an impartial standpoint.[90] I have tackled this problem elsewhere.[91] Suffice it to say here that most people are used to weighing up how much good or how much harm actions with plural impacts on different parties will do (and to one course doing more harm than another), that intrinsic value admits of degrees which can be impartially recognized as such, and that practical solutions can be found by employing principles such as the equal treatment of equal interests, by prioritizing basic needs, and among basic needs prioritizing those of the bearers of complex and sophisticated capacities (whether human or non-human). If goods were radically incommensurable and could not be ranked or prioritized, such comparisons could not get started;[92] but manifestly they can.

Another recurrent objection concerns biocentric consequentialism's recognition of some slight positive intrinsic value in the flourishing of viruses.[93] In practice, however, the value of the smallpox virus will be readily outweighed by the losses to worthwhile life it is likely to cause in human and non-human victims (and so it should be destroyed). Even so, in the unlikely event of a choice between giving a lifeless planet viral life and keeping it entirely lifeless, there is a case for the former, unless there is a prospect for later colonization by higher, more complex and sophisticated forms of life.

A further objection is supposed to turn on consequentialism's implication that self-defence is subject to justification in terms of foreseeable outcomes.[94] But since there are limits to measures that are justifiable even in self-defence, we cannot assume that actions regarded as self-defence need no further justification, or that consequentialism is misguided in suggesting otherwise. (I have discussed the scope and limits of self-defence from a consequentialist perspective elsewhere.)[95] The time has come to consider rival theories.

Alternative theories

Rival theories divide into theories that reject consequentialism and work from some other basis (**deontological theories**) and theories of a consequentialist kind that seek to relate obligation to value and disvalue in some other way than that just presented. (Social contract theories, being non-consequentialist theories, form a subtype of deontological theories for the purposes of this classification.) I shall consider deontological theories first.

Deontological theories make actions right for reasons other than their optimizing the foreseeable balance of good over bad. When this is applied to single actions without reference to rules, it is implausible that actions could be right without reference to the difference to this balance that the agent could make. But these theories are more plausible when they justify actions as right simply because they comply with principles or rules (for example, of keeping promises, or, to introduce an environmentally relevant case, of recycling paper or aluminium). For principles or rules such as these do seem to make actions that comply with them right, and deontologists suggest that this is not because of the overall consequences of the rules or of general compliance but simply because of the rules as such (rule-deontology).

However, rule-deontologists have no basis for answering certain vital questions: How do we identify right-making rules? What is it that makes these rules, or compliance with them, moral (as opposed to prudential or pragmatic)? How could we set about qualifying recognized rules, deselecting outmoded rules, or adding new rules? And what are we to do when rules clash (as, for example, the rules about keeping promises and about recycling paper or aluminium easily might)? Consequentialists can cope with these questions by relevant appeals to the balance of good over bad consequences; but rule-deontologists usually have nothing whatever to appeal to.[96] **Kantians** (followers of Immanuel Kant) appeal to the conceivability or (sometimes) to the desirability of everyone acting in the way an actual or proposed rule requires. But these are fairly clearly the wrong tests. It would be conceivable for all fertile humans to have children this decade, but nothing follows about the rightness or even the permissibility of a particular couple doing so, irrespective of their various relationships and of the prospects for any offspring of their union. And it would be undesirable (even if it were possible) for everyone on Earth to bathe in the Bristol Channel, but this does not make bathing there wrong, or a rule forbidding such bathing right. Nor can conflicts between rules be appraised by asking what would happen in the unlikely event of everyone complying with one rule and infringing the other. Far more satisfactory is the consequentialist appeal to the likely balance of foreseeable consequences.

Another kind of non-consequentialist normative ethics is **virtue ethics**. While all ethical theories recognize the key role of the virtues, virtue ethics is distinctive in representing as right those actions that a virtuous person would perform, and (unlike consequentialism) regards virtue as a more basic concept than rightness. In its less plausible versions, no criterion of an action's rightness is offered beyond its conformity with one or another virtue. But this view offers insufficient guidance to agents confronting choices between different virtues, or facing situations where displaying virtues such as wisdom or loyalty threatens significant ecological disruption, or leaves avoidable suffering unremedied, or avoidably makes the world worse than other options would have made it.

In its more plausible versions, virtue ethics sometimes represents virtues as traits of character which promote the survival both of the individual agent and of the human species, together with enjoyment and freedom from pain for those affected, plus social cohesion.[97] This aspect of virtue ethics amounts to an improvement on rule-deontology through supplying an indirect criterion of rightness, not too far removed from the kind of criteria recognized by consequentialism. But the adoption of this particular criterion presupposes an anthropocentric value-theory which disregards non-human interests,[98] even if virtues like compassion and courage could be expressed in ways involving some concern for such interests.[99] Besides, this same criterion seems to neglect the value of autonomy and of the development of other characteristic capacities. These difficulties could be remedied by adopting instead a non-anthropocentric and less impoverished value-theory, and thus moving much closer to the position defended here. But the resulting theory would at best be tenuously connected to the anthropocentric history and Aristotelian roots of virtue ethics, and the resulting criterion of virtue would barely comply with the traditional virtues which themselves usually comprise the mainstay for adherence to this philosophical position.

Besides, a further problem would remain for virtue ethicists of this kind. This problem concerns their view that what makes acts and practices right turns not on the differences made by these acts and practices but on the differences characteristically made by virtuous persons. The constant arrival of new ethical issues, often arising from technological developments (for example, in medicine, computing and robotics, as well as in agriculture and resource management), casts increasing doubt on whether being virtuous could be sufficient for making right decisions. While there are likely to be strong (possibly necessary) links between good traits of character and right decisions, consequentialists are to be applauded for making the concept of right decisions independent of that of character traits (and thus of virtues), and for explaining virtues as traits or qualities involving dispositions to make such decisions or comply with independently justified practices. (We return to the environmental role of attitudes in chapter 3 and to environmental virtues in chapter 5.)

The only other kind of non-consequentialists who have something plausible to appeal to are **contract-theorists** or **contractarians**. The common assumption of contractarians is that the rules that self-interested people in a fair bargaining position ('a level playing-field') would agree to are fair and just, and that compliance with them is right. (The people supposedly have to be self-interested to make what they agree to recognizably reasonable. Besides, we cannot ascribe to them moral motives, because what they agree to is being proposed as itself the foundation of moral behaviour and thus of moral motives too, and so if we were to ascribe to them moral motives, we would be begging the question about which these are.) Given this assumption, the above questions about rules could imaginably be answered by applying the test of what self-interested people in a fair bargaining position would agree to. In fact for many practical purposes this approach upholds many of the same rules as practice-consequentialism. But it has fatal flaws. For there is no reason to suppose that self-interested people would agree to rules (such as rules requiring preservation of non-human species) that benefit either future generations or non-human species. If people agreed to such rules, this would betoken that they were not self-interested.[100]

Nor can this problem be resolved by changing the assumption so that the test becomes what representatives of *all* the generations would agree to. This is because some of the rules and practices needing to be appraised and justified are rules governing relations between different generations, and it is rules and practices such as these that contribute to determining how many generations there will be. But only if the number of the generations could be known without resolving the question of which rules and practices are right, fair and just would it be possible to discover what it is that representatives of all the generations would agree to.[101] So this apparently ingenious modification of the contract theory fails to rescue it. Thus contractarianism is likely to produce inadequate guidance for our practice, since it is skewed towards the interests of the parties involved in the crucial agreement, and these quite certainly do not include non-humans, and cannot (for the reasons just given) include all future generations either. Consequentialists, however, are free to take fully into account the foreseeable interests of future generations and of non-humans.

Accordingly, non-consequentialist or deontological normative theories all turn out to be unsatisfactory, and to suffer from a range of flaws that are characteristically absent from consequentialism. Given the inadequacy of deontological theories, consideration should now be given to those consequentialist theories which, instead of appealing to all the foreseeable consequences (as **the Total View** does), appeal either to average quality of life, or to some prioritized subset of consequences, such as intended consequences, the effects of acts as opposed to omissions, or the outcomes for actual people (and other creatures) as opposed to possible ones.

Philosophers, economists and social planners sometimes favour maximizing the average per person of whatever makes life worthwhile (**the Average View**) rather than the total, for fear that maximizing the total might require increases to the present human population. I have argued elsewhere that it does not;[102] significant increases above the present population of 6 billion are more likely to add to unsatisfied basic human needs (see pp. 86–9) than to contribute positively to the balance of well-being over misery and suffering. (Related issues concerning the human future are discussed in chapter 4.) But in any case the average view has more serious problems, even if it can be re-expressed to include the well-being of non-humans as well as human beings. For maximizing the average quality of life would in some circumstances make it wrong to have children (unlike maximizing the total). This could arise if the prospects for the children were for lives not quite as happy or fulfilling as those enjoyed by current adults, even if the children's prospects were moderately favourable. Thus the Average View could mandate the extinction of a whole society, or even, in theory, of humanity itself.[103] It could also, in theory, mandate the extinction of any and every other species capable of varying degrees of quality of life. Hence it should be rejected.

But might the consequences that count be restricted to intended ones? Where theorists suggest that unintended consequences have no bearing on the morality of actions, they are confusing appraisals of agents and their character (where intentions are highly relevant) and appraisals of the rightness of actions. For good intentions do not make actions right. For example, the planners of the Chernobyl nuclear energy plant probably had good intentions. Nor does a lack of good intentions make actions wrong, despite the view of Kantians that deeds are morally worthless when the motive of duty is absent.[104] Thus companies which conserve energy or recycle materials mainly to enhance their own reputation are still usually considered to be acting rightly. Since agents have some degree of control over the foreseeable consequences of action (and inaction), whether intended or otherwise, disregarding unintended but foreseeable outcomes would exonerate agents of responsibility in cases where (for example) foreseeable environmental degradation could have been prevented. Hence not only intended consequences should be taken into account when the rightness of actions and policies is in question, but all the foreseeable consequences.

Other theorists suggest that it is the consequences of our actions only for which we are responsible, and not (or not as much) those of our omissions. (This is sometimes called the **Acts and Omissions Doctrine**.[105]) Occasionally this is argued on the supposed ground that omissions have no consequences. But this is manifest nonsense, particularly in environmental contexts. If it were true, omissions to regulate industrial processes that damage the health of workers or of adjacent communities would make no causal difference and as far as their impact is concerned be immune from criticism. What is more, policies of non-intervention to preserve ecosystems could not be advocated on the strength of the effects of adopting them, and thus of the difference that they make. More often it is argued that we cannot be held responsible for not doing everything that we omit to do, because doing all this would be beyond our powers. While this is true, it distracts attention from omissions to do what we could have done, such as omissions to take action on occasions when we could have prevented serious harm, have upheld important practices or have brought about a significant balance of good over bad outcomes. For such circumstances, there is no good reason to treat the foreseeable consequences of omissions as any different from those of comparable actions. In general, there is no good reason to distinguish, in terms of responsibility, between what people knowingly omit to do when it was in their power to do it and what they knowingly do when they could have done otherwise (or could have done nothing).[106]

One final suggested restriction of the range of relevant consequences should be considered here. This is the suggestion that none but actual people (and other actual bearers of moral standing) should be allowed to count, and that impacts on possible people and other possible creatures of the future have no bearing on moral rightness. This restriction would deny obligations grounded in (say) the happiness or the well-being of possible people who could be brought into being, and thus any related obligations to generate what might be considered too large a population. It seeks to achieve this by confining moral standing to people (and other creatures) who either exist already or who are going to exist whatever current agents may do (and is accordingly sometimes called **the Prior Existence View**). It also implies that the people of the twenty-second and subsequent centuries currently lack moral standing, since none of them are yet actual or can even be identified at present.

But this proves to be an unfortunate implication, as Derek Parfit has argued.[107] It means that the suggested restriction (and the related version of consequentialism) cannot criticize a policy which gives people of the current century a high quality of life by severely depleting resources, and which spells a greatly reduced quality of life for the people of all subsequent centuries. For the latter do not count at all. It cannot criticize such a policy even if one alternative is a policy of sustainability that would produce a slightly lower quality of life in the present which could be maintained into the indefinite future, to the great comparative advantage of every generation after 2100; if the gains apply to possible people only, they count for nothing, unlike the losses for the actual people of the present. But faced with these alternatives, most people would agree that the policy of sustainability is far preferable to that of depletion. This being so, the suggested restriction turns out to have unacceptable implications, and must therefore be rejected.

To summarize, none of the suggested restrictions on the range of foreseeable consequences that are morally relevant is acceptable, and the same applies to normative theories that deny that the balance of foreseeable consequences supplies the criterion of right and wrong. The relevant consequences are the foreseeable consequences of action and inaction upon all bearers of moral standing, as biocentric consequentialism insists. Here it has to be understood that impacts on basic needs outweigh lesser impacts, and that impacts on creatures with complex and sophisticated capacities such as autonomy and self-consciousness (in cases where these capacities are themselves at stake) outweigh impacts on creatures lacking them. Actions are right if they maximize the balance of good over bad consequences, or if they uphold practices, general compliance with which would promote such a balance (practices like keeping promises), and obligatory if the difference made by the action or practice is significant and greater than that of alternatives. Thus understood, biocentric consequentialism supplies a normative theory capable of coping both with inter-human ethics (including the relations of countries and of generations) and with inter-species ethics as well. Its implications will be expounded in greater detail in the following chapters.

> It is for readers to judge whether biocentric consequentialism comprises a consistent, convincing and potentially comprehensive theory. Try comparing it with biocentric egalitarian theories, with contractarianism, and with consequentialist theories such as the Prior Existence View.

Meta-ethical debates

Is there any objectivity to claims made in the fields of ethics in general or of environmental ethics in particular? Can there be claims about value that are not dependent on human valuations? Are there any obligations that are not based on one or another perspective? Questions such as these (**meta-ethical** questions) cry out for attention. For if there is no objectivity in ethical claims, then our preferred theory of normative ethics may after all be no more than a matter of opinion, whether it be deontological or consequentialist, anthropocentric, biocentric or ecocentric, and no more binding either. The same would apply to all our practical judgements about what should be done both locally and globally.

Similar issues have long been debated with regard to ethics in general. Thus some philosophers have maintained that claims about value and obligation are neither true nor false (or lack truth-value), not being the kind of claims capable of these properties (or not being truth-apt). Instead they have suggested that such claims either embody emotions and attitudes, or express prescriptions or commitments; supposedly, the speech-acts involved in these claims do not involve the making of statements at all. Further, since these claims never attain truth, they can never be objects of knowledge at all (**non-cognitivism**), nor attain objectivity except among people who share the same perspectives. Only the briefest of discussions of these matters is appropriate here, since the primary focus of this section concerns the debate about the related meta-ethical issues within environmental ethics.[108] (Readers wishing to focus on that debate could omit the coming three paragraphs.)

Reasons for doubting non-cognitivism include the following. First, non-cognitivists too readily assume that utterances that express emotions, attitudes, prescriptions or commitments cannot or do not at the same time involve statements. Talk about what is right, obligatory or valuable could well involve statements *as well as* (say) prescriptions. (Non-cognitivists who do not make the assumption just mentioned have an uphill task to substantiate their case without this basis for denying truth-values to such talk.)

Second, at least some such talk must have truth-value (be true or false, that is), contrary to non-cognitivist claims, as it can figure in valid deductive arguments such as the following:

> If you are acting rightly, you will be praised.
> You are acting rightly.
> Therefore you will be praised.

But such arguments can only be valid if each of the premises as well as the conclusion has a truth-value. Besides, the initial premise can only have a truth-value if each of its component propositions has a truth-value, including its antecedent. Hence 'you are acting rightly' must have a truth-value in both of its occurrences in this argument. Further, while the second premise could be used to make a prescription (or at least an evaluation), this is not the case with the same words when used in the initial premise, as this begins with an 'if'. Yet these words must have the same sense in both these premises, or the argument would not be valid. Hence the meaning of 'you are acting rightly' must allow of its use both with and without an 'if', and thus in making conditional statements as well as in expressing judgements, and cannot depend on its distinctive use in making evaluations or prescriptions, again contrary to the claims of non-cognitivism. (Generally, the assumption should not be made that the meaning of an expression varies with the speech-act being performed.) Non-cognitivist replies to this problem have failed to carry conviction.

Finally, the suggestion that there is no knowledge of what is right or of what ought to be done seems to involve such paradoxical implications as that no one knows the difference between right and wrong, and that no one can ever know what they ought to *believe*, a view that would in turn cast doubt on all factual knowledge as well as knowledge of value. So we have already found grounds for preferring **cognitivism** (which says that there can be knowledge of value, rightness and obligation) to **non-cognitivism** (which denies this).

Environmental ethicists, ever since the 1970s, have usually been **cognitivists** (in the above sense), at least where claims about intrinsic value in nature are concerned. Relatedly they have often been **objectivists** (holding that such claims are capable of being true or false, and capable of justification on an unrestricted interpersonal basis). In particular, environmental philosophers such as Holmes Rolston III have argued the intrinsic value of natural entities or their states to be objective, not least because this is held to be the basis of our objective duties to the natural world.[109] As was argued in chapter 1, it is difficult to deny that the health of living creatures has such value, at least if that of human beings and other sentient creatures has such value. And as was there explained, the intrinsic value of the well-being of non-human creatures is held by philosophers such as Rolston not only to be independent of human interests (non-anthropocentric), but also independent of human valuations (non-anthropogenic). Some arguments against the anthropogenic view were also presented there.

Among other philosophers who recognize intrinsic value in nature, some adopt a less objectivist position. Thus Taylor makes such claims dependent on adoption of a philosophical world-view which he calls 'the biocentric outlook on nature'.[110] Taylor proceeds to offer a justification for adopting this outlook; thus it is coherent, compatible with scientific findings and fit for rational acceptance, and therefore has some degree of objectivity.[111] But it remains one outlook among others,[112] some of which deny intrinsic value to non-sentient (or even non-human) creatures. All this effectively makes Taylor's overall theory effectively a form of non-cognitivism, components of which (including beliefs about intrinsic value) are tantamount to commitments as opposed to statements. To this extent, Taylor's theory resembles the non-cognitivism of Richard Hare, who regarded ethical language as prescriptions, some of which are rational,[113] including some that relate to the environment.[114] At the same time, Taylor's and Hare's kinds of non-cognitivism embody some recognition of the potential objectivity of value-claims.

But even such positions as these are still confronted with the general problems for non-cognitivism, such as those presented above, including the various implications of the view that no one knows the difference between right and wrong, or (come to that) between the valuable and the valueless. Alternatively followers of Taylor could maintain that some knowledge of values and obligations is possible, but that this possibility does not extend to his biocentrism or its claims about intrinsic value. However, the suggestion that no claims about intrinsic value can be known even though some knowledge of (say) basic duties is possible raises insuperable difficulties, not only about drawing the line at intrinsic value and about knowing the limits of knowledge, but also about how basic duties could be known if nothing could be known about intrinsic value, the most plausible basis of such knowledge. For, as was argued in chapter 1, intrinsic value supplies the basis of all other kinds of value, and it is difficult to see what basis other than value there could ultimately be for obligation or duty.

Taylor, Hare and others hold that 'oughts' (including claims about value and obligation) cannot be derived from facts or from 'is' propositions and conceptual truths alone. But many philosophers have argued that such derivations are far from impossible. A famous example is John Searle's paper 'How to Derive "Ought" from "Is"',[115] in which an obligation is derived simply from the fact of someone making a promise, plus the meaning of 'promise'. Unless reasons can be given why such inferences cannot be made about environmental matters, the so-called fact–value distinction cannot be supposed to prevent knowledge in this area, including knowledge of intrinsic value. Thus if things are intrinsically valuable when there is reason to promote, cherish or protect them for no reason other than their own nature (as was suggested in chapter 1), then there will be plenty of scope for good reasoning about the location of intrinsic value (as I have argued elsewhere).[116] Awareness of this scope underlies James Sterba's recent efforts to argue from biological facts about harm and benefit to a biocentric account of intrinsic value without resort to Taylor's biocentric outlook, or any correspondingly optional commitments or perspectives.[117]

Some philosophers, however, may remain unconvinced by cognitivist arguments such as these. Yet even adherents of non-cognitivist perspectives can share in reasoning about responsibilities and policies based on the idea of value being what there is reason to promote, cherish or protect, as developed elsewhere in this book outside the current section, despite disagreeing with its central meta-ethical stance.

A number of philosophers, however, appeal to the view that there can be no value without a valuer, and defend adjusted versions of belief in intrinsic value. Thus J. Baird Callicott adopts an anthropogenic theory of value; it is the valuations of human beings and other vertebrates that confer value on its bearers, which (he adds) can still be valued for themselves, and thus intrinsically, and at the same time non-anthropocentrically. While Callicott recognizes that such value is not technically intrinsic value, since it depends on something other than the natural or other entity that is thus valued (and therefore calls it 'truncated intrinsic value'), he suggests that this is the closest defensible kind of value to the intrinsic value that he used to defend in the 1970s, and that ethicists such as Rolston continue to defend. As such, he commends it as the best available basis for non-anthropocentric belief in the intrinsic value of nature.[118]

In reply to this anthropogenic (or, as Callicott sometimes puts it, **'vertebragenic'**) theory, an adapted version of an argument from chapter 1 can be deployed. For this position implies that if vertebrates had never evolved, there would have been nothing to confer value on the well-being of flourishing creatures nor to confer disvalue on their diseases or premature deaths, and that because of this there would have been no such value or disvalue. So there would have been no reason for agents of any kind (intelligent extraterrestrials included) to preserve or protect them. Besides, since (as was also argued in chapter 1) 'having value' does not mean or even imply 'being valued' but 'being valuable', there is little reason to think that the universe had to await the arrival of vertebrates for its flourishing lives to attain value.[119]

Callicott accuses Rolston of not taking into account the (**modernist**) **assumptions** on which his own case is based, such as the distinctions between objects and subjects, and between primary qualities (mass and position) and secondary qualities (like colour), and their implications, such as that value, like colour, cannot belong to objects, but must depend on minds. These implications are supposed to undermine belief in objective intrinsic value, and to require a distinctively **postmodern** understanding of that concept. However, the position of everyone who has a position (premodern, modern, or postmodern) depends on the assumption that there are both objects and subjects (an entirely unobjectionable form of dualism); and the theory that colours are mind-dependent by no means implies that value (or, to cite Callicott's example, goodness) is mind-dependent.[120] (It may also be doubted whether colours really are mind-dependent. Would no roses be red if there were no minds to perceive them? But this question is more of a problem for Rolston than for Callicott.) Hence Callicott's metaphysical objections to belief in objective intrinsic value present no grounds either for rejecting that belief or for endorsing an anthropogenic or vertebragenic theory of value instead.

One final rival view to belief in objective intrinsic value should be considered. This is the view of Robert Elliot that all intrinsic value is relative to and dependent on a valuational framework or perspective. Thus talk of health having intrinsic value is short for health having such value for the holders of a specific perspective, granted the criteria held within that perspective. Ultimately there are no criteria independent of perspectives (Elliot adds) for preferring the judgements of one perspective over another.[121] (Thus biocentrism might be one perspective, ecocentrism another and anthropocentrism a third; ultimately, there might be no grounds to choose between them.) This position is cognitivist (because it allows us to know that things such as health really are intrinsically valuable from particular perspectives), but at the same time reductionist, in that it supplies a **relativist analysis** of 'value', and denies that any value can be independent of the perspectives or valuational frameworks mentioned in this analysis.

Two sorts of problems for such a reductionist account can be mentioned here. One is a version of a familiar problem. This account makes value dependent on consciousnesses, since in the absence of conscious participants in perspectives there would be no value. (This could be taken to mean that if there were no consciousnesses in any possible world there would be no value at all.) From this point onwards, the objection proceeds along parallel lines to the objection to the anthropogenic approach. The second problem is that if there are no grounds independent of perspectives to prefer one perspective to another, then not only every value-claim but all reasoning too is undermined, because each and every perspective is groundless. This is relativism that goes too far. There is no problem about accepting that there are many perspectives.

But if examples are biocentrism, ecocentrism and anthropocentrism, there are good reasons for selecting between them. And there is no reason to assume that such reasons must already belong to one perspective or other, and thus beg the question, if only because this very assumption would then have to be perspective-dependent and would thus undermine itself.

Thus none of the alternative theories to belief in the objectivity of intrinsic value turns out to be superior to this belief, neither non-cognitivism nor the anthropogenic approach nor **reductionism**. There is thus every reason to adopt the view that intrinsic value is an objective property, and can be recognized as supplying inter-personal grounds for action, and for judgements about rightness and obligation.

> Before proceeding, readers should reflect on how far the meta-ethical conclusions expressed in the previous paragraph are persua-sive, and what difference they make to the standing of normative principles and their practical applications.

Summary

Lynn White's influential interpretation of biblical and traditional Christian attitudes to nature conflicts with strong evidence sup-portive of a stewardship interpretation, to which Peter Harrison's recent findings, where acceptable, add new perspectives. Under the influence of Aldo Leopold, environmental ethics was initiated in the early 1970s by Richard Routley, Arne Naess and Holmes Rolston; their work suggests that a broader understanding of moral standing or 'moral considerability' (Kenneth Goodpaster's phrase) is needed, but this can be harnessed to a biocentric as opposed to a holistic normative theory. Biocentric consequentialism is introduced and defended as a theory of normative ethics superior both to de-ontological (including egalitarian) and to non-biocentric theories, and to theories that exclude any of the foreseeable consequences of action. Finally, objectivist understandings of value-judgements and ethical principles are defended against other meta-ethical options.

Notes

1   Lynn White Jr, 'The Historic Roots of Our Ecological Crisis'.
2   White, ibid., p. 13.
3   White, ibid., p. 11.

4   Val Plumwood, 'Nature, Self and Gender: Feminism, Environmental Philosophy, and the Critique of Rationalism'.

5   White, 'The Historic Roots of Our Ecological Crisis', pp. 13 and 14.

6   White, ibid., pp. 11–12, and 14.

7   White, ibid., p. 12.

8   John Passmore, *Man's Responsibility for Nature*, p. 20.

9   Passmore, ibid., pp. 3–40.

10   See further Clarence Glacken, *Traces on the Rhodian Shore: Nature and Culture in Western Thought from Ancient Times to the End of the Eighteenth Century*; David Ehrenfeld and Philip J. Bentley, 'Judaism and the Practice of Stewardship'; Eric Katz, 'Judaism and the Ecological Crisis'.

11   For parallel but more detailed critiques of White's interpretation of the Bible, see Wendell Berry, 'The Gift of Good Land', and Robin Attfield, *The Ethics of Environmental Concern*, pp. 20–32.

12   René Dubos, 'Franciscan Conservation versus Benedictine Stewardship', p. 119. For further discussion of White's theory, see Eugene C. Hargrove (ed.), *Religion and Environmental Crisis*.

13   Dubos, 'Benedictine Stewardship', pp. 120–3.

14   See further Susan Power Bratton, 'The Original Desert Solitaire: Early Christian Monasticism and Wilderness'.

15   Passmore, 'The Treatment of Animals', p. 198.

16   C. W. Hume, *The Status of Animals in the Christian Religion*, pp. 94–8.

17   See Sean McDonagh, *To Care for the Earth, A Call for a New Theology*.

18   See Paul Gregorios, *The Human Presence*; Andrew Louth, *Maximus the Confessor*, pp. 63–77.

19   Thomas Aquinas, *Summa Contra Gentiles*, III:II:112(1).

20   White, 'The Historic Roots', pp. 14–16.

21   Dubos, 'Benedictine Stewardship', pp. 130–1.

22   Glacken, *Traces on the Rhodian Shore*, p. 213.

23   Dubos, 'Benedictine Stewardship', p. 134.

24   Dubos, 'Benedictine Stewardship', p. 136. Dubos's commitment to these views is evident from his co-authoring, with Barbara Ward, *Only One Earth: The Care and Maintenance of a Small Planet*.

25   A similar appraisal is in place of Peter Singer's 'Man's Dominion: A Short History of Speciesism', which comprises chapter 5 of his *Animal Liberation: A New Ethic for Our Treatment of Animals*. For a more detailed critique, see Attfield, 'Western Traditions and Environmental Ethics'.

26   Dubos, 'Benedictine Stewardship', p. 123.

27   Peter Harrison, 'Subduing the Earth: Genesis 1, Early Modern Science, and the Exploitation of Nature'.

28   Harrison, 'Subduing the Earth', pp. 94–5.

29   Harrison, ibid., pp. 96–8.

30   Harrison, ibid., pp. 98–102.

31   Harrison, ibid., pp. 102–7.

32   Harrison, ibid., p. 108.

33   Harrison, ibid., pp. 107–8.

34   Karen J. Warren, 'The Power and Promise of Ecological Feminism'; Steve Chase (ed.), *Defending the Earth: A Dialogue between Murray Bookchin and Dave Foreman*.

35   This charge is made against 'the stewardship model' in Matthew Fox, 'Creation Spirituality', p. 231.

36   Harrison, 'Subduing the Earth', pp. 108–9.

37   See Clare Palmer, 'Stewardship: A Case Study in Environmental Ethics'.

38   I have replied to this criticism in *The Ethics of the Global Environment* at p. 46, and to Palmer's other criticisms at pp. 44–59. See also Attfield, 'Christianity'.

39   See Al-Hafiz B. A. Masri, 'Islam and Ecology', and M. Izzi Dean, *The Environmental Dimensions of Islam*, pp. 74–7.

40   Cited by Khalil Karam, 'Ethics of Sciences: Extra-Atmospheric Space' (my translation).

41   Alain Pompidou, 'La politique spatiale: quelle ethique pour un homme en mouvement?' (my translation).

42   Richard Routley, 'Is There a Need for a New, an Environmental, Ethic?'.

43   Arne Naess, 'The Shallow and the Deep, Long-Range Ecology Movement: A Summary'.

44   Holmes Rolston III, 'Is There an Ecological Ethic?'.

45   Passmore, *Man's Responsibility for Nature*.

46   Plato, *Critias*, 111a–d, quoted in Eugene C. Hargrove, *Foundations of Environmental Ethics*, p. 29.

47   See Eugene C. Hargrove, *Foundations of Environmental Ethics*, pp. 14–47, and Robin Attfield, 'Has the History of Philosophy Ruined the Environment?'.

48   For Malthus, Emerson, Mill and Engels, see Passmore, *Man's Responsibility for Nature*.

49   G. P. Marsh, *Man and Nature*.

50   Aldo Leopold, *A Sand County Almanac and Sketches Here and There*.

51   Rachel Carson, *Silent Spring*.

52   See William T. Blackstone (ed.), *Philosophy & Environmental Crisis*, p. 1; Roderick Frazier Nash, *The Rights of Nature: A History of Environmental Ethics*, p. 125.

53   Joel Feinberg, 'The Rights of Animals and Unborn Generations'.

54   Routley, 'Is There a Need?', p. 205. Routley here quotes Leopold, *A Sand County Almanac: With Other Essays on Conservation*, p. 238.

55   Routley, 'Is There a Need?', p. 207.

56   Routley, ibid., p. 209.

57   Routley, ibid., p. 206. I have challenged this verdict in Attfield, 'Depth, Trusteeship and Redistribution'.

58   Passmore, *Man's Responsibility for Nature*, chs 2 and 7.

59   See Arne Naess and David Rothenberg, *Ecology, Community and Lifestyle*, p. 29.

60   Arne Naess, 'The Shallow and the Deep'.

61   Rolston, 'Ecological Ethic', section B.

62 J. Baird Callicott, 'Animal Liberation: A Triangular Affair'.
63 Callicott, ibid., p. 326.
64 Callicott, 'Animal Liberation and Environmental Ethics: Back Together Again'.
65 Joel Feinberg, 'The Rights of Animals'; see especially pp. 66–7.
66 Routley, 'Is There a Need?', p. 209.
67 Kenneth E. Goodpaster, 'On Being Morally Considerable'.
68 Goodpaster, ibid.; Robin Attfield, 'The Good of Trees'.
69 Feinberg, 'The Rights of Animals', pp. 55–7.
70 Peter Singer, *Practical Ethics*, 2nd edn, pp. 16–54.
71 This impression of his position is derivable from Holmes Rolston III, *Genes, Genesis and God*.
72 Thus Holmes Rolston III, *Environmental Ethics: Duties to and Values in the Natural World*, pp. 186–8.
73 This is the thesis that the planetary biosphere operates in a self-regulating manner, maintaining conditions suited for life. See James Lovelock, *Gaia: The Practical Science of Planetary Medicine*, and chapter 1 above. If the biosphere really were itself a living organism with a good of its own, then it too would qualify for moral standing; but Lovelock's hypothesis can be construed as holding no more than that it functions in some respects *as if* this were the case.
74 See further Robin Attfield, *The Ethics of Environmental Concern*, ch. 8.
75 Bryan Norton, *Toward Unity Among Environmentalists*; John O'Neill, *Ecology, Policy and Politics: Human Well-Being and the Natural World*; Tim Hayward, *Ecological Thought: An Introduction*; John Benson, *Environmental Ethics: An Introduction with Readings*.
76 Norton, *Toward Unity*, p. 240.
77 O'Neill, *Ecology, Policy and Politics*, p. 24.
78 Norton, *Toward Unity*, p. 241.
79 See Attfield, *Value, Obligation and Meta-Ethics*, pp. 82–94.
80 Thus Michael F. Smith, 'Letting in the Jungle'.
81 Peter Singer rejects speciesism in *Practical Ethics*, pp. 55–82.
82 Richard Sylvan (formerly Routley), 'A Critique of Deep Ecology'.
83 Attfield, *Value, Obligation and Meta-Ethics*, pp. 45–78; Val Plumwood, 'Nature, Self and Gender: Feminism, Environmental Philosophy, and the Critique of Rationalism'.
84 Such a theory is defended in Paul Taylor, *Respect for Nature: A Theory of Environmental Ethics*.
85 Goodpaster, 'On Being Morally Considerable'.
86 Attfield, 'Biocentrism, Moral Standing and Moral Significance'.
87 Taylor, *Respect for Nature*, ch. 4 and p. 263.
88 James Sterba, 'From Biocentric Individualism to Biocentric Pluralism'; *Justice for Here and Now*, ch. 6; *Three Challenges to Ethics*, ch. 2.
89 In theory there is an infinite range of options, at least when none is precluded on deontological grounds, as has been argued in Timothy Chappell, 'Option Ranges', *Journal of Applied Philosophy*, 18, 2001, 107–18. But rather than undertake the impossible task of deciding between an unending range of actions distinguishable only by

action-descriptions which shade into one another, it is possible for agents, when they have a choice, to choose from among finite ranges of options, typically quite small, that are interestingly different in their content and consequences.

90　O'Neill, *Ecology, Policy and Politics*, p. 23; Sterba, 'Biocentric Pluralism', p. 205.

91　Attfield, *Value, Obligation and Meta-Ethics*, chs 3 to 6, particularly ch. 6.

92　Thus Timothy Chappell, 'The Implications of Incommensurability'.

93　O'Neill, *Ecology, Policy and Politics*, p. 23.

94　Sterba, 'Biocentric Pluralism', p. 205. For an argument that none but foreseeable outcomes should be considered relevant, see James Lenman, 'Consequentialism and Cluelessness'. Lenman regards this as an argument against consequentialism, but in recognizing that consequentialism could be restricted to foreseeable outcomes, and that 'impure consequentialism' (or practice-consequentialism) may in any case be immune to his criticisms, he leaves the door open for versions such as that defended here.

95　See Attfield, *Value, Obligation and Meta-Ethics*, pp. 130–1.

96　See Attfield, ibid., ch. 7. Deontological works for which this forms a problem include W. D. Ross, *The Right and the Good* (Clarendon Press, Oxford, 1930), and Tom L. Beauchamp and James F. Childress, *Principles of Biomedical Ethics*; see pp. 37f.

97　See Rosalind Hursthouse, *On Virtue Ethics*, pp. 201 and 210, and 'Virtue Ethics vs. Rule-Consequentialism: A Reply to Brad Hooker', p. 43.

98　Brad Hooker, 'The Collapse of Virtue Ethics', p. 35.

99　Hursthouse, 'Virtue Ethics vs. Rule-Consequentialism', pp. 46–50.

100　See Attfield, *The Ethics of Environmental Concern*, pp. 102–7 and 141–2. A different form of contractarianism is presented in T. M. Scanlon, *What We Owe to Each Other*, which makes better provision for animals than most other forms. However, in excluding impacts on possible people and on non-sentient creatures from the core of morality, this approach seems to marginalize some foreseeable consequences of action that should on occasion supersede those foreseeable impacts that Scanlon's theory makes central. This suggests that his approach based on what we owe, or what we can justify, to each other is no more satisfactory a basis for ethics than other contractarian approaches.

101　See Attfield, *Value, Obligation and Meta-Ethics*, pp. 14–16.

102　For detailed discussion of the Repugnant Conclusion objection to consequentialism, see Attfield, ibid., pp. 149–73; see also *The Ethics of Environmental Concern*, pp. 132–6.

103　See Richard Sikora, 'Is it Wrong to Prevent the Existence of Future Generations?'; Derek Parfit, *Reasons and Persons*, pp. 420–2, Attfield, *The Ethics of Environmental Concern*, pp. 98–9 and 118–19.

104　See Peter Lucas, 'Environmental Ethics: Between Inconsequential Philosophy and Unphilosophical Consequentialism', p. 367.

105 Thus, for example, Jonathan Glover, *Causing Death and Saving Lives*, p. 92.

106 See Attfield, 'Supererogation and Double Standards'. For a recent defence of the Acts and Omissions Distinction, see Timothy Chappell, 'Two Distinctions that do make a Difference: The Action/Omission Distinction and the Principle of Double Effect'.

107 See Parfit, *Reasons and Persons*, pp. 362–3.

108 I have discussed these matters more fully in *Value, Obligation and Meta-Ethics*, chs 12–14.

109 See Holmes Rolston III, *Environmental Ethics: Duties to and Values in the Natural World*.

110 Taylor, *Respect for Nature*, pp. 44–5.

111 Taylor, ibid., pp. 158–67.

112 Taylor, ibid., pp. 167–8.

113 See R. M. Hare, *Moral Thinking: Its Levels, Method and Point*.

114 Examples can be found in his essay 'Moral Reasoning About the Environment', in R. M. Hare, *Essays on Political Morality*, pp. 236–53.

115 John Searle, 'How to Derive "Ought" from "Is"'.

116 Attfield, *Value, Obligation and Meta-Ethics*, ch. 3.

117 See Sterba, 'From Biocentric Individualism to Biocentric Pluralism'; also *Three Challenges to Ethics*.

118 Callicott, 'Rolston on Intrinsic Value: A Deconstruction', *Environmental Ethics*, 14 (1992), pp. 129–43.

119 For a more detailed discussion of Callicott's anthropogenic theory, see Attfield, 'Evolution, Theodicy and Value', pp. 283–5.

120 See Attfield, *Value, Obligation and Meta-Ethics*, pp. 21–3; also Attfield, 'Postmodernism, Value and Objectivity'. Arran E. Gare, in *Postmodernism and the Environmental Crisis*, adds at p. 87 that postmodernism is ecocentric; however, such ecocentrism has been appraised above.

121 Robert Elliot, 'Intrinsic Value, Environmental Obligation, and Naturalness'; *Faking Nature: The Ethics of Environmental Restoration*, pp. 30–41. This position is discussed in Robin Attfield, 'Postmodernism, Value and Objectivity'.

Further Reading

Harrison, Peter, 'Subduing the Earth: Genesis 1, Early Modern Science, and the Exploitation of Nature', *Journal of Religion*, 79 (1999), 86–109; casts new light on stewardship.

Attfield, Robin, *Value, Obligation and Meta-Ethics* (Éditions Rodopi, Amsterdam and Atlanta, GA, 1995); see chs 2–6 (on value), 7–9 (on normative ethics), 12–14 (on meta-ethics). A more detailed study of normative and meta-ethical questions.

Elliot, Robert, *Faking Nature: The Ethics of Environmental Restoration* (Routledge, London and New York, 1997); Elliot's perspectival reductionism is defended at pp. 30–41.

Attfield, Robin, *The Ethics of the Global Environment* (Edinburgh University Press, Edinburgh, and Purdue University Press, West Lafayette, IN,

1999), chs 2 (on normative ethics) and 3 (on stewardship). Ch. 3 defends a possible secular version of stewardship.

Rolston, Holmes III, *Environmental Ethics: Duties to and Values in The Natural World* (Temple University Press, Philadelphia, 1983); see pp. 112–17 for Rolston's appraisal of the anthropogenic theory.

Some Useful Websites

http://www.jri.org.uk/ The John Ray Initiative; has information on events relating to stewardship.

www.srforum.org The Science and Religion Forum; runs conferences on science and religion; also publishes 'Reviews' on works in this field.

http://ethics.acusd.edu/Applied/Environment/index.html An Environmental Ethics directory.

3 Some Critiques of Environmental Ethics

Several criticisms of **environmental ethics** in general and of the normative theory defended here will be introduced and discussed in this chapter. While some maintain that normative theories need look no further than to human interests, or at least to the interests of sentient creatures, others suggest that the role and impact of ethical theories in general can at best be negligible. In reply to these various criticisms I shall argue that normative theories that transcend **anthropocentrism** and **sentientism**, far from being futile or vacuous, make a distinctive difference, and that the role and impact of **normative ethics** are significant (not least, though not only) through **ethical consumerism** and ethical investment, and have the potential to become more significant still. Finally, in the light of specific criticisms of **biocentric consequentialism**, its implications for population levels and for environmental protection are further clarified and defended.

Environmental ethics, motivation and the good life

The first critique of environmental ethics needing to be considered involves a defence of **anthropocentrism** that appeals to what is involved in a good human life. It suggests that appeals to what is involved in a good human life allow environmental ethics to stir people to action (a valuable part of the truth about motivation), and also, less plausibly, that in the absence of such appeals no one would ever be motivated to do as normative principles suggest that they should. At the same time it sometimes suggests that non-anthropocentric theories actually fail as theories, supplying neither inspiration nor guidance nor even coherence.

All this is most explicitly claimed by Janna Thompson in 'A Refutation of Environmental Ethics'.[1] Thompson, however, is not rejecting environmental ethics as a subject, but rather those approaches that are non-anthropocentric or (more accurately) non-sentientist (locating moral standing and intrinsic value in non-sentient as well as in sentient beings), for this is what she means by 'environmental ethics'. As I have explained in chapter 1, I regard it as misleading to define 'environmental ethics' in such a way that anthropocentric and sentientist approaches are excluded, for this implies that the valuable contributions that (for example) Thompson herself has made to environmental philosophy (noted, for example, in chapter 6 below) have no connection with environmental ethics at all.

Yet Thompson could still be right on the substantive issues that she raises. Natural entities, she suggests, are valuable because they enhance our lives. In part, our lives can be enhanced through the spiritual enrichment involved in living in harmony with nature; other enhancements consist in our appreciation of natural processes for what they are, and, she could readily add, in our appreciation of the beauty of the natural world. If so, she argues, there is no need to postulate intrinsic value in nature to account for its having value in a non-instrumental sense.[2]

Thompson also criticizes all the varieties of non-sentientist environmental ethics, claiming that no non-arbitrary reasons are available to justify claims about the intrinsic value of the well-being or flourishing of living organisms, and that once value is located in entities that have a good but lack a point of view there is no reason not to locate value in just anything and everything. Such a theory, however, would be vacuous, and would give no guidance for our practice.[3] But this part of Thompson's case is more effective against some theories than others, and is unconvincing as a refutation of its comprehensive range of intended targets. For as Kenneth Goodpaster has argued, it makes no sense to ascribe moral standing to things that lack a good of their own (like rocks and machines), since they cannot be harmed or benefited (as opposed to merely being damaged or reconstructed),[4] and for the same reason it makes no sense to claim to find intrinsic value in their states, since none of their states begins to compare with such recognized intrinsic goods as well-being or health.

Hence there are good reasons to hold that some aspects of nature have intrinsic value and that others lack such value, while there are further reasons to hold that some have greater intrinsic value than others (see the discussion of creatures capable of autonomy in chapter 2), and relatedly that specific actions and policies that recognize intrinsic value (and the difference between greater and smaller degrees of it) are preferable to ones that do not. And there are equally good reasons against treating everything as intrinsically valuable without discrimination. So non-anthropocentric and non-sentientist theories (such as the one presented in chapter 2) need not be arbitrary, vacuous or incoherent, and are well capable of supplying practical guidance (for example, along lines that will become apparent in subsequent chapters, and to which the biocentric component of the normative theory presented here proves to make a tangible difference). Having presented a fuller reply to Thompson elsewhere,[5] I must now return to her more positive case.

This kind of case is supplemented by David Cooper and by John O'Neill. Cooper would (rightly) be unhappy with the goal of harmony (or even identification) with nature, for human survival depends on consuming natural items for food, drink and shelter, and also because 'for all our continuity with it, nature is also "the Other" to the human world of culture'.[6] Nature's otherness allows human society to adopt deliberate, distinctive cultural patterns and relationships, and also allows human individuals to discover or rediscover a sense of perspective as nature's processes (such as the flight of a falcon) unfold heedless of our often petty concerns. But appreciation of nature's otherness, including a recognition that animals and trees are not mere implements or resources, is itself 'an ingredient in the good life', facilitating a sense of proportion, and rescuing us from self-centred arrogance.[7] (We may note that this recognition of nature's otherness also involves a rejection of teleological anthropocentrism,[8] alongside adherence to normative anthropocentrism.) These themes add significantly to Thompson's remarks, for there are probably millions of people who benefit in these ways, and no account of human good can afford to disregard them.

O'Neill for his part relates the objective goods of natural entities to human well-being by developing an **Aristotelian account of human flourishing**, for which human good involves the development of characteristic faculties and capacities, granted the presence of suitable objects and circumstances. Thus 'the flourishing of many other living things ought to be promoted because they are constitutive of our own flourishing'.[9] Besides, the flourishing of these creatures ought to be promoted as an end in itself, he accepts, and not just as a means to human satisfaction or fulfilment. This is compatible with an Aristotelian ethic, and should be done because such care is in fact *constitutive* of a flourishing human life, just as, according to Aristotle himself, caring for friends for their own sake is *constitutive* of the flourishing of the friend who cares about them. The Last Man's act of vandalism shows him to be living a life below the level that is best for a human being.[10] Likewise, John Benson holds that the Last Man does real harm – to himself.[11]

These claims about what constitutes a flourishing human life, as O'Neill recognizes, have to be defended. The most promising approach, he suggests, is an appeal to the claim that a good human life requires a breadth of goods, far richer than, for example, egoism could recognize. The connection with care for the natural world turns out to consist in the fact that the recognition and promotion of natural goods as ends in themselves involve just such an enrichment.[12] Further, when our powers of perception are extended through disinterested study of natural creatures, as in science and art, characteristic human powers are developed thereby,[13] and this is a component of human well-being.[14] O'Neill recognizes that this is an anthropocentric ethic, but regards it as not objectionably so, since non-human creatures for which people care are not being treated as means or instrumentally. According to this ethic, adults would teach children to care for many (but not all) natural entities for their own sake, but the ultimate object would be not the good of the natural objects of such care but the good of the children. Human good would supply the sole basis for concern for nature, and thus the sole underlying motivation for such care as well.

There is more to ethics than these promising approaches allow

Although the position introduced at the end of the previous section seems to inherit the characteristic shortcomings of anthropocentrism (as discussed in chapter 2), it captures some important truths. One is its Aristotelian emphasis on an account of human flourishing involving the development of human capacities, including the capacities for disinterested love, care and friendship. O'Neill would need to supply far more argument to make it seem plausible that all our obligations could actually be derived from our living a flourishing life; but any credible ethic needs a defensible conception of such a life, and O'Neill's account contributes to such a conception, particularly with respect to his claim that a good human life requires a breadth of goods. Having argued elsewhere for a detailed version of an Aristotelian conception of human flourishing, incorporating non-distinctive or generic goods such as physical health as well as distinctive human excellences such as practical wisdom,[15] I welcome O'Neill's general account of human good. It well supplements that of Thompson and (though O'Neill's was written earlier than Cooper's) that of Cooper. Besides, incorporating physical and emotional as well as intellectual capacities in an account of human good also contributes to avoidance of the pitfall, against which Plumwood warns, of crediting unduly polarized distinctions between reason and emotion, mind and body, or humanity and nature.[16]

There is also good reason to welcome aspects of O'Neill's and Cooper's treatment of the problem of motivation for caring for nature. For the recognition and promotion of natural goods really can comprise an enrichment, as well as contributing a sense of proportion and a heightened sensitivity, and so the argument that caring for nature benefits human beings has substance for at least some cases. This argument also has its limits, just as there are limits to the argument against ethical egoism that caring for others characteristically produces net benefits for the carer. (For while it characteristically produces benefits, there are also predictable and persistent costs, and so the claim that it characteristically produces net benefits is an exaggeration.) Yet there is merit in this argument, which supplies one possible answer to the question 'Why should I care?'. As Cooper argues, alienation from the natural world, rather like alienation from the social world, is prone to accompany and betoken the kind of unhappiness and rootlessness that became so prevalent in twentieth-century society, while sensitivity to fellow creatures tends to promote imagination and openness, and hence a fuller and more satisfying (and thus a more flourishing) life.[17] To conclude from this that 'regard for other species' is 'an ingredient in a good human life'[18] would overstate matters, for many animal-lovers remain alienated from human society or positively misanthropic; yet its tendency to accompany roundedness and fulfilment should not be denied.

However, the theories holding that care for natural goods is constitutive of a flourishing human life (**the constitutiveness theory**) and that this is why we should care for and promote these goods (**the motivation theory**) are open to many serious criticisms. Thus while recognition and promotion of natural goods enriches our lives, so too could their recognition without their promotion, and so too could awareness of quite different ranges of objects of wonder, from mineral gemstones to synthetic gemstones, or again of human performances from sport to ballet. If what is needed for enrichment and a flourishing life is a breadth of goods, cultivation of natural goods is just one of the options, which could be replaced by cultivation of a range of languages or a range of sports or artistic activities, and which could accordingly be discarded as soon as a conflict with other human interests arose. Similarly, spiritual fulfilment does not invariably require it either, as a whole range of other modes and varieties are available. (It is much easier to assert that something is necessary for spiritual fulfilment than to supply the kind of argument needed to validate such a claim.) Relatedly, while the development (or 'extension') of our powers of perception normally contributes to human flourishing, this does not require the objects of perception themselves to be flourishing; indeed some branches of science, such as pathology, require the opposite. Even the science of ecology, for which a study of well-functioning systems is central, can develop the powers of its participants in studies of declining or disappearing species, or of the detrimental effects of climate change.

Besides, human flourishing, as I have argued elsewhere,[19] does not require the development of every one of a person's characteristic human capacities, although it does plausibly require that of most. Although blindness and deafness are liabilities, we would not deny that someone was flourishing or leading a rounded and fulfilling life simply because she was either blind or deaf. And even if we are lovers of classical music or of sculpture, we would surely have to allow that people could be flourishing who are unmoved by (or blind to) sculpture, or deaf to the delights of classical music. So even if the attainment of certain kinds of perception, sensitivity or contemplation relating to nature comprise fulfilments or developments of capacities that would contribute (in conjunction with a range of other fulfilments) to a person's flourishing, it cannot be inferred from their atrophy or their underdevelopment that a person is failing to flourish; for a range of their other powers (of physical prowess, of wit, of musical or artistic performance, or of other kinds of sensitivity such as empathy for friends) might be sufficiently developed as readily to undermine this conclusion. But if so, **the constitutiveness theory** fails, both in itself, and as underpinning for the motivation theory, since neither natural goods nor care for them are, strictly speaking, constitutive of a flourishing human life. To affirm that they are thus constitutive is, I suggest, wishful thinking. Indeed I can think of a philosopher apparently leading a flourishing life who professes no interest whatever in such natural goods.

Similarly, while a reflective awareness of nature's otherness can provide the benefits already mentioned, a comparative unawareness of it (as in failure to reflect on the world of nature at all) need not spell lack of perspective or absence of a sense of proportion. For these benefits could be derived from other sources, such as human conversation, experience of life's vicissitudes, or simply humorous exchanges. Such unawareness certainly need not betoken egoism, from which we may be rescued, for example, through participation in all kinds of inter-human relationships. ('Comparative unawareness' is mentioned here since every speaker of any language probably has some awareness of the contrast between the givenness of nature and the somewhat less inflexible realm of human choice.) Hence, while some basic awareness of nature's otherness may be a precondition of human life and thus human flourishing, explicit or reflective awareness of this otherness cannot be regarded as constitutive of or essential to human flourishing, even though it can importantly contribute to such a life. Once again, there is certainly no reason apparent here why everyone should care or needs to care about natural goods or to seek to promote them; yet this is what environmentally enlightened versions of anthropocentrism ultimately need to show.

The gap between arguments from human flourishing and reasons to care about natural goods becomes apparent in further ways. Let it be granted that some natural goods are constitutive of particular people's flourishing. (This could be because of the contingency that they care about a particular childhood haunt or pet animal, and would become desolate or even fall apart if the haunt were destroyed or the pet were to die.) Even so, not enough natural goods are plausibly constitutive of the flourishing of enough people for this to comprise a sufficiently pervasive reason for their protection or preservation. For even if all so far explored places and all known species were cared about (by at least someone), it is fairly certain that unexplored places (such as the ocean depths and the waters beneath the Antarctic icecap) and undiscovered species (including the species in these places, and probably towards some 30 million others located in places such as tropical forests and coral reefs) are not constitutive of anyone's flourishing (see pp. 42–3). (Many such species are likely to be rendered extinct without even being discovered, given current rates of species loss.) Nor, in many cases where just a few people care about a species, is regard for these people likely to comprise a strong enough ground to outweigh the benefits likely to arise to humanity from building on the habitat or site on which the species depends for its survival. Some of the grounds for preserving species, admittedly, turn on future interests (to be discussed in chapter 4). But the present point remains clear: the particular argument from natural goods being constitutive of the flourishing of current human beings cannot supply grounds for preserving enough non-human creatures. O'Neill suggests no more than that it supplies grounds for the preservation of 'a large number';[20] but its scope turns out not remotely to correspond to the range of creatures that environmentalists and environmental ethicists would standardly wish to preserve.

The same gap emerges if we reflect on the future of the non-human species of the planet after the demise of humanity. While the future of humanity may stretch to millions of years, that of non-human life could possibly extend to trillions. But the post-human flourishing of non-human creatures is unlikely to be constitutive of the flourishing of many people, present or future, if of any (see p. 42). So the argument from human flourishing (including that of future people) supplies insufficient grounds to facilitate their post-human survival and flourishing through human protection of non-human species from extinction in the last few generations of human existence. Human actions could well make a difference to the survival of many kinds of non-human life across vast eras of the post-human future, but arguments from human flourishing would seem to have little or no bearing on such actions.

Yet a further problem for environmentally enlightened anthropocentrism is to account for the near-universal judgement that the **Last Man** (let us suppose him to be the last sentient being too) acts wrongly if in his last hour, for the sake of no benefit to himself, he destroys a healthy tree. Vandalism, admittedly, is a bad human trait, but there has to be something valuable about the object vandalized for vandalism to take place, and this would seem to have to consist in the intrinsic value of the tree, or of its continuing to flourish. O'Neill and Benson, however, suggest that the Last Man's act shows that he is not flourishing (O'Neill) or actually harms himself (Benson).[21] Of these responses, Benson's claim about harm is the claim that an anthropocentrist needs to make, for O'Neill's suggestion that the Last Man is 'living a life below what is best for a human being' does not show what is wrong with what he does.

But can Benson's claim be upheld? The Last Man's act may show his lack of sensitivity towards the natural world, but this tells us little or nothing about whether he is flourishing, or whether his well-bring is intact. (We know, from the description of the thought-experiment, that he has only a short time to live, and thus may be grieving at the loss of everything that has given life its meaning, but this is beside the point of whether his well-being deteriorates as a result of his action.) The above reasoning about whether understanding for and care of natural goods is constitutive of human flourishing suggests that his flourishing could well be unaffected, despite the wrongness of his action. If so, anthropocentrists would have to abandon the effort to find some harm to humanity resulting from that action, and sentientists would likewise have to abandon efforts to locate consequential harm to sentient creatures (since there remain no other sentient creatures). Yet if the action of the Last Man is wrong, there must be reasons why it is wrong, independent of human or even sentient interests, reasons that anthropocentrism and sentientism, however enlightened, cannot supply.

A related issue arises without any need for a thought-experiment, that of how to account for the wrongness of cruelty to animals, and neglect of the animals in one's charge. Anthropocentrists have to claim that this is entirely grounded in human welfare, and largely in the difference made either to the flourishing or the character of the human agent concerned. But we do not need to know whether the agent's well-being or character suffers or degenerates to know that such cruelty or neglect is wrong, and this would seem to be because the animals' suffering matters in itself, irrespective of effects on the agent. While this is not an objection to sentientism (and thus to Thompson's position), it is a formidable problem for anthropocentrist efforts to make human well-being, however broadly construed, the sole criterion of ethics.[22] O'Neill, Cooper and Benson are right to remind us of the breadth of human flourishing and of its far-reaching environmental implications, but environmental ethics (and normative ethics in general) has reason to appeal directly to non-human flourishing as well.

There is more to human motivation too

The motivation theory holds that the reason why we should care for and promote natural goods consists in human flourishing (of which these goods are supposedly constitutive), and is often defended on the basis that there can be no other reason for doing this. But this basis should itself be questioned. In one version it suggests that reasons for action always turn on the well-being of the agent herself. But if so, it would make little sense to appeal (as environmentalists regularly do) to the well-being of future generations, and it would be difficult to understand people who devote themselves to the well-being of other people, or of other species, or of causes that transcend their lifetime. It would also be difficult to make sense of genuine friendship, with its concern for the friend for her or his own sake. While, as Aristotle held, such friendship may be constitutive of human well-being, this kind of friendship cannot be entered into or fostered solely for the sake of one's own flourishing. Maybe, as Ernest Partridge has argued, human beings have a need for **self-transcendence**, for commitment, that is, to concerns and causes that transcend their own interests.[23] But commitments of this kind are not standardly undertaken to gratify this need, and could not in the normal course of events be undertaken on this basis. For if they were undertaken on this basis, this very need could not be gratified. Motivation, then, does not have to appeal to the well-being of the agent. (Much less, as O'Neill remarks, does it need to appeal to identification with what the agent cares about; we can be just as concerned about what we regard as other than ourselves as with our selves, however broadly 'selves' are construed.)[24]

A less implausible version of the claim that human flourishing underlies all motivation holds that reasons for action always turn on the well-being of one or another human being, who need not be the agent in question. This version is less implausible because (unlike the other) it can explain motivations like friendship, patriotism and loyalty to a good many campaigns and causes. But it fails to account for behaviour motivated by concern for the welfare of animals (except where there are social reasons for such concern, such as the contracts of a veterinarian with her human clients). For example, it fails to account for the motivation of members of the pressure group Compassion in World Farming. Similarly it fails to account for the disinterested concerns of preservationists, who are not invariably seeking to preserve their own local environment, but often seek to protect spatially distant ones, and not invariably for the sake of any humans that may be affected at that.

As O'Neill recognizes, there is widespread concern for natural creatures for their own sake. While it is true that this does not of itself show that the well-being of these creatures has intrinsic value, the above discussion shows that there must be reasons for this concern independent of the well-being of the people with the concern, and that there can be reasons altogether independent of the well-being of human beings. Further, the analogy with friendship suggests that there can be unconditional concern (which need not be grounded in one's own good) for the good of the other: of the friend, or, in this case, of the creatures concerned. We do humanity a disservice when we pretend that nothing can stir us to action apart from members of our own species and their well-being.

Nor must theories of motivation be confined to the interests of sentient species, or of species with a point of view. For example, the concerns of preservationists are not so restricted; and the Last Man thought-experiment (also discussed above) suggests that there is something of intrinsic value in the continued flourishing of a tree. There is also Donald Scherer's thought-experiment. Compare a planet without life ('Lifeless') with a planet harbouring organisms with capacities for photosynthesis, reproduction and self-maintenance ('Flora').[25] Even if neither has any potential to benefit any sentient beings elsewhere in the universe (not even through aesthetic enjoyment), most people take the view that, even if there is no value in Lifeless, there is value in Flora, and understand this as a reason to preserve Flora in the event of human plans to disrupt or destroy it. Flora cannot benefit these same people or other sentient beings, and yet its inhabitants are held to carry intrinsic value in a sense (such as that introduced in chapter 1) that comprises a reason or ground for action. (What point, indeed, can be attached to any use of 'intrinsic value' in which such value does not supply a reason or ground for action?) Perhaps, then, we also do humanity a disservice if we pretend (with sentientists) that nothing can stir us to action apart from the interests of humans and other sentient beings.

It may be concluded that a non-anthropocentric and non-sentientist normative ethic is needed to accommodate the full range of reasons by which human beings are capable of being motivated. Far from being uniformly incoherent or vacuous or yielding no clear guidance, theories of normative ethics of these kinds are actually needed if natural goods are to be recognized and treated seriously, and if the pool of human motivation is not to be misrepresented as lacking depth. It can also be concluded, with Thompson, O'Neill, Benson and Cooper, that human well-being (involving as it does the development of most if not all characteristic human capacities) supplies a broad (albeit not all-encompassing) basis for many kinds of environmental concern, available even to the most resolute anthropocentrist.

Readers are encouraged to form a view on whether an ethic that is not anthropocentric can motivate action, and whether it is possible to care about the good of non-human creatures, and also on the breadth of range as well as the limits of environmentalist arguments based on human well-being alone.

Can environmental ethics make a difference?

We now consider a different challenge, confronting most if not all forms of normative environmental ethics. It has been suggested by Barnabas Dickson that environmental ethics has and can have little or no impact on practice, whether at the level of public policy, of business decisions, or of consumer choice. Proponents of environmental ethics ('ethicists') pay insufficient attention to the socio-economic context in which environmental problems arise and are tackled. The context in which action takes place in contemporary developed societies diminishes almost to vanishing point the influence of ethical principles and attitudes, or so Dickson suggests.[26] So we need to consider whether environmental ethics is (as David Hume famously suggested once of reason in general) inert in matters of practice, or (as Hume's critics have maintained about reason) capable of making a difference.[27] Dickson's claims, however, embody a specific basis of which (unlike Hume's) a discussion here is necessary and appropriate.

Dickson begins by identifying and criticizing two assumptions or claims which he ascribes to a number of ethicists, including Leopold, White, Passmore and myself. The first such assumption is that certain general attitudes to nature play an important role in the causation of problems; these attitudes, which purportedly legitimate the heedless exploitation of nature, are dubbed 'legitimating attitudes'. While ethicists disagree about which these attitudes are, they agree that people's attitudes have a significant causal role. (A preliminary discussion of the role of beliefs and attitudes in generating environmental problems has already been presented in chapter 1.) The second assumption is that 'bringing it about that people adopt environmentally benign attitudes will play an important part in realising solutions'.[28] Besides the ethicists mentioned already, this assumption is also ascribed to J. Baird Callicott, Alastair Gunn and Eugene C. Hargrove. Once again, Dickson recognizes that these and other ethicists differ about which attitudes are benign, but finds them united about the key role of attitudes in solving environmental problems.[29]

Dickson's criticism of the first ethicist claim, in so far as it relates to the present and not only to the past, is that it pays insufficient attention to the social context of modern societies. For in modern societies most people are not directly involved in many of the interactions with the natural environment on which they depend. At most they will be involved in a few, and will often have little influence on these interactions.[30] (Must there not therefore be some individuals, such as company directors and leading bankers and cabinet ministers, who have a large influence on production, and others who jointly, through their work or potentially through industrial action, have a significant influence? Dickson seems later to recognize this,[31] but writes here as if the arguably significant attitudes of these producers can be disregarded.) Rather, most people consume the products of these interactions, and it is by consuming that they provide a signal to producers that consumer demand can be expected to continue. Hence the first ethicist claim should be understood as holding that legitimating attitudes have their effect by causing consumption that in turn causes producers to continue producing in environmentally harmful ways. (Should it not also be understood as concerning people's influence as voters, as Dickson later acknowledges,[32] and also as participants in campaigns, as signers of petitions, as suburban gardeners, as senders of e-mails, as shareholders, and as participants in pension-funds?) But this highly **mediated** (that is, indirect or distanced) relation between individual consumption and harmful consequences means that individuals are unlikely to see themselves as responsible for these consequences.[33]

Dickson goes on to suggest that in modern society the mediated relation between individuals and the natural environment considerably reduces people's sense of responsibility for their consumptive actions. Thus individual people interact with the environment indirectly (through other agents), as one among many other consumers, at a spatial distance, with spatially dispersed consequences, and in ways of which they are largely unaware; and all these aspects weaken the sense of responsibility that they might have felt for direct, unshared impacts on visible neighbours in their immediate vicinity.[34] Consumers of coffee (to borrow and develop Dickson's own example)[35] produce impacts on coffee production only indirectly, alongside other consumers, and on plantations and producers in several distant countries, of whom they can know little. If the producers are exploited, or competition undermines their earnings, or cash-crop production destroys rainforests, or reduces food for local consumption, or raises prices for such food, or even contributes to famine, the consumers are unlikely to feel responsible, even if such possible impacts ever come to light at all. The world economic system is perennially liable to have such effects, and consumers can scarcely be blamed for their participation. But I return to the consumption of coffee below.

Dickson's claim, however, concerns what people *feel* about responsibility (he actually says it concerns the '**phenomenology** of action', and thus agents' perceptions of their actions and responsibilities), rather than about responsibility itself. In a revealing chapter, Jonathan Glover has discussed the phenomenon of 'moral distancing' as a defence mechanism enabling people to inflict pain and suffering at a distance, and discusses as a case in point the doctrine of acts and omissions, according to which agents are less responsible for the foreseeable consequences of their omissions than for exactly similar foreseeable consequences of their actions.[36] Dickson too alludes to this doctrine, once again in explicating the feelings of modern consumers;[37] but if, as Glover argues and as I have argued elsewhere[38] and at p. 51, this doctrine is an illusion, then the issue has to be reopened of whether any of the kinds of mediated relation between action and consequences genuinely affect responsibility itself, rather than perceptions of responsibility. For example, no one could seriously defend the claim that spatial distance and spatial diffusion either make causal outcomes less genuine or exonerate agents of causing them.

Yet the issue is supposed to be the causal responsibility of individuals and their attitudes for environmental problems through their acts of consumption, and to this issue consumers' lack of sense of responsibility makes no difference. Even indirect consequences remain consequences, and when they are foreseeable (as when ill-timed official announcements predictably inaugurate an economic slump) we may even be morally responsible for them. Further, as Derek Parfit has argued, in modern society many actions, each of which has only a small or even an imperceptible effect, can jointly have serious foreseeable outcomes, responsibility for which is shared by all the individual agents concerned.[39] But importantly, the issue is not whether or in what degree they are morally responsible. If it were so, then the fact that they could not possibly be aware of all the distant and diffused side-effects of their actions (let alone omissions) would be highly relevant, for this fact makes many of these outcomes unforeseeable, and therefore not ones for which the agents could be held morally responsible or blamed. (Yet when campaigning organizations, like those mentioned below, bring these outcomes to light and publicize what they discover, agents can no longer claim exoneration simply by appealing to ignorance, once that ignorance is no longer beyond their control.) Since the issue is causal responsibility, the agents' ignorance is beside the point. Besides, it cannot be replied that this ignorance is relevant on the basis that in its absence these consumers would act differently. For this reply would concede that the beliefs and attitudes of consumers make a significant causal difference, which is the point at issue.

Can values contribute to change?

The second ethicist assumption is that 'bringing it about that people adopt environmentally benign attitudes will play an important part in realising solutions'.[40] According to one version, a small group of decision-makers are to be persuaded to adopt these attitudes. One objection is said to be that the 'small group' is hard to identify, but this is not a serious objection at all. The real objection is that the context of managers' decisions in modern economies includes pervasive pressure to keep costs down; failure to do this puts profits and sometimes one's job at risk. Hence even managers with the right attitudes will often be unable to adopt environmentally benign solutions. Supposedly, the ethicist 'remedy' would only work if this systematic and powerful pressure were absent.[41]

But this verdict treats the ethicist case as suggesting that environmentally benign attitudes are a sufficient condition of realizing solutions (which may be why the second ethicist assumption is re-expressed as the claim that 'the solution of environmental problems rests on the adoption of a more ethical orientation towards the environment').[42] Dickson well shows the falsity of any view that makes attitudes a sufficient condition of solutions, but it is not clear that any philosopher has held such a view, although the quotations from Callicott suggest that he comes close to this position.[43] The adoption of environmentally benign principles and beliefs could still (in theory) be a necessary condition of solutions, or more plausibly a condition necessary in some situations (and thus part of a necessary condition). Solutions might well be impossible if no one were trying to reach them, and if no one were trying to reach them (broadly) on the basis of the right sort of attitudes or policies, if not of basic principles. Beliefs and attitudes could thus interact with material economic forces in influencing events, as was claimed in chapter 1, and as I shall shortly illustrate.

Dickson's point about pervasive pressures also shows that environmentalists' efforts to convert corporate decision-makers to their policies are constantly beset with difficulty, but this is hardly news to campaigning environmentalists. Fortunately it is not the whole story either. For consumer pressure in the market place often obliges corporations to adopt environmentalist policies out of self-interest, just as threats of exposure by pressure groups can have a similar effect, quite apart from the effects of governmental regulation. Indeed corporate decision-makers are newly acknowledging awareness of ethical pressures from consumers, and a good proportion of institutional investors in the UK and the USA, such as USS (Universities Superannuation Scheme) are adopting, under pressure from their members, the practice of '**Socially Responsible Investment**'. This practice involves efforts to induce the corporations in which these investors invest to adopt (for the sake of their reputations and with a view to retention of market confidence) a stance of corporate social responsibility, not least with regard to their environmental impacts.[44] There are also occasions when developments in green technology give rise to new opportunities for creative initiatives, generating entire new industries concerned with recycling or pollution-abatement or renewable energy generation. Besides, awareness of environmentalist opinion sometimes supplies a tie-breaker between benign and more harmful policies. Sometimes these decisions cause new problems in other communities or other countries, a possibility of which Dickson warns.[45] But the partial and ambiguous nature of some solutions does not indicate that environmental activism is bound to fail, or that it cannot exercise significant influence.

According to the other version of the second ethicist assumption considered and criticized by Dickson, attitudes of the electorate in a democracy can inaugurate state policies, taxes and regulation of an environmentally benign variety,[46] and can thus contribute to desirable solutions. This approach recognizes the scale of the task for campaigners, and the need to tackle the framework in which corporations operate, and also circumvents the problem (supposedly faced by the other version) of requiring possible self-sacrifice on the part of key environmental agents. However, the economic pressures against choosing environmentalist options will be strong and pervasive, both from firms that stand to lose money, and from workers and unions fearing loss of jobs. Electorates may be persuaded that environmental policies would spell a downturn in the economy, particularly if the threats are 'direct and immediate', while 'because of the mediated relationship with the environment' the benefits 'seem more distant'.[47] Here, then, Dickson succeeds in showing the potential relevance of mediated impacts. Yet the other side of the same coin is the potential relevance of disclosures from campaigners and campaigning journalists of the reality of these impacts, however mediated; large numbers of consumers and of voters could be swayed in either direction. While it must be granted that the economic system generates huge problems for environmental campaigners, no one has shown that these problems are insuperable, and indeed Dickson eventually acknowledges that 'there is evidence that the electorate can be persuaded to go some way towards adopting environmental values' and modern states to introduce related policies and constraints.[48]

Dickson does not ultimately claim that either of the two versions of the second ethicist assumption or claim is untrue or unworkable, but suggests that ethicists are in error through representing changes in individual attitudes as crucial, and ignoring systematic pressures which could in practice undermine either or both of the versions of the second 'assumption'.[49] (He is probably right here, at any rate about some ethicists. Others, however, have attempted to take systematic and structural factors fully into account.)[50] However, the admitted viability of this assumption suggests that there is nothing intrinsically objectionable about holding it, and nothing objectionable at all as long as the problems and pressures are recognized. Similarly, if attitudes can play this role in solutions, it would be surprising if they cannot play any part in the generation of problems, although the second ethicist claim could in theory be held in the absence of the first.[51] For all that Dickson seeks to argue to the contrary, the claim that certain general attitudes to nature play an important role in the causation of environmental problems remains tenable, as long as their 'important role' is understood to be generally that of part of a necessary condition for the incidence of these problems (as was also suggested above in connection with solutions), rather than that of singly necessary or singly sufficient conditions. (While there is, as Dickson suggests,[52] an empirical or verifiably factual component to this claim, its core, with regard to the strength of the relation claimed between attitudes and environmental problems in particular, is defensible on an **a priori** or non-empirical basis. For no empirical basis is required for the claim that actions are typically explicable through beliefs and attitudes, or for the claim that all actions have causal impacts of some kind on the world. Granted also that environmental problems are problems arising from human interactions with the natural environment, there will have to be some human actions, and related beliefs and attitudes, that give rise to any such problem.)

One of Dickson's conclusions is that 'environmental ethics does not have a contribution to make to the solution of environmental problems'. This is 'because the solution of environmental problems may not rest on ethical change' (to which environmental ethics might have contributed).[53] Dickson is right if, by 'rest on ethical change' he means 'be secured by ethical change' (as a sufficient condition). But to show that normative environmental ethics has no contribution to make to environmental solutions, he would need to show that environmental ethics can make no difference at all (not even as part of a necessary condition), perhaps because economic structures determine everything. But he does not show any of this.

Besides, through conceding that both versions of the second ethicist claim may be workable, he has effectively conceded, to contrary effect, that the attitudes on which normative environmental ethics might be expected to exercise an influence really can make a contribution to the solution of environmental problems, both through the decisions of key decision-makers in corporations, labour unions and banks and through the decisions of governments and civil servants as influenced by the attitudes of electorates.

Environmental ethics, then, is not destined to be inert outside academic institutions. Furthermore, the examples cited are not the only routes through which beliefs and attitudes can prove significant. But I cannot say more here about routes such as the lobbying of pension funds, or even the crucially important route of environmental education.

To turn away briefly from high theory and corporate decision-making, we can now return to the example of purchasing and consuming coffee. For, besides key decision-makers, governments, and their electorates, consumers too are capable of taking into account the outcomes of consumption, however mediated, and acting accordingly. The workers on tea and coffee plantations in India, Sri Lanka and East Africa frequently receive very poor wages and live in squalid conditions, all of which are in some ways the mediated (indirect, distant, diffused, cumulative and/or inaccessible) consequences of consumer decisions and of the related economic structures. This information, however, has been publicized by **NGOs** such as Christian Aid and Traidcraft, which have also established cooperatives whose workers receive a fair reward for their work, funded by consumers in developed countries who purchase fairly traded tea and coffee at above-market prices.

Such consumers, in conjunction with Oxfam, CAFOD and Friends of the Earth, have also formed the International Federation for Alternative Trade and the Trade Justice Movement to promote fairly traded commodities and related campaigning. Fairly traded tea and coffee (and other commodities too) are available for purchase in a widening range of outlets in Britain, Canada, Switzerland, the United States and other developed countries, and this gives consumers concerned about the global impact of consumption opportunities to contribute to **fair trade**, and also to enhanced environmental health for the producers. Sales of fairly traded coffee have increased annually from the mid-1990s, and in 2001, according to Reuters News Service, were approaching 1 per cent of world sales. While no one expects these efforts to overthrow the world system of production, many consumers have taken up these opportunities and have thereby given many producers their only hope for the future.

Furthermore, NGOs have campaigned to ameliorate environmental impacts and to enhance conditions of production in many other cases. Thus the World Development Movement managed to persuade Del Monte to allow independent trade unions in its banana plantations in Central America, and has been lobbying other large banana companies to curtail the aerial spraying of their plantations with herbicides and pesticides. Compassion in World Farming has successfully campaigned for a Europe-wide ban on the rearing of chickens in battery cages, and is seeking to ban the export trade in live animals across the European Union, and in Britain to replace slaughter with vaccination as government policy for combating foot-and-mouth disease. Animal-welfare and environmental NGOs have persuaded the countries of the International Commission on Whaling to ban commercial whaling, and are putting pressure on companies that fish for tuna to use methods that avoid harm to dolphins. Friends of the Earth and human rights campaigners, having secured widespread public support, recently persuaded the construction company Balfour Beatty to withdraw from building the Ilisu Dam that (among other environmental impacts) would have flooded an ancient Kurdish town in eastern Turkey and deprived Syria and Iraq of vital water supplies.

Nor are these cases isolated. Pressure groups are often able to enlist consumer opinion to address the outcomes of consumer choice, however indirect, distant, diffused, cumulative and/or inaccessible. They reasonably assume (just as consequentialists do) that we have responsibility, as agents, for foreseeable impacts that we cause to happen, however unintentionally, and also for foreseeable outcomes that we allow to happen by default. They further assume that consumers have no desire to generate suffering or environmental harm in any of these ways, and that the related moral responsibility can be constructively exercised to solve problems both of environmental degradation and of injustice. While consumers cannot tackle all the interactions with nature related to their consumption, yet in an ever-expanding range of cases precisely this task can often be undertaken. In these cases, consumer indifference can reasonably be held after all to be perpetuating the problems (as the first ethicist claim suggests), and consumer participation can contribute crucially to solutions (as the second claim can now be construed as suggesting).

Campaigning of this kind can even make an impact on economic structures. Thus the Jubilee 2000 Campaign to secure the cancellation of developing countries' unrepayable debt seems actually to have proved crucial in persuading several countries to renounce bilateral debt of this kind, and even to achieve some amount of debt alleviation on the part of multilateral bodies like the World Bank. In the most spectacular event of this 'Drop the Debt' Campaign, 100,000 people surrounded the English city of Birmingham during the G8 Summit held there in 1998. This campaign was as relevant to environmental as to developmental issues, for the need to service debts has frequently induced indebted countries to cut down their forests to fund interest payments. Relatedly, Susan

George has demonstrated a strong correlation between indebtedness and large-scale deforestation.[54]

While current international schemes for debt alleviation are admittedly inadequate, they are much less inadequate than the system that was in place before the Jubilee 2000 Campaign began. Thus lobbying about the terms of international trade cannot reasonably be discredited as a mere ploy to salve people's consciences as consumers and beneficiaries of that trade. It reflects the application of ethical principles both to the circumstances and to the structures of production, in which most interactions with nature take place. In doing this, it takes structural issues and their far-reaching implications seriously, and at the same time (fortunately) does not despair about whether the application of values can contribute to change. To assume that **normative ethics** can make no difference would involve forgoing in future many gains to nature and to humanity achieved by campaigning NGOs, of which only a few from the last five years have been cited here.

Readers are invited to form a view on whether psychological distance limits responsibility, and whether the application of ethics can generate significant change. Supply examples (for or against this possibility) of your own.

Does a consequentialist environmental ethic have unacceptable implications?

Besides critiques of the capacity of environmental ethics to motivate action and influence change, a range of further challenges should be considered that suggest the guidance generated by normative theories of environmental ethics is wrong-headed and open to objection, particularly where such theories adopt a consequentialist form. Consequentialists hold that moral obligations and moral rightness turn on the foreseeable consequences, intended and unintended, or both actions and omissions, and it was largely on this basis that environmental ethics was argued in the last two sections to have a contribution to make to environmental campaigning and change. Yet it is sometimes argued that consequentialist ethics mandates policies that could prohibit assistance to starving people or to developing countries, or produce overpopulation, or authorize large-scale extinctions of non-human species. While critics would be hard-pressed to present all three charges simultaneously, each of these charges deserves attention. For they are all serious charges, and the success of any one of them could serve to undermine aspects of the argument of the previous sections, and would also undermine the normative theory (biocentric consequentialism) adopted in chapter 2.

The first challenge arises from the lifeboat ethics of Garrett Hardin, who argues that countries resemble lifeboats, and that well-equipped lifeboats should not (indeed are obligated not to) render assistance to the ill-equipped, crowded lifeboats that represent developing countries with populations close to their **carrying capacity**. The consequences of rendering assistance will be increases to population, increased starvation and also greater destruction of the environment. Thus assistance makes matters worse, and on a consequentialist basis is entirely unallowable. The same applies to taking people from struggling boats on board well-equipped boats; for the well-equipped boats will then either reach or exceed their own carrying capacity, and all on board will drown. The way to minimize evils and maximize survival is to refuse assistance, and to prohibit immigration too. While Hardin actually endorses these implications,[55] they form a challenge for all who believe in humanitarian assistance, particularly those who endorse consequentialist ethics.

However, Jesper Ryberg has shown that these conclusions can (and should) be rejected without discarding consequentialist ethics. This is partly because of two theories about population, each of them defensible, despite rejection by Hardin. One is **the child-survival hypothesis**: when the chances of child-survival are increased through improved nutrition and medical facilities, the average number of pregnancies and births tends to decrease, because parents perceive that enough children will live through and beyond their own old age. The related **demographic transition theory** maintains that when standards of living in poor countries improve, these countries tend (like developed countries before them) to undergo a transition from high death rates and fertility rates to low ones.

If these two theories are right, then the bad consequences predicted by Hardin can foreseeably be avoided. But in any case it is unclear that assistance must make matters worse. For assistance rendered on a sustainable basis could raise the carrying capacity of a poor country, and thus sustainably support more lives with satisfied basic human needs, without involving commitments to ever increasing assistance and without causing a spiralling of population growth, starvation, or environmental destruction. Consequentialists who recognize positive value in the satisfaction of human needs and the fulfilments that it facilitates would have to recognize this policy as desirable, at least if, with Ryberg, they reject Hardin's claim that such a policy would prove ruinous to the donors. (On the same basis, there would also be a case for allowing some amount of immigration, at least to facilitate the education and training necessary for these developments, but Ryberg does not mention this.) What makes all this possible is the fact that 'With respect to countries, the carrying capacity is changeable.'[56]

Ryberg's remark about carrying capacities reflects a distinction made by William Aiken. The biological concept of carrying capacity (the capacity of a particular territory to support no more than a certain fixed number of a given non-human species) should not be confused or conflated with that of a territory's carrying capacity with respect to human beings. The human carrying capacity of a country depends on factors such as markets and their regulation, and can be increased by practices such as aid and trade. Hence for human beings 'carrying capacity' is a socio-economic concept; and claims that a country has exceeded its carrying capacity are not so much contributions to social science as covert judgements that no international measures can or should be undertaken to allow it to support its population. Such claims may even express a desire to protect more affluent places,[57] or a refusal to take steps to facilitate sustainable development in that country, or to assist its efforts to protect its environment. Hence Hardin's lifeboat scenario, dependent as it is on the struggling lifeboats symbolizing countries that have exceeded their human carrying capacity, is fundamentally flawed. Consequentialism, then, precludes neither famine-relief, nor development aid, nor international measures to make economic and social **development** sustainable and to protect Third World species, and may well, in certain circumstances, call for such policies.

Nevertheless it is sometimes argued that consequentialism requires perpetual additions to the human population of the planet with a view to maximizing the total of happiness, and that this would involve overpopulation, with predictable attendant evils such as environmental degradation. There is a corresponding objection to consequentialism (which Parfit has named **the Repugnant Conclusion**),[58] according to which a very large population of uniformly but barely happy people (happy enough for life to be worth living, but by a narrow margin only) has to be regarded by consequentialists as preferable to a smaller population of very happy people. (Once it is recognized that other species have moral standing, this preferability has to be understood as conditional on the happiness of the larger population not being outweighed by harm done to other creatures.) But this objection need not be considered in detail here, concerned as it is with nothing that could ever happen on Earth. (There never have been on Earth populations of uniformly but barely happy people, with no one leading a life not worth living, no one more than marginally happy, and no great harm being done to other species – and predictably never will be.) It is concerned rather with possible worlds with enough planets and enough space to support such a population, and enough resources to ensure that no lives cease to be worth living, and also that no great harm is done to other species. (And this is a context so different from familiar settings as to be capable of significantly changing our responses about what is desirable and preferable.) Having shown elsewhere that this theoretical objection is not fatal to consequentialism,[59] I will concentrate here on the objection that relates to our own planet.

Although the objection was introduced as concerning simply levels of happiness, it cannot have any impact on kinds of consequentialism harnessed to a broader theory of value than one focusing on happiness and unhappiness alone (such as biocentric consequentialism) unless it is re-expressed to concern not only happiness but also whatever makes life worth living or has intrinsic value. In this re-expressed form, it claims that consequentialism requires perpetual additions to the human population of the planet with a view to maximizing the total of intrinsic value. We have seen that such an ethic can in some circumstances support famine-relief and development assistance that could either raise a developing country's population or at least prevent it falling through starvation and malnutrition. But the objection goes on to suggest that such an ethic also has to advocate continual population increases up to the point where further increases would contribute more to misery than to quality of life (or to whatever makes life worth living), and implies that getting to this point involves reaching a disastrously high population total (disastrous not least for the environment).

This is, of course, the contrary of what Hardin was taking consequentialism to involve; his view is that it requires that no action be taken that could increase population and the associated evils supposedly attaching to any such increase. Even though Hardin's view has been seen to be unsustainable, his implicit view that the evils associated with population increases justify an upper limit to such increases deserves serious consideration. We should note that the re-expressed objection would have to involve the addition of lives of a positive quality (lives worth living), since otherwise there would be no net increase of intrinsic value. And we should also observe that because this would involve the satisfaction of the additional people's basic needs and the development of most of their characteristic human capacities, there are limits to the numbers of these additional people in all circumstances where resources are limited.

Population increases will not always increase misery or the number of people whose basic needs are not satisfied, for sometimes there will be sufficient space and resources for these evils to be avoided. For this reason, the underlying problem is not in principle one of numbers. Just say there were habitable space-colonies where additional people could live fulfilling lives without causing environmental harm. There would surely be nothing wrong with generating these people with a view to populating these colonies, and thus with adding to the total human population and at the same time increasing the balance of value over disvalue. Or just say trillions of people could lead worthwhile lives, but spread out in time, with no more than 6 billion living simultaneously, all of them respecting the environment. Again, this would surely be a welcome scenario.

In the real world, however, space and resources are restricted. Where space and resources are in short supply, and there are already people whose basic needs are not satisfied and who are thus unable to develop their **essential human capacities** (as there are in the world as it is), population increases are likely to increase the number of people in this sorry plight, whether by worsening the situation of existing people or because some of the newly born children never overcome their very poor start in life. There might still be an overall increase in happiness, partly through the joys of parenthood and partly through the fulfilments attained by some of their children. But when values and disvalues beyond happiness and unhappiness are taken into account, increases in the number of people whose lives are not worth living count heavily against policies that generate such population increases. In these circumstances, then, consequentialism does not require us to increase human populations.

This suggests that consequentialism does not mandate policies that would produce overpopulation. Overpopulation involves a population level that either undermines the quality of life of many people through overcrowding, or consumes resources in ways that cannot be made good through inter-communal exchanges such as trade, or seriously disrupts the environment. But (granted a biocentric version of consequentialism) these are all serious evils, which, as foreseeable consequences, count heavily against policies liable to produce them. This is just as true at the planetary level as at the level of single territories or countries. Granted that the planetary human population is almost certain to continue increasing for some years, there are strong consequentialist reasons why the total should be stabilized at a sustainable level that would as far as possible avoid the evils just mentioned. (This is the point where, in view of the limits to certain planetary resources such as land and supplies of fresh water, numbers re-enter the frame. I have argued elsewhere that the total human population should if possible be stabilized at around 8 billion, or, if necessary, at as low as possible a level above that.[60] If space and resources were different, and environmental damage could be avoided, the sustainable total would not need to be set as low as this. But when ethicists reflect on policies, facts must be faced.)

Would biocentric consequentialism preserve enough species?

It has, however, been specifically argued by Alan Carter that biocentric consequentialism could authorize large-scale extinctions of non-human species. Biocentric consequentialism is held to imply that 'maximising the number of humans who have most of their essential capacities developed to some degree should be accomplished at the expense of all creatures which lack the greater capacities possessed by most humans (such as in self-consciousness and autonomy) when this would be the most practicable means of achieving that goal'.[61] (Essential human capacities are ones in the absence of which from most members of a species it would cease to be a species of humans; self-consciousness and autonomy are good examples of such capacities.) Carter also takes biocentric consequentialism to imply that we ought to maximize the number of people who have most of their essential human capacities developed to some degree,[62] a belief that we have already seen to be mistaken. However, facilitating the development of essential human capacities might still seem to threaten 'the extinction of many inessential species',[63] granted that there is greater intrinsic value in the satisfaction of the basic needs of creatures endowed with self-consciousness and autonomy (including most humans) than in that of creatures which lack these interests (see chapter 2), and that there could be competition (for example, for territory) between the humans and the relevant non-humans concerned.

While Carter does not specify which species are 'inessential', the context suggests that he means 'inessential for human interests and for the continued existence of current ecosystems'. He accepts that human interests require human societies to live sustainably, that biocentric consequentialism can recognize this, and that this involves preserving ecosystems. But he seems to hold that there are many species whose preservation is not indispensable in this regard. These will include the 'inessential species' that he thinks biocentric consequentialists could be committed to replacing with creatures having more value in their lives, such as humans. Although it is less than certain that there are any such 'inessential species', I will assume their existence in order to evaluate Carter's argument.

However, quite apart from human interests, biocentrism recognizes intrinsic value in the flourishing of members (present and future) of non-human species, a value that would be lost if current humans or those of the near future extinguish their kind. Countless possible future creatures which might have lived would in this way be prevented from coming into being. The large numbers of possible future species-members multiply the value of current members, considerably strengthening the case against extinction. Biocentrism, then, can oppose extinctions on the basis of value in non-human nature.

Carter, however, anticipates this reply. The loss of future members of inessential species would not, he suggests, outweigh (for biocentric consequentialism) the value of the human fulfilments made possible by the human occupation of their habitats which threatens these species with extinction. Granted that the basic needs of current humans who could occupy the habitat in question outweigh those of the current members of the endangered species there, then in every generation the same will apply, and human needs will outweigh those of the members of the currently endangered species that would have lived at that time if their species had not been driven to extinction.[64] Here the initial premise is wrongly expressed, for biocentrists would not accept that the value of flourishing human lives as such outweighs the flourishing lives of every other species. But this premise could be re-expressed to convey that the basic needs of creatures with relatively complex and sophisticated capacities such as self-consciousness and autonomy take precedence over those of other creatures. This revision at least allows Carter's argument to get started.

But his argument still miscarries, for it cannot be assumed that what holds for the present generation holds also for all future generations too. For both humans and other species possessed of complex and sophisticated capacities could well become extinct long before their fellow species (if the latter are not extinguished first by human beings). So there could be billions of generations of other creatures living without competition from humans or other sophisticated species. The value of these possible creatures is relevant to current decisions about whether to colonize or otherwise take over the habitats of their current counterparts (their possible ancestors), and would not be outweighed by conflicting human interests from the same generation. So the above assumption is both unreliable and misleading, and it remains possible for current and foreseeable human interests to be outweighed by those of less sophisticated species. Thus once again the biocentric aspects of biocentric consequentialism underpin a strong case against the extinction even of so-called 'inessential' species. Further, there is no reason whatever for environmentalists to find biocentric consequentialism disappointing, as Carter suggests they may.[65]

Clearly a parallel argument could be constructed for the preservation of most non-human species; in addition, arguments for preserving non-human species with complex and sophisticated capacities are also available, turning on the high intrinsic value of their flourishing in the present. Alongside these arguments, there are strong preservationist arguments from human interests, some scientific, aesthetic, nutritional, recreational, or symbolic, and some concerning creatures constitutive of the flourishing of particular human beings or human cultures. In some cases, such as the smallpox bacillus, the likely harms of the survival of the species probably outweigh all other considerations, but the need for this kind of verdict is likely to be rare.

Thus the normative ethic defended in the previous chapter has ample resources for supporting the **preservation** of almost every species, is not overthrown by challenges ascribing to it unacceptable implications, and proves capable, in addition, of supplying useful practical guidance relevant both to action and to policy.

Are criticisms of consequentialism on target when they claim that it either prohibits aid to struggling countries or mandates overpopulation or authorizes the destruction of wild species and habitats? Can biocentric consequentialism escape criticisms to which other kinds of consequentialism are open?

Summary

Janna Thompson, David Cooper and John O'Neill ably and ingeniously relate environmental ethics to human good, but make it turn on this alone. But there is more to ethics and to human motivation than their theories allow. In reply to Barnabas Dickson's arguments that environmental ethicists exaggerate the impacts of attitudes on problems and of ethical beliefs in potential solutions, arguments and evidence are given for attitudes and beliefs forming part of the necessary conditions of solutions; environmental ethics is thus capable of making a significant difference. Further objections, that consequentialist ethics could prohibit assistance to developing countries, or (as Alan Carter has recently suggested) require overpopulation and/or authorize large-scale extinctions of non-human species, are shown to miscarry; biocentric consequentialism is thus vindicated in matters of population and preservation, as well as of general practicality.

Notes

1   Janna Thompson, 'A Refutation of Environmental Ethics'.
2   Thompson, ibid., p. 160.
3   Thompson, ibid., pp. 148–59.
4   Kenneth E. Goodpaster, 'On Being Morally Considerable'; 'On Stopping at Everything: A Reply to W. M. Hunt'.
5   See Robin Attfield, *The Ethics of Environmental Concern*, 2nd edn, pp. 205–7.
6   David E. Cooper, 'Other Species and Moral Reason', p. 146.
7   Cooper, ibid., p. 146.
8   See Glossary. Despite this rejection, Val Plumwood would probably hold that the argument depicted here remains an ethical approach that has not sufficiently reviewed its various presuppositions. (See Plumwood, 'Nature, Self and Gender: Feminism, Environmental Philosophy, and the Critique of Rationalism'.) With this judgement I would in large measure agree.
9   John O'Neill, *Ecology, Policy and Politics: Human Well-Being and the Natural World*, p. 24.
10   O'Neill, ibid., p. 24.
11   John Benson, *Environmental Ethics: An Introduction with Readings*, pp. 18–28.
12   O'Neill, *Ecology, Policy and Politics*, pp. 24–5.
13   O'Neill, ibid., p. 81.
14   O'Neill, ibid., p. 161.
15   See Attfield, *A Theory of Value and Obligation*, chs 3 and 4; *Value, Obligation and Meta-Ethics*, chs 4 and 5; and 'Meaningful Work and Full Employment'.
16   Plumwood, 'Nature, Self and Gender: Feminism, Environmental Philosophy, and the Critique of Rationalism'.
17   Cooper, 'Other Species and Moral Reason', p. 145.
18   Cooper, ibid., p. 145.
19   Attfield, *Value, Obligation and Meta-Ethics*, pp. 45–62.

20 O'Neill, *Ecology, Policy and Politics*, p. 24.
21 O'Neill, *Ecology, Policy and Politics*, p. 24; Benson, *Environmental Ethics*, pp. 18–28.
22 Evidence is newly emerging that Karl Marx was not committed to anthropocentrism; see Lawrence Wilde, ' "The creatures, too, must become free": Marx and the Animal/Human Distinction'.
23 Ernest Partridge, 'Why Care about the Future?'.
24 O'Neill, *Ecology, Policy and Politics*, pp. 149–51.
25 Donald Scherer, 'Anthropocentrism, Atomism, and Environmental Ethics'.
26 Barnabas Dickson, 'The Ethicist Conception of Environmental Problems'.
27 David Hume, *A Treatise of Human Nature*, II.III.III. Relevant criticisms of Hume can be found in Julius Kovesi, *Moral Notions*, M. F. Cohen, 'The Practicality of Moral Reasoning', and in Renford Bambrough, *Moral Scepticism and Moral Knowledge*.
28 Dickson, 'The Ethicist Conception', p. 132.
29 Dickson, ibid., p. 135.
30 Dickson, ibid., p. 138.
31 Dickson, ibid., pp. 143–5.
32 Dickson, ibid., pp. 145–7.
33 Dickson, ibid., p. 139.
34 Dickson, ibid., pp. 139–42.
35 Dickson, ibid., pp. 140–1.
36 Jonathan Glover, 'Moral Distance', ch. 20 of his *Causing Death and Saving Lives*, pp. 286–97.
37 Dickson, 'The Ethicist Conception', p. 140.
38 Glover, *Causing Death and Saving Lives*, pp. 92–102; Attfield, *Value, Obligation and Meta-Ethics*, pp. 117–28.
39 Derek Parfit, *Reasons and Persons*, pp. 70–86.
40 Dickson, 'The Ethicist Conception', p. 132.
41 Dickson, ibid., p. 145.
42 Dickson, ibid., p. 143.
43 Dickson, ibid., p. 133. Dickson is quoting from J. Baird Callicott, 'Environmental Philosophy is Environmental Activism: The Most Radical and Effective Kind'.
44 Peter Moon and Raj Thamotheram, 'Corporations Become Socially Responsible: Businesses around the World are Acting on the Growing Backlash against Global Capitalism'. See also the six contributions on 'Ethics and Corporate Responsibility' in Rosamund M. Thomas (ed.), *Teaching Ethics, Volume Three: Environmental Ethics*.
45 Dickson, 'The Ethicist Conception', p. 148.
46 Dickson, ibid., p. 146.
47 Dickson, ibid., p. 147.
48 Dickson, ibid., p. 147.
49 Dickson, ibid., p. 147.
50 See Attfield, *The Ethics of Environmental Concern*, p. 17; *Environmental Philosophy: Principles and Prospects*, pp. 221–35; and 'Environmental

Ethics, Overview', where I wrote, at p. 79: 'The problems have to be understood against the background of the current inequitable international economic order, and are unlikely to be solved unless this order is radically restructured. Ethical theories in which all this is neglected are likely to prove transitory.'

51   Dickson, 'The Ethicist Conception', pp. 135–6.
52   Dickson, ibid., pp. 128, 147, and 148.
53   Dickson, ibid., pp. 148–9.
54   Susan George, *The Debt Boomerang: How Third World Debt Harms Us All*, p. 10.
55   Garrett Hardin, 'Lifeboat Ethics: The Case against Helping the Poor'; also Garrett Hardin, *Living Within Limits*.
56   Jesper Ryberg, 'Population and Third World Assistance'. The quoted sentence appears at p. 215. *See further* Peter S. Wenz, *Environmental Ethics Today*, pp. 30–1.
57   William Aiken, 'The "Carrying Capacity" Equivocation'.
58   Parfit, *Reasons and Persons*, pp. 381–90.
59   Attfield, *Value, Obligation and Meta-Ethics*, pp. 149–73; see also Attfield, *The Ethics of Environmental Concern*, pp. 133–6.
60   Attfield, *The Ethics of the Global Environment*, pp. 122–4.
61   Alan Carter, Review of Robin Attfield, *The Ethics of the Global Environment*, at p. 151.
62   Carter, ibid., p. 151. I discuss the supposed implications of this and other aspects of Carter's review in greater detail in 'Biocentric Consequentialism, Pluralism and "The Minimax Implication": A Reply to Alan Carter', forthcoming in *Utilitas*. For a more detailed discussion of essential capacities and their relation to well-being, see Attfield, *Value, Obligation and Meta-Ethics*, pp. 45–75.
63   Carter, ibid., p. 152.
64   Carter, ibid., pp. 152–3.
65   Carter, ibid., p. 152. I have long argued on the basis of biocentric consequentialism that the total colonization of the land surface of the planet by humanity is just as unacceptable as it would be disastrous: see *The Ethics of Environmental Concern*, pp. 80–1 and 191–2, *Environmental Philosophy: Principles and Prospects*, pp. 57–9, and *The Ethics of the Global Environment*, pp. 54–5 and 70–1.

Further Reading

O'Neill, John, *Ecology, Policy and Politics: Human Well-Being and the Natural World* (Routledge, London, 1993). Communitarian, Aristotelian, anthropocentric ethics, with critiques of biocentrism and consequentialism.

Thompson, Janna, 'A Refutation of Environmental Ethics', *Environmental Ethics*, 12 (1990), 147–60. Seeks to refute non-sentientist environmental ethics.

Dickson, Barnabas, 'The Ethicist Conception of Environmental Problems', *Environmental Values*, 9 (2000), 127–52. Poses a central challenge to all environmental ethics.

Glover, Jonathan, *Causing Death and Saving Lives* (Penguin, Harmondsworth and New York, 1977), ch. 20, 'Moral Distance', pp. 286–97. Contests the views that either motivation or obligation need be attenuated by spatial, causal or psychological distance.

Carter, Alan, Review of Robin Attfield, *The Ethics of the Global Environment*, in *Mind*, 110 (2001), 149–53. Biocentric consequentialism, even if the best monistic theory available, is held to be as defective as the rest.

Some Useful Websites

www.ciwf.co.uk Website of Compassion in World Farming.
www.christian-aid.org.uk Website of Christian Aid.
www.traidcraft.co.uk Website of Traidcraft.
www.foe.co.uk Website of Friends of the Earth, UK.
www.cafod.org.uk Website of CAFOD.
www.ptree.co.uk Website of People Tree: Fair Trade & Ecology Catalogue and Magazine.
www.ethicalconsumer.org Website of Ethical Consumer Magazine.
www.ifat.org Website of International Federation for Alternative Trade.
www.usshq.co.uk Website of USS; *see* article from the *Independent* of 12 December 2000.

4 Taking the Future Seriously

This chapter considers the nature and basis of our **future-related responsibilities**, or responsibilities with regard to future generations. After reflecting on the differences that the present generation can make, it considers and appraises principles that might give shape to such responsibilities, and possible grounds for restricting their extent. I proceed to argue that environmental responsibilities cannot entirely be based on human interests, even when future interests are fully taken into account, that **environmental injustices** in the present affect our responsibilities with regard to the future, and that **future interests** (like other currently unrepresented interests) should be represented in present decision-making.

The scope and limits of future-related responsibilities

When we think about the future, we need to think about transactions and relations between successive generations. Relations between the generations impinge upon environmental ethics not only in the sense of relations between overlapping generations of different ages (generations such as grandparents, parents and children) but also, more particularly, in the sense of relations between generations living at different times, including future generations, whose numbers, quality of life and very existence depend, in part, on current decisions and policies. Future generations, of course, include children conceived in the coming months and born next year, and so they sometimes foreseeably overlap with contemporary generations; but they also include all the others who will or could inherit our environmental heritage and problems in the coming centuries. But these heirs of our environmental legacy are more liable to be forgotten than the contemporary young. So the discussion of inter-generational relations here will concern relations between present agents (both individual and corporate) and future generations, rather than relations between older and younger contemporaries as such. Since relations of equity between the generations turn out to have considerable ethical significance (as is already apparent from the brief discussion of population issues in chapter 3), this chapter will concern inter-generational equity and the responsibilities of present agents with regard to people and fellow creatures of the future.[1] Many of these turn out to arise from environmental problems triggered by the activities of the present generation and of the generations of the recent past.

The discourse of generations could still prove misleading, if either the present generation or any other generation, whether worldwide or in any one region or country, is regarded as an undifferentiated or even a united group, with evenly distributed powers and responsibilities. For example, powerless people of the present, for whom life is precarious and survival is the main priority, surely have very few responsibilities with regard to the future, whereas people and organizations possessed of some degree of affluence or power probably have much greater than average responsibilities.[2] Indeed, the importance of rectifying current imbalances of power will be returned to in connection with the social and environmental heritage of future people. Yet transactions and relations between generations can still justify reflection on the responsibilities of the present generation as such, as long as we avoid an idealized and unrepresentative model of generations as unified agents possessed of an unhistorical internal solidarity.

Probably the greatest among the possible impacts, and therefore the first to be mentioned, would be the extinction of humanity and of most animal species. This could arise through a nuclear winter, or through bacteriological warfare unleashed (maybe) by terrorist movements or oppressed peoples, as well as through factors currently beyond human control such as a collision of our planet with an asteroid. Other possible causes (all of them anthropogenic) include some kind of pandemic crossing species boundaries, or a collapse of the ozone layer, or a collapse of some other environmental constant on which we rely for our survival. So there is a serious, albeit remote, possibility that there will be no human beings or other animals from a few decades hence; and clearly the effect on people and animals of the further future would be the obliteration of the very possibility of existence.

More difference would be made to more future creatures by the avoidance of such catastrophes than by most other imaginable measures. This does not make it irrational to have other, more positive, priorities besides the avoidance of such catastrophes, since another outcome to be avoided is securing the future but only at the cost of an abysmally low quality of life. Indeed, this outcome might be even worse than there being no human future at all. Nevertheless, the avoidance of catastrophes which would eliminate future generations emerges as a high priority for almost any defensible environmental ethic.

There are, however, other priorities of matching importance, relating to the human population, whether population growth is itself regarded as the problem, or the problem lies in its causes such as economic systems and poverty. What is clear is that there will at some point be a serious problem if the human population increases to a level at which it cannot be recurrently sustained by the life-support systems and productive capacities of the planet; and that even before this point is reached there will be problems whenever increases of the human population significantly conflict with the preservation of biodiversity. Accordingly, as was suggested in chapter 3, a stable and sustainable level of the human population should if possible be attained, partly on environmental grounds. If the total population ever exceeds this level, it will inevitably have to reduce again if humanity is to avoid the horrors of food wars, massive malnutrition and near-global famine, and also if the genetic stock of the planet's species is not to be severely depleted. Thus if any obligations exist with regard to future people, they include effort to prevent there being too many of them at any one time. Or rather, since the importance of preventing the extinction of humanity has already been stressed, our responsibility includes effort to prevent there being at any one time either too many or too few of them.

If these are genuine responsibilities, there will almost certainly be others. Renewable resources (such as forests and fishstocks), for example, are likely to be needed by some if not all future generations, and should be preserved in a renewable condition. (This also applies to many replicable cultural resources such as symphonies, pictures and books.) It applies equally to the various 'ecosystem services' (such as the purification of air and water through natural systems) which have benefited all generations hitherto, and which are now often at risk.[3] Likewise, recently generated environmental problems should not be inflicted on future generations, or should at least be limited to manageable proportions, as Jane Lubchenko has recently written in an article judiciously entitled 'Entering the

Century of the Environment'.[4] Besides, the environmental injustices which currently involve the transfer of **pollution** and unhealthy work to poor neighbourhoods and poor countries (see pp. 115–19) are likely to be perpetuated unless action is taken in the present to redress them,[5] and institutional changes are adopted to prevent their recurrence and to bequeath more equitable social and international relations to posterity.

It is sometimes suggested that such responsibilities will comprise negative duties (duties to prevent harm) rather than positive ones to enhance well-being, since we are in no position to guarantee a high quality of life among our successors, but can prevent their environments from becoming intolerable and making life unlivable. This view, however, ignores our obligations to solve or mitigate ongoing environmental problems, and to bequeath fair institutions and social environments. It would also clash with the findings of chapter 2, reached in the context of discussion of the Prior Existence View (pp. 51–2), concerning the preferability of policies of sustainability to policies of resource-depletion. For if policies of sustainability would (as in Parfit's thought-experiment) make a positive difference to coming generations, this prospect could underpin responsibilities in the present.[6] These responsibilities would consist not so much in the prevention of harm, but rather in providing for the quality of life of whichever people live in future times to be higher (perhaps considerably higher) than it would have been if different policies had now been adopted. So future-related responsibilities are not confined to negative ones.

It is sometimes further assumed that obligations are always owed to someone or something in particular. This has even been taken to imply that there are no obligations regarding people beyond the immediate future, since the people of that period are possible people whose identity is currently unknown, whose very existence depends on current choices, and who can have no rights prior to their existence, or thus in the present. Hence no obligations can be owed to them.[7] But the same thought-experiment of Parfit shows, to the contrary, that there can be obligations with regard to whoever lives in a certain future period, despite their identity being currently unknown and hitherto undetermined, and hence that obligations are not invariably owed to someone or something in particular. (Acts could instead be obligatory which it would be wrong to omit to do, and omissions could be obligatory when the act omitted would itself be wrong.) This important conclusion further undermines the Prior Existence View,[8] and also shows that the scope of future-related obligations need not be restricted to duties to identifiable individuals, nor to duties with regard to the immediate future. (These conclusions, incidentally, explain why I have avoided unrestricted talk of obligations *to* future generations, or of duties *owed to* them, since future-related responsibilities are not, strictly, obligations *to* the possible people of the future, just as such possible people may not strictly have *rights* in the present. However, we can correctly speak of responsibilities or obligations *in their regard*, and this is the practice that I have followed.)

While much remains to be said about the scope of future-related obligations, we should pause to reflect on their basis, and also on the adequacy or otherwise of the various normative theories that are sometimes applied to such responsibilities.

Some bases for future-related responsibilities

What are the grounds of such responsibilities? Can we be confident that there are such grounds? Consequentialism, with its stress on meeting needs and making the greatest possible difference to the foreseeable balance of value over disvalue, has already been defended in chapter 2, and clearly involves obligations relating to all foreseeable generations. But the current focus on **future-related responsibilities** and on **equity between generations** makes it appropriate to reinforce the consequentialist case through the consideration of further grounds for such responsibilities, grounds coherent with consequentialism (or so I maintain) but not presupposing its acceptance.

One such argument concerns the symmetry of space and time, and thus of spatial and temporal distance. It is widely accepted that agents able to affect spatially distant people have responsibilities with regard to those people. This view is recognized within all systems of universalist ethics, including Kantian deontology, contractarianism, appeals to non-derivative human rights, and the various kinds of consequentialism. (It was also central to the arguments in chapter 3 about the ethics of consuming commodities produced in distant places.) But what holds for spatially distant people applies equally to the temporally distant people of foreseeable future generations, or so it may reasonably be held; to discriminate on the basis of time is just as arbitrary as discriminating on the basis of space. If so, then (granted the widely accepted view about spatial distance) current agents have responsibilities with regard to people of foreseeable future generations, however distant.

The apparent differences between those far away in time and those far away in space turn out mostly not to be differences, and not in any case to be relevant. Thus some degree of uncertainty about the effects of actions performed here and now turns out, on reflection, to be relevant to both cases, without making such effects unforeseeable. The unknown identity of the future people affected by our acts and omissions of here and now is mirrored in the case of spatially distant people, but does not plausibly undermine responsibility. The fact that agents other than ourselves will also have an impact on future people is another feature shared by future people and distant people alike. And the admittedly differentiating fact that the identity of future people has in many cases not yet been determined, unlike that of spatially distant people, does not seem to make a relevant difference to our responsibility with regard to whichever people actually come into being at future times. Parallel arguments are in place about responsibilities with regard to other species and their future members. Hence future-related responsibilities such as those suggested above seem to have an unquestionable basis, whether or not biocentric consequentialism is endorsed.

A related analogical argument, with related conclusions, has been presented by Richard and Val Routley.[9] The Routleys were arguing for future-related responsibilities in the present, and on this basis against nuclear energy generation, and also against a range of normative theories concerning obligations to the future. All this makes their argument highly relevant here.

Imagine a manufacturer consigning a package containing a highly toxic and explosive gas in a very thin container for delivery to a distant destination by a long-distance Third World bus or coach. This bus 'is nearly always full to overcrowded, with passengers hanging off the back, and, as in Afghanistan, passengers riding on the roof, and chickens and goats in the freight compartment'. It 'sets down and picks up many different passengers in the course of its long journey and the drivers change many times'.[10] The container will not last for the full journey if there is a breakdown and the interior becomes overheated (as is likely to happen if the bus strikes a large pothole), or if a passenger should for any reason interfere with the package.[11] 'If the container should break the resulting disaster would probably kill at least some of the people and animals on the bus, while others could be maimed or contract serious diseases.'[12] This act of the manufacturer would widely be regarded as appalling, which nothing could excuse, let alone the claim that possibly no disaster will ever happen.[13] Even if otherwise the manufacturer's firm would go out of business and his village undergo economic loss, this fails to justify his action.[14]

But the act of storing nuclear waste products in the current state of technology closely resembles this act of consigning faultily packaged lethal gas to a vulnerable vehicle, and the future people liable to be affected closely resemble the passengers, except that they cannot leave the bus. Parallel arguments to those of the manufacturer (such as economic necessity) are seriously put forward in the case of nuclear energy generation, but with no greater validity, particularly as there is no known safe way to store nuclear wastes.[15] Without appealing to any particular normative theory, this analogical argument makes a strong case for responsibilities with regard to people of the distant future (indeed of the next million years), and also against putting them at risk from nuclear waste products in particular. It also graphically captures the relation between spatial and temporal distance. Just as there are responsibilities with regard to all the people of the bus route, close or distant, so responsibilities are generated with regard to all the future people liable to be affected, whether immediate or distant, because of their very vulnerability.

The Routleys also make use of their argument to criticize normative theories that deny future-related responsibilities or that recognize obligations to the immediate future only. One of their targets here is Rawlsian contractarianism, which supplies an insufficient basis for such responsibilities;[16] but the same conclusion has already been reached in chapter 2 (about contractarianism in all its varieties), and needs no further defence. One of their general criticisms of contractarianism and kindred theories, however, helps explain the inadequacy of theories of this whole general type. Theories that make obligations dependent on an actual agreement or contract, or on voluntary participation in an actual community, or in relations involving love or sympathy, effectively make obligations contingent on voluntary commitments of a kind which people could avoid entering, as if they had no existence in the absence of such voluntary ties.[17] Such relations could not hold between people widely separated in time (nor, for many circumstances, in space), and so these theories tacitly imply that there could be no responsibilities transcending such distances.

Yet we have no need to know whether the manufacturer has made agreements with the bus passengers or participates in or loves one or another community in order to be assured of his having responsibilities towards distant members of the travelling public. Hence future-related obligations should not be represented as contingent on the existence of contracts, or on participation in communities (as communitarians hold), or on emotional attachments. It could be granted here that such relationships sometimes supply people's motivation to care about the future (or at least the near future), whether through a sense of fairness and a wish to

pass on to others benefits received by yourself, or through dedica-
tion to valued communal practices that you hope will outlive you,
or through love of your children and grandchildren. But future-
related obligations cannot be supposed to depend on such matters,
or people with few relationships would have few (if any) future-
related responsibilities or obligations, contrary to our reactions to
thought-experiments about human extinction and about overpopulation, and also to our reactions to the bus analogy. (For a more
detailed discussion of kinds of communitarianism, see chapter 6.)

Unlike the Routleys, however, John Passmore maintains that our
obligations are to immediate posterity only. This apparently tempt-
ing view is supported by what Passmore represents as a convergence of several theories, including Rawlsian contractarianism and
the consequentialism of the nineteenth-century philosophers Jeremy
Bentham and Henry Sidgwick.[18] The Routleys, however, show that
neither Rawls (who adopts a Just Savings Principle in the interests
of all future generations) nor Bentham nor Sidgwick is actually
committed to this conclusion.[19] Consequentialists, in particular, cannot accept it, granted that some current actions (storing nuclear
wastes is a contemporary example) could have a foreseeable direct
impact on the distant future without necessarily affecting people of
the more immediate future at all. Accordingly, the **convergence
theory** turns out to amount to advocacy of disregarding costs to
people of the non-immediate future.

Passmore also deploys in support of the same conclusion his
chain argument, supposed to make obligations to the distant
future superfluous. According to this argument, each generation
has obligations to the next, based (Passmore suggests) on love of
offspring, and since every successive generation has such obligations, obligations to the distant future turn out to be unnecessary,
because all relevant acts and omissions have already been included
in the chain of obligations.[20] But the Routleys have no difficulty in
showing that direct obligations with regard to the distant future
are needed to prohibit actions with delayed impacts not affecting
the immediate future (like planting bombs due to detonate in a
thousand years), and also policies detrimental to the distant future
but beneficial to the immediate future[21] (like Parfit's depletion
example, discussed at pp. 51–2). Passmore's chain argument and
convergence conclusion should thus be rejected alike, and responsibilities recognized with regard to all the generations to which
present action and inaction can make a difference.

Contrary to the stance of the Routleys, my claim is that such
responsibilities are fully consistent with consequentialism (see chapter 2), which (perhaps unsurprisingly) copes with the future impacts

of present action at least as well as its rivals. It is sometimes suggested that equity between generations is better safeguarded by explicit deontological principles requiring equal opportunities for successive future generations.[22] But the equal opportunities required by such principles could not in practice be delivered (not even for individual countries, let alone worldwide), granted our current ignorance of future circumstances and their partly unpredictable nature. Issues of equity are more adequately captured by giving equal consideration to equal interests, present or future, in so far as those interests are foreseeable, and devising policies on this basis. But the principle of the equal consideration of equal interests is precisely the presupposition of consequentialists, and would be employed as such where decisions are made and policies devised on a consequentialist basis.

While the consonance of this principle with principles of intra-generational (social and international) justice would need further argument, such as I have offered elsewhere,[23] **equity between generations** seems not to raise special problems for the consequentialist, except for problems such as those of overburdening the present and of special present obligations, discussed in the next section. Thus the equal consideration principle ensures that proportionate consideration would be given to more populous generations, where this would make a difference, rather than larger and smaller generations receiving the same consideration, as some suggested principles of equity between generations mistakenly advocate.[24]

It is sometimes suggested that the uncertainty of the future means that consequentialist interpretations of inter-generational equity give no guidance.[25] But this is implausible in view of the pervasive importance of planning for the foreseeable needs of future people in terms of energy, fresh water and food supply, a theme to be returned to in chapter 5. For such planning is widely recognized to be both feasible and beneficial. The mere fact that we may never know for certain whether such efforts will prove successful, presented as a problem for consequentialism by Andrew Dobson,[26] has no tendency to cast doubt on consequentialist accounts of what we should do on the basis of probability in the present, as Alan Carter has remarked,[27] or thus on the adequacy of consequentialism itself.

Even if people of the past have post-mortem interests in the completion of their projects, and this has some bearing on future-related responsibilities, as John O'Neill has argued,[28] the equal consideration principle can readily accommodate these interests too by considering them on a par with the completion of the projects of other people in the present. I conclude, then, that consequentialism is the normative theory that supplies the most credible basis for future-related obligations.

Some grounds for restricting future-related responsibilities

Before we return to the question of whether environmental responsibilities could be entirely grounded in human interests including those of the future, we need to review some suggested grounds for restricting the significance of future interests. One of the reasons for doing this is to consider the possibility that this significance is not as great as has so far been suggested, or as is widely supposed. This involves discussion of theories that might cast doubt on responsibilities focusing on the distant future and on the conclusions of the two previous sections, and also consideration of the case for discounting future interests.

Besides the theories of this kind that have been discussed already in this connection (in this chapter communitarian and contractarian theories and Passmore's convergence theory and chain argument, and in chapter 2 the average theory and the Prior Existence View), it is worth considering the bearing of theories of non-derivative rights and of Kantian theories on future-related obligations, and also some further suggestions about the underlying reason for future-related responsibilities. To consider rights theories first, even though there are deep problems (which have already been mentioned) with the very concept of the rights of future people, environmentalists often argue from the rights of our children and grandchildren, (for example) to inherit species and ecosystems intact. This approach seems entirely in order, on the analogy of ordinary bequests to family members and of the entitlements of legatees, and seems capable of extension to foreseeable further descendants, and also to the next generation or two as a whole.

It is important, therefore, to stress the limits which this approach would set to future-related obligations, which may also be seen as limits to this approach itself. For when the future-related responsibilities of current agents are considered, most future people have to be regarded as possible people. Whether one or another set of possible people is the set that comes into being is yet to be determined. If we think of the set of people alive in 100 years' time, while it is highly likely that there will be such people, not all the possible people of that time could live, as possible people include more than one set of occupants of the same space. So attempts to talk of the rights of possible people miscarry, through generating contradictions. For example, if all the possible people of that time were to have rights against potential ancestors to be given life at that time, these conflicting rights would generate contradictions with regard to current responsibilities to honour such rights. Yet if we restrict talk of future rights to the rights of those who will actually live, we do not know which (out of the possible people of that time) these ones will be. Hence there are no identifiable people of the future (beyond those already conceived) who would be wronged if future-related obligations are neglected and not discharged, and this makes such rights-talk largely futile.

It still makes sense, as has already been argued, to recognize the moral standing of future people, including all those who could be affected by current action or inaction. But when we speak of future people whose identities are currently unknown and almost certainly undetermined, talk of such people (and of doing our best for them) concerns not particular people but rather whoever there will be at that time. This is equally true when we use phrases such as 'the generation of 2100' or (in the same sense) 'our grandchildren of 2100'. Hence we should not be misled by such phrasing into imagining that talk of such generations is similar to talk of the younger generation in the present, or of our current children and grandchildren, whose identities are known, and who are thus the bearers of rights. In other words, those future-related responsibilities that are grounded in discoverable rights are restricted to the short-term future, and if there are more extensive future-related responsibilities, they are not grounded in rights, but in something else, such as the needs or the interests of possible people as bearers of moral standing.[29]

But we have seen from a number of examples including the bus analogy that there is a very strong case for future-related responsibilities much more extensive than ones relating to the short-term future only. If so, then these responsibilities cannot be grounded in rights. This does not, of course, suggest that there is anything amiss with discourse about rights in general, or with many current obligations being grounded in rights (although, for consequentialists, rights will not comprise their ultimate basis). All that follows is that normative ethics cannot wholly turn on rights, and that at least some responsibilities must have some other grounding.[30] (Parfit has well defended a closely similar stance in reply to a defender of future people's rights.)[31] These implications are consistent with the kinds of consequentialism that recognize rights but regard them as grounded in outcomes of positive or negative value, or in rules or practices with such a grounding. They are also consistent with the intactness of the rights of existent children and grand-children. Indeed there is nothing amiss with environmentalist appeals to the rights of our children and grandchildren, as long as the rights of identifiable people and the moral standing of possible but unidentifiable future people are not conflated or confused, and as long as our responsibilities with regard to the latter are not held to be attenuated simply because they are not grounded in rights.

Much the same applies to Kantian principles mandating agents to treat persons as ends, and never as means only. There is much to be said for rules of this kind, but they cannot underpin normative ethics as a whole, not only because they say nothing about the treatment of non-humans, or at least of most non-humans, but also because it is unclear what would be meant by treating the possible but unidentifiable people of the future as ends rather than as means, particularly when each possible person lives in a very restricted range of futures if they come into existence at all. As we have seen, there are no identifiable people who would be wronged if obligations relating to the distant future are not discharged. This does not show that there are no future-related obligations, but it does suggest that any obligations relating to the distant future are not grounded in respecting given individuals or in treating them as ends. Otherwise future-related obligations would be restricted to the short-term future, which (as we have seen) is implausible.

Another suggested basis for concern for future generations is that the prospect of continuation of shared communal practices into the future, generation after generation, is what gives life its value and makes it meaningful in the present. Much present activity would come to seem hollow and pointless if practices such as sports, music or academic life were known to be about to disappear for ever, or if the early extinction of humanity were in prospect. Hence it has been suggested that the reason for concern for the future lies in the value of the activities of the present.[32] If so, then future-related responsibilities would clearly be limited to those future people who continue current activities, and thus to limited tracts of time and of cultural space. While this view harbours some profound psychological insights, I have argued elsewhere that even if early human extinction were in prospect, cultural activities would still not become entirely meaningless, and, more importantly for present purposes, that the value of current activities cannot be the sole basis of future-related responsibilities.[33] The latter argument can be presented as follows.

Imagine that all our current activities are about to be annihilated through global nuclear warfare, together with all human beings currently alive, but that humanity could be resuscitated after several centuries if computers are now programmed to preserve human embryos in safe underground silos, and later to defreeze them and nourish them to adulthood at a time when the contamination has abated. If the only ground for future-related concern were the value of current activities, then there would be no reason, let alone obligation, to programme the computers accordingly, merely to prolong the career of humanity in the absence of our cherished activities. But most people would regard this view as untenable. It seems, then, that we assume that there will be value in the activities and lives of future generations, even if they are vastly different from our own, as well as in present activities. Love of ongoing activities that make life worthwhile emerges as one of our motivations for future-related concern (alongside love of children and grandchildren, of country, and of our familiar natural environment), and this is a valuable contribution of the theory under consideration. But future-related responsibilities are neither grounded in these values alone, nor confined in scope to the continuation of practices valued by ourselves.

Caring for posterity can instead be understood, at least in part, as motivated by the human need to identify with ideals and causes larger than ourselves and our own circumscribed (and sometimes petty) interests, or by the need for self-transcendence, as Ernest Partridge has called it.[34] While this can take the form of identification with particular current cultural activities with a prospect of continuation into the future, it can take broader forms, as in the line of the ancient playwright Terence 'I am a human being, and I count nothing human alien from myself'. I am not suggesting that we can only care about what we identify with (see chapter 3). Yet self-transcendence can be a powerful motive, sometimes involving care for the future of humanity as well as for its present needs (despite the claims sometimes made that human beings are incapable of such care), and for its own sake rather than our own. Indeed, the prevalence of this apparent need is presented by Partridge as evidence against psychological egoism (the view that everyone is motivated by self-interest).[35]

The problem, however, is that self-transcendence might come to be regarded as the sole reason for future-related responsibilities, which would turn out all over again to be restricted in scope to whatever satisfies this present need (for example, the perpetuation of human life, albeit in a form barely worth living). If so, these very responsibilities could even be suggested to be an expression of self-interest (in the form of our need for self-transcendence). This latter suggestion, however, is barely coherent, for self-transcendence contrasts with self-interest, and its pursuit collapses when self-interest is its motive.

What needs to be avoided is any suggestion that self-transcendence is the one and only ground of future-related responsibilities, which then would themselves have to be tailored accordingly. But such a view makes the mistake of confusing motivations with grounds. While self-transcendence is an important motivation, and in this sense supplies an important answer to the title-question of Partridge's essay 'Why Care About the Future?', the grounds (and relatedly the scope) of future-related responsibilities cannot be made to depend on whether it is present or absent. If each flourishing life (in the future as well as in the present) has intrinsic value, this value is not contingent on present motivations (nor, come to that, on anything else). Even if the phenomenon of self-transcendence went into abeyance (as can happen during epidemics of minor ailments such as coughs and colds), these responsibilities would remain no less real.

Restricting future-related responsibilities by discounting

Nevertheless, future-related responsibilities are standardly treated in the public policy of most countries and organizations as restricted, and this belief is embodied in the practice of **discounting**. Future benefits and costs are discounted at the social discount rate (often of 5 per cent), and this is applied to successive future years on a compound basis, such that the costs and benefits of three years hence are calculated at 95 per cent of 95 per cent of 95 per cent of current values, and such that the benefits and costs of thirty years hence and beyond count for little or nothing. Various justifications of this practice have been supplied, ranging from the progressive uncertainty of the future, via opportunity costs, and the possibility of compensating future sufferers of present policies, to the importance of not overburdening the present generation, and to the special obligations owed to present people. Appeal is also made to the sheer fact of time preference (people's desire to receive benefits sooner rather than later), but this seems irrelevant when it is proposed to reduce the significance of the deaths or disabilities of future people, whose suffering can be presumed to be just as great as that of present people in the same situations.

Appeal is also made to the supposed implications of refraining from discounting. Thus Andrew Dobson appeals to the argument of Peter Laslett and James Fishkin that since resources are finite and the number of future generations potentially infinite, and since dividing by infinity produces zero, an equal sharing of resources between generations would mean that each generation literally receives nothing.[36] One reply to this argument, from Alan Carter, is that the number of future generations could not possibly be infinite, since the laws of entropy reliably predict that the conditions necessary for life will eventually cease to hold.[37] This reply already shows that the argument fails to establish its conclusion, although the problem of sharing remains. A further reply is that renewable resources need not be divided and consumed at all, but that (if maintained in a renewable condition) they can be used without attenuation by each successive generation. Further, non-renewable resources, such as fossil fuels, are in many cases likely not to be required indefinitely, because new technologies are likely to replace them (for example, generating energy from renewable sources). Thus the issue is not one of sharing these resources between an indefinite succession of generations but of conserving them for the foreseeable needs of the next century or two and of devising benign technologies to replace them. Conventional discounting, however, effectively pays so little heed to the needs of thirty or more years hence that inadequate provision is made even for the needs of our grandchildren, let alone for their grandchildren's needs.

Philosophers who consider the standard justifications of discounting usually conclude that they too are inconclusive.[38] For example, uncertainty does not increase uniformly with remoteness in time, and some future costs are as certain as current ones. Likewise opportunity costs are only sometimes relevant, such as (for example) when the opportunities foregone are genuinely comparable with the (undiscounted) foreseeable costs for future decades, and when the consumption of resources actually conserved would not have threatened sustainability. The possibility of future compensation is irrelevant when the prospect of such compensation being paid is slender, or where (as with death) compensation is impossible. As for the argument from excessive burdens, while obligations admittedly have an upper limit, the practice of discounting is hardly necessary to rescue the current generation from the risk of it being exceeded, since a rule constraining the sacrifices to be expected of any generation (and capable of recognition on consequentialist grounds) would achieve this more directly and with fewer unintended side-effects. Besides, special obligations can be recognized without marginalizing future generations in order to make the recognition of these obligations possible, just as duties to family and friends are not normally held to involve disregard for strangers.

Generally, none of the justifications justify discounting across the board. As Partha Dasgupta has argued,[39] it is not actually wrong in principle. However, discounting can at most be seen as valid on occasion due to one justification or another, but only for those cases where particular justifications apply. For example, consequentialists can and should have regard to uncertainty of outcomes, but far from all future outcomes are uncertain; and uncertainty should also be recognized for uncertain outcomes in the present as much as in the future. Since none of the justifications apply to all outcomes, future-related responsibilities turn out not to be restricted on the basis of any of them, except where (in particular cases, such as cases of uncertainty) they are shown to be relevant. These responsibilities also turn out to be much greater than current practices of discounting assume.

Having read thus far, you should ask yourself what, in your view, is the extent of future-related responsibilities, what is their basis, whether any of the suggested grounds for restricting them deserves sympathy, and whether any across-the-board social discount rate is acceptable. However, the issue of whether responsibilities with regard to future human beings form the sole basis of environmental concern is tackled in the coming section.

Do human interests and environmental responsibilities converge?

Future-related responsibilities, then, are as great as consequentialism suggests, and greater than much current practice assumes or presupposes. Yet caring about them lies no more beyond our powers than being moral itself does. They are not to be regarded as restricted on any of the various grounds considered in the previous section, except where (for example) the uncertainty of outcomes makes planning for the future impossible.

Since responsibilities grounded in future human interests are of this order (and supplement the already considerable responsibilities grounded in current human interests), the possibility re-emerges that an anthropocentric ethic is sufficient to cover the full range of environmental responsibilities, and that in practice nothing is added by appeals to non-anthropocentric considerations such as the value of the flourishing of non-human species. The preservation of ecosystems and species, for example, can readily be justified (or so it may again be suggested) on the basis of human interests. Even if a non-anthropocentric ethic might offer different reasons, they are reasons, it might be suggested, for exactly the same responsibilities. Bryan Norton has suggested just such a convergence, which would apparently make non-anthropocentric normative theories superfluous. To quote again the passage about the evolutionary context of humanity cited in chapter 2, 'Policies serving the interests of the human species as a whole, and in the long run, will serve also the "interests" of nature, and vice versa', because 'no long-term human values can be protected without protecting the context in which they evolved'.[40] But does this **convergence claim** fare any better than Passmore's convergence theory, criticized above?

Here it is appropriate to develop and amplify the brief responses to this position already presented in that context. My initial response there was that these policies could fail to protect inaccessible tracts of nature, or distant tracts of the future, and also that much more than 'our culture's distant future'[41] might be at stake. Since this chapter concerns the future, I will focus here on the possible failure of policies serving the interests of humanity to protect distant tracts of the future in which much more could well be at stake than 'our culture's distant future'.

As was mentioned in a parallel context in chapter 3, the future of humanity may stretch to millions of years, but the future of non-human species (including some already in existence and others that might evolve from them), and thus of non-human life on Earth, could possibly extend to billions or even trillions. Yet in many cases the continued flourishing of non-human life after the demise of humanity could easily be prevented by human action either in the present or in coming centuries, through extinctions of species or of their habitats that break the genetic chains that would have generated such flourishing life in the post-human period. Species are becoming extinct at an alarming rate,[42] and many of these extinctions could be making a large difference to the possibility and character of life on Earth long after the last human being has expired. But this particular difference has little or no bearing on human interests. Even the argument that human interests do not cease with death, but continue through the fulfilment or non-fulfilment of the relevant person's projects[43] (which might seem to make the indefinite continuation of maximum biodiversity an element in the human interests of those who have made this project their own) wears thin when applied to a post-human future standing outside the entire career of humanity. It is implausible that the continued existence and flourishing of invertebrates for billions of years, desirable as we may recognize it to be, remains in the *interests* of those who advocated it during their lifetimes. Indeed the context of O'Neill's argument for post-mortem interests was the continuation of projects within society across the next few human generations, rather than across future biological time.

It is rather non-human interests which supply a large part of the case for the preservation of current non-human species with a view to their continued existence and flourishing after the demise of humanity, and this case may well make a difference by supporting stronger policies than human interests support alone. Even so, the reply could be advanced that there happens to be a sufficient human interest in preserving just the same range of species as non-human interests support, and thus that no policy difference is at issue after all. But this reply does not ring true. Norton's argument, for example, concerns preserving the context in which humanity and human values evolved.[44] But, while it is always difficult to specify where the outer limits of a context lie, it is clear that the context in which humanity evolved did not include the creatures of the bed of the deep ocean and the creatures living 2 miles below the icecap of Antarctica; and yet these creatures as well as those of regions inhabited by human beings are increasingly at risk of extinction through the side-effects of human action. (Hence the mention in chapter 2 of 'inaccessible tracts of nature'.) Even if the anthropocentrist reply moves from the context of human evolution to the range of species now known to humanity, it can be remarked that a large proportion of the species undergoing extinction are among the majority of species that have not been as much as identified. Yet unidentified species are clearly seldom the focus of the kind of human concern likely to foster interventions aimed at forestalling their extinction. As was argued in chapter 3, such species will hardly be constitutive of anyone's well-being.

Advocates of Norton's convergence claim could still appeal to scientific interest and aesthetic appreciation as grounds for preservation based on human interests, and it cannot be denied that these grounds are relevant to the preservation of all Earth's species. But the suggestion that these grounds are sufficiently strong in the absence of others to sustain policies of preservation is unconvincing. For the human interest in scientific study and in aesthetic appreciation has to be offset against other human interests, including some (such as the interest in social and economic development) that satisfy human needs, as well as others (such as the quest for profit) which often fall short in this regard. Thus when economists assign costs to species extinctions, such as those presented by Björn Lomborg[45] in reviewing the costs to humanity of accepting rather than resisting global warming (together with the multiple extinctions of species that this policy would involve), these resultant costs can prove modest and easily tolerated. While Lomborg's costings are (rightly) disputed,[46] the conclusion stands that human interests alone (scientific curiosity included) form an insecure basis for policies involving the preservation of most species and habitats, justifying on some views the preservation just of pivotal species (rivets within ecosystems), or (on other views) that of just those habitats beyond the scope of planetary self-repair. In these circumstances, the case from non-human interests, including those of the distant future, importantly adds to the preservationist case, and supports stronger policies. It also supplies the context of decisions about preservation, since life on Earth, and not just human life, is at stake. Thus human interests are insufficient to underpin the preservation of biodiversity (at least where species are concerned), even when future human interests are given due recognition.

Human interests also form an unreliable guide in matters of population. For, to use 'sustainable' in the conventional sense of 'capable of being continued indefinitely', human interests could easily support the highest sustainable level of the human population, even if this were to mean the loss of wild habitats, as long as the wild inhabitants of these habitats were not crucial to or constitutive of human interests. But if non-human interests also matter, and matter enough to outweigh the value of a number of human lives, then a somewhat lower target for stabilization of the human population would be appropriate. (We return to these themes in the next chapter.)

But a related issue should also be mentioned here. For the case for a lower-than-maximal level of the human population also supports limiting the human use of the surface of the planet, whereas if the maximum sustainable human population is our goal, then, subject to certain ecological constraints, total use is what might defensibly be aimed at. But the prospect of the whole surface of the planet being manipulated to serve human purposes strikes most people who consider it as appalling, and also as incompatible with good stewardship. While human interests (such as the need to encounter wildness) could supply some of the reasons for these reactions, a non-anthropocentric value-theory would much more readily explain what is objectionable about a **total-use scenario**.[47]

It is worth mentioning here that yet a further area where non-human interests made a difference is that of genetic engineering. Granted that possible people of the future have moral standing, the same must apply to possible non-human creatures that we could bring into being. If so, then the quality of the lives that these creatures would lead is relevant to the issue of whether they should be brought into being. Thus if their lives would be more painful or more stunted than the lives of other creatures that could have come into being instead, this is a significant consideration against bringing them into being in the first place (and a consideration completely independent of human interests). While genetic engineering does not seem intrinsically wrong, and needs to be appraised case by case with regard to its good and bad outcomes (and nothing further can be said about it here), it is important that the interests of possible creatures are not overlooked. In some cases these interests are likely to warrant different policies from human interests.

Thus Norton is right to stress the extent and strength of future human interests. But these interests fail to underpin sufficiently strong policies on biodiversity preservation, population levels, colonization of the Earth's surface, and probably genetic engineering. Norton's convergence claim, like Passmore's convergence theory, proves unpersuasive.

Saving the future from environmental injustice

Current human interests can clearly conflict with those of the future, and this can be true with regard to current environmental problems, which can require resources to be diverted from the kind of long-term issues discussed in previous sections of this chapter. Yet the same problems often relate to future interests in other ways, for if they are not remedied, future generations will inherit them, often in exacerbated form.

Among the environmental problems generated during the twentieth century, many can be classified as cases of **environmental injustice**. As Jane Lubchenko relates, '[t]he consequences of environmental degradation are often borne disproportionately by racially and economically disadvantaged groups,'[48] and this happens both within countries and in the international relations between countries. Thus to borrow her example, 'intensive shrimp farming in Southeast Asia, India and parts of South and Central America often brings economic benefit to a few owners (large multinational or national corporations) in the short term but in the longer term destroys mangrove forests needed by indigenous peoples to provide food, fiber, and ecosystem services such as water purification, sediment trapping and flood control'.[49] These are examples of injustice because bad outcomes of social practices are disproportionately suffered by groups who are most vulnerable and least able to purchase better treatment, to move away or in some cases even to protest. They are also among the human-generated challenges that Lubchenko (writing as President of the American Association for the Advancement of Science) urges scientists and technologists to research and tackle in the twenty-first century.

James Sterba classifies an aspect of the same phenomenon as 'environmental racism', which he defines as 'the imposition of unfair risks to health and well-being on people of colour'.[50] Some of his examples are cases of discrimination within American society; thus 'three out of every five black and Hispanic Americans live in a community with toxic waste sites'. Another concerns the overseas exportation of residues: 'The developed countries ship an estimated 20 million tons of waste to the Third World each year.' Specific instances are particularly disturbing: 'In 1987, dioxin-laden industrial ash from Philadelphia was dumped in Guinea and Haiti. In 1988, 4000 tons of PCB-contaminated chemical waste from Italy was found in Nigeria, leaking from thousands of rusting and corroding drums, poisoning both soil and groundwater.' Nor are these the only cases.[51] As Carl Talbot observes, environmental racism has become globalized in a practice amounting to 'toxic imperialism'.[52] While these problems satisfy the definition of 'environmental problems' offered in chapter 1 above, awareness of them requires us to revise our usual image of typical environmental problems so that, alongside wilderness loss and threats to the distant future of non-human species, we include the siting of hazardous processes and the dumping of toxic wastes in disadvantaged areas and countries, with consequent threats to human health and well-being – issues that have often been ignored by mainstream environmental campaigning groups and organizations.[53]

The prospect of systemic global trade in toxic substances with a view to their disposal in Third World countries came to light when a leaked memorandum from Lawrence Summers, chief economist of the World Bank, was published in *The Economist* in 1992 under the title 'Let Them Eat Pollution'. This memo advocated an increase of the trade in toxic waste between developed countries and the Third World on economic grounds. Thus the smaller loss of earnings resulting from damage to health by pollution in low-wage economies and the 'inefficiently low' levels of pollution in African countries in particular were presented as grounds for an increased level of pollution in those countries.[54] Even if the original memo was written with tongue in cheek, it correctly assumed that the practice of toxic export and disposal was a real and growing phenomenon, and that little justification could be offered other than the bizarre principles ostensibly propounded by Summers. Andrew

Dobson warns of the possible spread of this practice, to the likely detriment of future generations, if countries (and those charged with the disposal of nuclear wastes on their behalf) are guided by communitarian rather than universalist principles, and their sense of transgenerational community awareness fails to extend to future generations of peoples with which they feel insufficient ties of similarity and solidarity in the present.[55]

People disproportionately exposed to such practices and to local polluting processes include not only minority communities and the poorer Third World countries, but also women, particularly women in the Third World. As Talbot has written, 'Degraded agricultural land and poor and limited access to food, potable water, health care and energy supplies . . . have their initial and greatest impact on the lives of women and their children. This is borne out by the enormous disparities in infant and maternal rates of ill health, malnutrition, and mortality between the developed world and the Third World.'[56] Third World women have responded through forming groups not only to defend natural habitats (as in the Chipko Movement in India and the Green Belt Movement in Kenya)[57] but also to campaign for more equitable trading conditions for women and to oppose toxic processes and tips.[58] Some ascribe the prominence of women in the environmental movement to their biological role of reproduction and care for their families, and to a related concern for a clean and healthy environment, while others regard these tendencies as gender-related social roles. In any case many women undeniably suffer environmental injustices as a result of their gender, and a significant number have become active in **the Environmental Justice Movement**, campaigning for recognition and redress for environmentally disadvantaged communities.[59]

For ethicists addressing such problems, Sterba's sifting of principles offers a valuable basis, albeit one in need of considerable supplementation. Sterba first suggests a 'Principle of Procedural Justice': 'Everyone, especially minorities, should participate in the selection of environmental policies that affect them.'[60] Sterba recognizes that this principle is incomplete, since principles governing the weight to be given to minorities' votes would also be necessary. More importantly, even if this principle might imaginably be made effective within one state or federation (such as the American context of Sterba's reflections), its application to international policies with distant and/or widely dispersed effects would be likely to remain problematic until and unless some form of global governance is brought into being to regulate this kind of international trade, and until in addition member countries become willing to consult affected parties. There is an even greater problem with regard to affected parties of the future, who cannot in principle be consulted, an issue to which we shall return. Since the Principle of Procedural Justice would be likely to reduce suffering and injustice and to make decision-making less biased towards powerful groups and lobbies (and is hence justifiable on a consequentialist basis), it should be supported, but without high expectations concerning its capacity to solve the problems under consideration here.

Similar considerations apply to the principle Sterba next considers, Richard Bullard's suggestion that 'Every individual has a right to be protected from environmental degradation'.[61] The greatest problem here concerns individuals of the future, whose very futurity makes their protection difficult to achieve, and many of whom would have no rights in the present. Yet if nothing is done on their behalf, the individuals of the twenty-second century stand to inherit considerable environmental degradation with no possibility of redress against those of their predecessors who caused it. Our future-related responsibilities, as well as our responsibilities to vulnerable people of the present, imply (at least) that the latter should not be subjected to toxic dumping or other environmental degradation generated by others. In so far as this conclusion is based on future-related responsibilities, its basis is not future rights, but the future needs of the successors of the vulnerable people and communities of the present, whose lives will otherwise be blighted in advance of their conception by contamination over which they will have no control.

Sterba finally maintains that environmental risks to health and well-being should be shared either proportionately to the pollution and contamination one produces, or preferably in proportion to the amount of resources one consumes.[62] While vulnerable communities should certainly be spared such risks as far as possible, these principles are problematic, since much pollution is caused by poor people who lack access to environmentally-friendly technology and have little choice about methods of production, and there is just as little choice about (for example) much consumption of electricity, since electricity is usually generated from non-renewable rather than renewable resources. Remedies therefore involve both the use of greener technologies, and at the same time a reduction of inter-human exploitation and greater social justice in the present, particularly with regard to vulnerable communities and poor countries, much as the Environmental Justice Movement advocates.

Building social justice and sound institutions in the present constitutes a large part of our responsibilities with regard to the future. This is because successive generations will be enormously encumbered if they inherit unfair or corrupt institutions, and their own ability will be curtailed to play their part in meeting their own and others' needs, protecting planetary systems and making provision for their successors. While some adverse impacts of current action on the distant future are not mediated through more immediate future generations (as the Routleys show with respect to nuclear waste disposal projects), most such impacts operate by cultural transmission down the generations. Hence what we can do for future people (both distant and more immediate) consists largely in equipping them with social and international frameworks within which the opportunities and problems of the day can be addressed, and conveying to them the value of the just and worthwhile practices that give such frameworks their point. It is largely because environmental injustice, environmental racism and toxic imperialism are polar opposites of such frameworks and practices that they need to be contested in the present, and (if they continue to haunt us) in successive generations.

Representing the future in present decision-making

Since future generations stand to be affected by current decisions, but cannot influence them, provision should be made for their interests (as voiceless parties) to be represented in current decision-making. The kernel of this idea was voiced in one of the earliest essays in environmental ethics, Joel Feinberg's 'The Rights of Animals and Unborn Generations', when he wrote in a favourable tone of proxies able to speak on behalf of those not yet present to claim a livable world as their right. He went on to distinguish the role of these 'spokesmen' from that of 'custodians' (perhaps equivalent to the 'stewards' or 'trustees' of chapters 1 and 2 above), since they are (or would be) the 'genuine representatives of future interests'.[63]

Feinberg may have had in mind environmentalist campaigners and the various environmentalist organizations (in contrast with the rest of us, with our 'housekeeping role as temporary inhabitants of this planet',[64] but, presumably, an often defective grasp of future needs). But to appoint these as representatives of **future interests** would have its dangers, as we have seen with regard to their partial blindness in the past to environmental racism and injustice, which need to be resisted partly on the basis of these very future interests. Even the elected representatives of contemporary constituents are liable to charges of being out of touch; and the problems are (to say the least) magnified where, short of time-travel, the constituents cannot be visited, and, having as yet no settled identities, can only be imagined as kinds rather than as individuals. Yet to disregard the interests that they are virtually certain to have because of the problems of representing them would be to default on the ample responsibilities identified in this chapter.

Dale Jamieson has drawn attention to another problem, the very large numbers of future people, and the likelihood that they far outnumber current people. Future votes, Jamieson has suggested, would be sufficient to veto most developments conducted for the sake of current interests.[65] But the votes of future people are not in question, because (apart from the infants and children already alive) we can have no idea what form future preferences will take. Granting this is clearly compatible with taking seriously future needs, since people's basic needs are independent of their preferences. But if so the issue of numbers re-emerges in a different form. Just say proxies are appointed to decision-making assemblies to represent future generations. Should they wield an overwhelming vote, or even a veto, because of the magnitude of future needs and numbers?

The importance of representing living adults, and thus people capable of being consulted and of appointing and removing their representatives, requires that such proxies should wield neither an overwhelming vote nor a veto. Besides, if there are to be legislators who are *not* proxies for future people, it is undesirable that their role should be understood as representing the present *as opposed to* the future, and as not involving recognition of future interests, as might easily become the case with legislators who are not proxies if the proxies were equipped to wield significant political clout. The central role of such proxies would therefore be to advise their fellow-legislators of future impacts and future needs, to oppose indiscriminate practices such as that of discounting future interests, and to advocate appropriate policies. This they would probably be best placed to do if they had the status of legislators rather than advisers, and thus were equipped with votes of their own; but their votes would form a minority in any given legislature.[66]

The issue remains of how such proxies should be selected. The selecting body might be a panel of environmental campaigning groups, and other bodies concerned about the future such as the World Futures Studies Federation and organizations of planning professionals, subject to approval by the legislature. (In this way the departure from democracy involved in the appointment of proxies to a legislature would be minimized.) By way of checks and balances so as to avoid the dangers of significant future interests being disregarded, they should also be subject to re-selection (and thus de-selection) at least as often as other legislators. And to avoid individuals making a political career out of representing the future, they should cease to be eligible for re-selection after their second term of office. The proxies should be assisted by research teams, charged with discovering future needs in areas such as supplies of food and energy, the curtailment of global warming and other forms of pollution, on the analogy of research conducted at international level by the World Commission on Environment and Development (which produced *Our Common Future*, the 'Brundtland Report' in 1987).[67]

Since the rationale for representing future generations is to represent the interests of otherwise voiceless parties affected by decisions of the legislature in question, there is a comparable case for representation of non-human species (present and future), a case fully supported by biocentric consequentialism. In view of the overlapping interests of future generations and of non-human species (and in spite of the partial non-convergence of these interests), this might best be done if the same proxies were to represent both sets. If so, the panel selecting proxies should include animal-welfare organizations as well as environmental ones, each again subject to approval on the part of the legislature. There is an analogous case for proxies in international decision-making fora, such as the European Parliament and the United Nations.

While there is, in addition, some kind of case for the representation in national legislatures of contemporary foreign nationals affected by the decisions taken, there is also a strong case against this, in that the governments of the relevant states are already charged with representing these interests in international negotiations and international decision-making bodies. Nevertheless the proxies charged with representing future generations and possibly non-human species could reasonably be expected to take into account the full '**environmental footprint**' of their own legislature's decisions, that is the full territorial swathe of space as well as of future time affected thereby. Those charged with representing other species and the human future could hardly afford not to be internationalists.

The introduction of constitutional measures of this kind could make a significant contribution towards decision-making bodies taking future interests seriously. But even in the absence of their introduction, legislatures are still subject to future-related responsibilities. The greatest potential impact of ethical principles lies where power is concentrated; while ethics can affect the decisions of individual consumers (see chapter 3), it is at the levels of corpora-tions, governments and international bodies that the application of these principles could have greatest effect. Legislatures, with the aid of researchers dedicated to studying future needs, have clear responsibilities to adopt policies responsive to these needs, without waiting for the kinds of constitutional reform that could reconfigure the political context and predispose it in favour of such policies. Lester R. Brown and Sandra Postel have suggested that such judge-ments should be based on whether they 'diminish the prospects of the next generation',[68] but this is too limited a perspective. Rather, they should be based, alongside current human interests, on whether they enhance or diminish the prospects of the future of humanity, and of non-human species too.

Issues on which you should now be able to reach a view of your own include whether environmental responsibilities can be based entirely on human (including future) interests, to what extent envir-onmental injustices in the present affect our responsibilities to the future, and in what form, if any, future interests (and other interests that have hitherto gone unrepresented) should be represented in current decision-making.

Summary

The current generation can make large differences to the numbers and quality of life of future generations. Considerations of the sym-metry of spatial and temporal distance, like the bus analogy of the Routleys, uphold responsibilities with regard to such generations (distant ones included), count against normative theories that make obligations depend on feelings or relationships, and cohere with consequentialist grounds for such responsibilities. Rival theories fail to uphold these responsibilities and/or distort or restrict their content, as does the practice of non-selective discounting. Despite Bryan Norton's convergence claim, future human interests fail to underpin sufficiently strong policies on biodiversity preservation, population levels and colonization of the Earth's surface, in the absence of arguments from non-human interests. Future-related responsibilities are shown to include resisting environmental injus-tice in the present. Future interests (and non-human interests too) should ideally be represented in current decision-making.

Notes

1   This and the next three paragraphs are based on Robin Attfield, 'Environmental Ethics and Intergenerational Equity'.
2   Robin Attfield, 'Differentiated Responsibilities', forthcoming in Markku Oksanen and Juhani Pietarinen (eds), *Philosophy and Biodiversity*.
3   Jane Lubchenko, 'Entering the Century of the Environment: A New Social Contract for Science', pp. 492–3.
4   Lubchenko, ibid., pp. 491–2.
5   Lubchenko, ibid., p. 494.
6   Derek Parfit, *Reasons and Persons*, pp. 362–4.
7   Thomas Schwartz, 'Obligations to Posterity', and 'Welfare Judgments and Future Generations'. For an ingenious reply to Schwartz, see Alan Carter, 'Can We Harm Future People?'
8   Parfit, *Reasons and Persons*, p. 363.
9   Richard Routley and Val Routley, 'Nuclear Energy and Obligations to the Future'.
10 Richard Routley and Val Routley, ibid., p. 133.
11 Richard Routley and Val Routley, ibid., pp. 133–4.
12 Richard Routley and Val Routley, ibid., p. 134.
13 Richard Routley and Val Routley, ibid., p. 134.
14 Richard Routley and Val Routley, ibid., p. 135.
15 Richard Routley and Val Routley, ibid., p. 135.
16 Richard Routley and Val Routley, ibid., pp. 140–1, 149, and 166–73.
17 Richard Routley and Val Routley, ibid., pp. 139–41.
18 John Passmore, *Man's Responsibility for Nature*, p. 91.
19 Richard Routley and Val Routley, 'Nuclear Energy', pp. 146–9.
20 Passmore, *Man's Responsibility for Nature*, pp. 87–90.
21 Richard Routley and Val Routley, 'Nuclear Energy', p. 145.
22 Brian Barry, 'The Ethics of Resource Depletion'.
23 See Attfield, *Value, Obligation and Meta-Ethics*, ch. 9.
24 See Attfield, *The Ethics of the Global Environment*, pp. 81–6.
25 Alan Holland, 'Sustainability: Should We Start from Here?', p. 67.
26 Andrew Dobson, *Justice and the Environment: Conceptions of Environmental Sustainability and Theories of Distributive Justice*, pp. 128–9.
27 Alan Carter, 'Distributive Justice and Environmental Sustainability', p. 456.
28 John O'Neill, *Ecology, Policy and Politics*, ch. 3.
29 For another view, see Joel Feinberg, 'The Rights of Animals and Unborn Generations'.
30 See further Parfit, *Reasons and Persons*, pp. 364–6.
31 Parfit, 'Comments', pp. 854–62, replying to James Woodward, 'The Non-Identity Problem'. A similar stance to Parfit's is ably defended in Alan Carter, 'Can We Harm Future People?', at p. 436, in reply to Robert Elliot, 'The Rights of Future People'.
32 David N. James, 'Risking Extinction: An Axiological Analysis'.

33   See Attfield, *The Ethics of the Global Environment*, pp. 64–7. The next paragraph here recapitulates a thought-experiment first presented at p. 66 there.

34   Ernest Partridge, 'Why Care about the Future?'.

35   Partridge, ibid.

36   Andrew Dobson, *Justice and the Environment*, pp. 105–6 and 113–14; Peter Laslett and James Fishkin, 'Introduction: Processional Justice', at p. 6.

37   Alan Carter, 'Distributive Justice and Environmental Sustainability', pp. 453–5.

38   Parfit, 'Energy Policy and the Further Future: The Social Discount Rate'; Parfit, *Reasons and Persons*, pp. 480–6; John Broome, *Counting the Cost of Global Warming*, pp. 52–112. See also Richard and Val Routley, 'Nuclear Energy and Obligations to the Future', pp. 149–61.

39   Partha Dasgupta, *Human Well-Being and the Natural Environment*, pp. 89–103.

40   Bryan G. Norton, *Toward Unity among Environmentalists*, p. 240.

41   Norton, *Toward Unity*, p. 241.

42   See Attfield, *The Ethics of the Global Environment*, ch. 8.

43   Thus O'Neill, *Ecology, Policy and Politics*, ch. 3.

44   Norton, *Toward Unity*, p. 240.

45   Björn Lomborg, *The Skeptical Environmentalist*.

46   These costings have been widely disputed by environmentalists. See the University of Aarhus website mentioned below.

47   This scenario was introduced in support of similar conclusions in Richard Routley and Val Routley, 'Human Chauvinism and Environmental Ethics'. The current paragraph is based on Attfield, 'Ecological Policies and Ecological Values'.

48   Lubchenko, 'Entering the Century of the Environment', p. 494.

49   Lubchenko, ibid., p. 494.

50   James Sterba, *Justice for Here and Now*, p. 141.

51   Sterba, ibid., p. 141.

52   Carl Talbot, 'Environmental Justice', p. 101.

53   Sterba, *Justice for Here and Now*, p. 142.

54   Talbot, 'Environmental Justice', p. 101.

55   Andrew Dobson, *Justice and the Environment*, p. 106.

56   Talbot, 'Environmental Justice', p. 98.

57   Mary Mellor, *Breaking the Boundaries: Towards a Feminist Green Socialism*, pp. 79–81.

58   Talbot, 'Environmental Justice', p. 98.

59   Talbot, ibid., p. 98.

60   Sterba, *Justice for Here and Now*, p. 142.

61   Robert Bullard, 'Overcoming Racism in Environmental Decision-making', p. 15.

62   Sterba, *Justice for Here and Now*, p. 143.

63   Feinberg, 'The Rights of Animals', p. 65.

64   Feinberg, ibid., p. 56.

65   Dale Jamieson, 'Future Generations'.

66 See further Robin Attfield, 'Discounting, Jamieson's Trilemma and Representing the Future'.
67 World Commission on Environment and Development, *Our Common Future*.
68 Lester R. Brown and Sandra Postel, 'Thresholds of Change', in Lester Brown (ed.), *State of the World*, at p. 4. The basis of such appraisals is well spelled out in Joseph R. Des Jardins, *Environmental Ethics: An Introduction to Environmental Philosophy*, 3rd edn, p. 85.

Further Reading

Lubchenko, Jane, 'Entering the Century of the Environment: A New Social Contract for Science', *Science*, 279 (23 January 1998), 491–7. A leading scientist reviews the environmental challenges (including environmental injustice) of the new century.
Routley, Richard and Routley, Val, 'Nuclear Energy and Obligations to the Future', *Inquiry*, 21 (1978), 133–79. Normative and applied ethics illuminated by a graphic example.
Partridge, Ernest (ed.), *Responsibilities to Future Generations: Environmental Ethics* (Prometheus Books, Buffalo, 1981) Useful collection; Partridge's own chapter has insightful discussion of self-transcendence.
Des Jardins, Joseph R., *Environmental Ethics: An Introduction to Environmental Philosophy*, 3rd edn, (Wadsworth/Thomson Learning, Belmont, CA, 2001), ch. 4. A clear and valuable discussion.
Young, Michael D., *For Our Children's Children: Some Practical Implications of Inter-Generational Equity and the Precautionary Principle* (Resource Assessment Commission, Canberra, 1993). Discusses a range of intergenerational principles.

Some Useful Websites

www.anti-lomborg.com A University of Aarhus website with critiques of Lomborg's *The Skeptical Environmentalist*.
www.igc.apc.org/econet/ Website of The EcoJustice Network.
www.worldfutures.org Website of World Futures Studies Federation.
www.phil.uga.edu/faculty/wolf/gauss.htm A University of Georgia website; has further discussion of sustaining renewable resources.

5 Sustainable Development, Population and Precaution

While the goal of a sustainable level of population (in the sense of a level capable of being sustained indefinitely) was included among the implications of consequentialism in chapter 3 and among future-related responsibilities in chapter 4, it is important to clarify and appraise the concept of **sustainable development**. This concept is widely recognized as offering possible solutions to many of our developmental and ecological problems. It is also important to trace the bearing of sustainable development (as interpreted and defended here) on inter-generational equity, on environmental sensitivity, on **population ethics** and on liberal democracy, and to relate it to **the Precautionary Principle**. These are the concerns of the current chapter.

The concept of sustainable development

The concept of **sustainable development** has come to be used in multiple senses. This variety of usage is partly due to the success of the Brundtland Report (1987), which advocated sustainable development as its central theme,[1] and subsequently the adoption of its message (in diluted form) by the United Nations Conference on Environment and Development (**UNCED,** or 'the Earth Summit') held at Rio de Janeiro in 1992.[2] Since then, all signatories have been committed in theory to sustainable development, and in practice have bestowed this name upon a wide range of policies, not all of them either developmental or sustainable. Yet the partial political success of a concept should not be held against it. The concept of peace, to take a parallel case, has not been and should not be abandoned just because it is so frequently reinterpreted or misused.

Both development and sustainability had been much debated as goals prior to the Brundtland Report. Development, indeed, is the subject of several fields of study and research, including development ethics. Although those debates cannot be entered into here, the United Nations definition of development, drawn from the Declaration on the Right to Development of 1986, is worth quoting. According to this Declaration, development is:

> a comprehensive economic, social, cultural and political process, which aims at the constant improvement of the well-being of the entire population and of all its inhabitants on the basis of their active, free and meaningful participation in development and in the fair distribution of the benefits resulting therefrom.[3]

Development, then, aims at enhanced quality of life, including the reduction of poverty, and is to be contrasted with growth, which often lacks these aims (and often fails to fulfil them). Not all development need be desirable or praiseworthy, as aims are not always satisfied, despite the best of intentions. Ethical qualifications could also be necessary if development were to conflict either with the preservation of biodiversity or with equity between generations; an active generation could in theory develop out of poverty but impoverish its successors and severely degrade their environment.

The **sustainability** of a practice or of a society is basically its capacity to be practised or maintained indefinitely, and the main point of the early advocacy of sustainable forms of society (on the part of Herman Daly and others) was the importance of recognizing limits to certain forms of growth, including ecological limits.[4] If sustainable practices are to be capable of forming part of a sustainable world system, then as well as not undermining themselves they will not undermine other practices or systems that would otherwise be sustainable, including a potentially sustainable global system; otherwise there would be nothing unsustainable about an internally sustainable society that exported unsustainability to other parts of the world, whether in the form of pollution or of economic exploitation. Sustainability theory, it should be added, has generally been neutral between anthropocentrism and non-anthropocentrism. Preservationists could criticize it on this basis, but its supporters could claim that it can be reconciled with preservationism. What has been less clear is whether it can be reconciled with social justice, of the kind stressed by developmentalists.

The claim of the Brundtland Report was that development could be combined with sustainability, and practical policies were depicted for achieving this on a global basis. Sustainable development was defined as development that 'meets the needs of the present without compromising the ability of future generations to meet their own needs',[5] and this definition has become central among accounts of sustainable development. However, even if a prior definition of development such as that supplied above is assumed, the Brundtland definition leaves sustainable development *under*defined. Thus sustainability appears merely to concern refraining from impeding future generations meeting their needs rather than introducing and establishing benign practices which they could maintain and pass on to their successors. There is no overt recognition here of limits, even though the report goes on to show such recognition in the next sentence;[6] and there is no overt recognition of environmental aspects of sustainability, although the report goes on to discuss 'socially and environmentally sustainable development',[7] and even to recognize non-anthropocentric values.[8] While the report later makes good several of these deficiencies, its central concepts were not made as clear as they might have been.

Subsequently, sustainable development was redefined in a United Nations Environment Programme report (*Caring for the Earth*) as 'improving the quality of life while living within the carrying capacity of supporting ecosystems',[9] and this has become the other widely recognized core definition, as Michael Jacobs observes.[10] This definition recognizes environmental limits and is explicit in relating development to quality of life, but omits mention of meeting needs and misleadingly appears to endorse the applicability of the concept of carrying capacity to human populations (on which see chapter 3). Nature's intrinsic value, as opposed to its instrumental potential, also goes unrecognized. Yet its implicit mention of environmental limits helpfully suggests that sustainable development is implicitly environmentally sustainable, as is also recognized in the Brundtland Report.[11]

The undemandingness of the two classical definitions may help to explain the ability of governments to endorse sustainable development at Rio, even though they might have disagreed about its detailed content. Jacobs rightly rejects the view that the concept can be made to mean whatever one likes,[12] but goes too far in suggesting that it is an essentially contestable concept, a normative concept with no more than a vague primary meaning 'coalesced around the Brundtland and *Caring for the Earth* definitions'.[13] For, while sustainable development is neutral with regard to issues such as the intrinsic value of non-human creatures, there is every reason to take its core to comprise varieties of development that are environmentally and socially sustainable (that is, capable of being maintained indefinitely), where 'development' is understood as defined in the United Nations Declaration cited above. 'Development', that is, is understood here as a comprehensive economic, social, cultural and political process, which aims at the constant improvement of the well-being of all the inhabitants of a territory on the basis of their active, free and meaningful participation in this process and in the distribution of the resulting benefits to satisfy their basic needs. ('Constant improvement' need not mean perpetual increments to welfare extending across the indefinite future, but could mean 'improvement from present levels to a level where needs are met, which is itself constantly maintained thereafter' in the sense that no generation falls below it.)

This formulation still leaves plenty of room for interpretation and debate (not least of the kinds that Jacobs goes on to specify), but also motivates and thus elucidates that debate by supplying the kind of core that makes the debate intelligible and worth having. (The core meaning as recognized by Jacobs seems too tenuous and too protean for this role.) Besides, sustainable development is not essentially a normative concept, since those using the terms 'sustainable development' need not be expressing approval, and we can make sense of people being opposed to sustainable development itself, whether on grounds (supposedly) of its inadequate environmental sensitivity, or (arguably) of insufficient provision for the future in terms of inter-generational equity, or (even) of its silence on social and international exploitation in the present. However, the comparatively specific and demanding nature of sustainable development (as defined here) also explains why sustainable development is not easily achieved, but this does not make discussion about how to approximate to it in practice any the less worthwhile.

Debates about sustainable development

Jacobs is right, however, that the primary concept facilitates debates about alternative conceptions of sustainable development, and introduces four 'faultlines of contestation' and corresponding sets of alternative interpretations. The first concerns the degree of environmental protection required. While all sides agree that economic development and environmental protection must be integrated, the 'weak' version of sustainable development involves a trade-off between growth and such protection, whereas the strong interpretation accepts environmental limits, sometimes based on the carrying capacity of ecosystems[14] and sometimes on a precautionary approach (see pp. 144–6) in face of dangers of damaging and irreversible change. Julie Davidson adds clarity by characterizing the strong or radical interpretation as typically recognizing intrinsic value in the natural environment, for this recognition could (and does) supply a ground for environmental limits.[15] The radical version would here seem more consistent than the weak one (since growth is not as such a goal of sustainable development), but is not itself a mandatory interpretation, since sustainable development is not essentially committed to radical interpretations of carrying capacities, nor to recognition of intrinsic value in nature. However, adherents of a resilient version of the precautionary approach and/or of belief in the intrinsic value of many natural entities would have reason to prefer the strong or radical interpretation, irrespective of their beliefs about the carrying capacity of ecosystems. I return to 'weak' and 'strong' versions of sustainability below.

The second faultline concerns social and international equity, which, as Jacobs attests, is central in Southern (Third World) perspectives, where raising living standards for the poor is a pressing concern, and where the distribution of global resources (including finance) in such a way as to facilitate this is understandably demanded (as at the recent Johannesburg Summit of 2002). But these perspectives tend to be ignored in government and business circles in the North, where sustainable development tends to be regarded as an environmental issue only. (UNCED estimated ten years ago that an annual transfer of $125 billion from North to South was needed to enable developing countries to develop sustainably.)[16]

Here the Southern version seems much more consistent with the Brundtland Report and the Rio Declaration, except perhaps where the issue is local sustainability in Northern localities; and even then the environmental footprint of a locality needs to be understood in an international context, in case the price of apparent domestic sustainability is unsustainability elsewhere. Southern versions confront such problems as how sustainability can be prioritized where widespread poverty urgently needs to be alleviated,[17] but they contrive to reconcile these goals, not least out of concern that the environmental needs of the poor be addressed. The issue of equity supplies a strong reason to resist the tendency to replace talk of 'sustainable development' with talk of 'sustainability'; the fact that these phrases are often used interchangeably disguises the more important fact that their meanings are not the same.

The third faultline concerns participation, where governments and businesses favour a top-down interpretation, restricting the range of parties consulted and limiting the scope of consultation to implementation rather than objectives and policies. Contrastingly, the more radical perspective favours bottom-up participation of a much more inclusive and unrestricted kind. While participation is not mentioned in the *Caring for the Earth* definition of sustainable development, it is implicit in previous United Nations statements on development such as the *Declaration* cited above, in the Rio Declaration, and in *Agenda 21* (the global action plan signed by the governments represented at Rio).[18] It is also implicit in the Brundtland definition (despite Jacobs' suggestion to the contrary)[19] in so far as the pivotal notion of development presupposed statements such as that of the *Declaration* that made participation by the entire population of the essence. *Agenda 21* in particular requires the participation of every sector of society;[20] hence the bottom-up interpretation has an interpretative edge.

Jacobs' fourth faultline concerns the scope of the subject area of sustainable development. While government and business circles tend to restrict sustainable development to environmental protection, other circles often relate it to issues of health, education and social welfare. This expanded application of the concept can be traced back to the centrality of 'quality of life' in the *Caring for the Earth* definition, and can be justified on the basis that sustainable development applies not only to the environment but to social and economic practices and structures in general. While this broadening of the scope of sustainable development makes it open to the criticism that it becomes a less specialized and distinctive concept, it is difficult to deny that its scope is any narrower than the range of aspects of development capable of being or becoming sustainable.[21] Certainly, where the structures of society need to be overhauled to tackle poverty, as in many Southern countries, there is little alternative to understanding sustainable development in such a light. No less long-term a view of sustainable development need be taken; but what has to be recognized is that long-term sustainability often cannot be initiated without attention to drastic short-term social change in the near future.

Jacobs adds that radical responses to the four faultline issues (the strong, egalitarian, bottom-up and broad interpretations of sustainable development) tend to be held together by the same people, holders of 'the sustainable development world-view'. Correspondingly the weak, non-egalitarian, top-down and narrow interpretations are also prone to coincide in the positions of central government and business interests.[22] Given the entrenched official support for sustainable development, this allows of 'the articulation and dissemination of a radical world-view under the shelter of government and business approval'.[23] Julie Davidson develops these ideas, suggesting that a business-as-usual approach should be rejected in favour of sustainable development as both a political philosophy and 'a new way of living';[24] I shall be returning to her views about this conception of the good life and its relation to liberal political theory. Jacobs further remarks that one of the motivations for adopting what he regards as the sustainable de-velopment world-view is concern for justice, including inter-generational justice, while another is environmental concern.[25] To investigate how well sustainable development addresses these concerns, we need to consider the debate about weak and strong sustainability.

Sustainable development and the debate about sustainability

A hard-fought debate has also taken place in the field of environ-mental economics between theories of 'weak' and 'strong sustain-ability'. Jacobs (himself a participant in that debate)[26] regards this as effectively the same debate as that between 'weak' and 'strong sustainable development', except that (unlike that debate) the **sustainability** debate concerns concepts of capital.[27] Yet a debate about sustaining capital resources and whether technology com-prises a substitute for 'natural capital' seems far removed from one about whether (say) equity and participation are implications of sustainable development. So the debate about capital (as discussed here) is going to need to be transcended to ensure that sustainable development issues are adequately addressed.

The principal source of this debate is the concern, implicit in definitions of sustainable development, that future generations should have resources (both technological and natural) to meet their own needs, comparable to those available in the present. Exploitation of non-renewable natural resources and destruction of renewable resources would reduce the resources available unless equivalent resources become available through technology. If human-made capital (machines and technological know-how) can usually be substituted for natural resources, and this substitution is actually carried through generation by generation, then this seems to supply the secret of sustainable resources, or 'sustainability'. But if such unlimited substitution would undermine either natural systems or social systems, then sustainability involves limits to substitution, and the preservation of more natural resources (or capital) in their natural form. The former stance is usually referred to as 'weak sustainability', and the latter stance 'strong sustainability'. Faced with the question of what sustainability is supposed to sustain, both theories answer 'capital'. Both theories also seem to offer prospects of supplying a measure of capital, both natural and human-made, and thus of making talk of sustainability more readily operational.

However, Alan Holland has shown that the prospects of measuring natural capital are illusory. Thus the value of resources such as a tree or a block of stone in terms of their potential uses varies from place to place and culture to culture depending on markets and on the technology available, and so would-be measures of their potential for development purposes would have to be endlessly relativized to the state of knowledge and of demand at one time or another,[28] and thus become pointless. Even so, sustainability might remain important as a qualitative concept; future generations would be unlikely to thank their predecessors if they were deprived of resources simply because the economic value of natural resources could not satisfactorily be measured. It could be particularly important to discover what limits there may be to the substitution of technology for natural capital, in keeping with the concern for environmental protection underlying both the Brundtland Report and *Caring for the Earth*.

To the extent that the question of substitution can be asked about natural resources (construed as natural capital), the answer must surely be that there are limits to substitution, at least in practice.[29] No human-made substitute for the ozone layer is likely to protect terrestrial species from skin-cancer; and there must be limits to global warming if existing ecosystems are not to be transformed, and existing coastlines and islands are not to be inundated. Even if a technological replacement for the ozone layer is possible in theory, and even if the absorption of carbon dioxide by the oceans could be increased by technological means, the risks and possible side-effects involved in these implicit global experiments make it massively wrong to undertake them. While much substitution is compatible with systems remaining intact (as when forests are replanted), some natural systems need to be left intact and unsubstituted if there is to be any cultural arena at all in which acts of substitution can be contemplated, debated or rejected.

Nevertheless, conducting the debate about sustainability in these terms remains unsatisfactory. If the criterion justifying substitution consists in the resources available for human purposes, then, as Wilfred Beckerman argues, it cannot be justified to hold back from investment in human-made capital (such as building houses or a school) that might have benefited the poor simply to save some species of beetle.[30] If it is right instead to build the houses or the school a short distance away and save these species, there must be some ground other than human interests. The strangeness of conducting the entire debate in these anthropocentric terms also emerges from the examples of a tree and a block of stone selected above. For the economic debate about sustainability and **substitutability** treats both of these alike as 'natural capital' (and treats whales and tigers in exactly the same way), ignoring the fact that trees, whales and tigers are living creatures with a good of their own, and cannot be regarded as nothing but resources (or, therefore, as nothing but capital). Besides, as Holland remarks, economic sustainability is in no way guaranteed to remove existing injustices, and risks actually perpetuating them.[31] Unlike policies of sustainable development, it has no obvious implications for intra-generational (social and/or international) justice.

These shortcomings of understanding sustainability in terms of capital (whether natural, human-made or total) can be avoided if sustainability is construed in some different manner, better able to uphold ethical and environmental concerns as well as economic ones. Sustainable practices and societies, certainly, require both raw materials and suitable technology, sufficient for the needs of each generation (for example, for the production of electricity), and thus may positively demand the introduction of new, greener technology to replace the polluting technology of the present. But valuing nature solely on the basis of its value for human utilization is misguided, and involves a narrow form of anthropocentrism. Even within an anthropocentric perspective, recognition of nature's aesthetic value is sufficient to show the defectiveness of this approach. (It is seriously possible that people need natural beauty in some degree for the sake of their mental health;[32] but the economic value of the difference made is unlikely to be recognized in calculations of nature's value.)

In place of a 'natural capital' interpretation of sustainability, Holland suggests a 'physical stock' interpretation, involving an inventory of numbers of known species and of their members, and of quantities of fossil fuels.[33] While the publication of such inventories might encourage preservation, surveys of 'indicator' species and habitats might instead be used to monitor environmental sustainability,[34] both in terms of the survival of particular species and of their diversity (a valuable suggestion). However, where the question concerns what is to be sustained, we need to question the view of Holland and others that nature in general (including inanimate nature) is intrinsically valuable and to be sustained as such, and to look deeper for an answer, since theorists both of sustainability and of sustainable development have standardly envisaged society or societies as included in what should be made sustainable.

Part of the answer to this question lies in sustainable social practices and systems, as the core definitions of sustainable development suggest. (Not all sustainable social systems are equitable, and so social sustainability cannot be supposed to guarantee that all values are honoured, but social sustainability may still be necessary if sustainability theory is to be reconcilable with inter-generational equity.) Another part concerns the sustaining of major ecosystems (such as the carbon and nitrogen cycles, and the proportion of carbon dioxide in the atmosphere), for without this the prospects that development or society can be run in an environmentally sustainable manner are slim.

Yet a further part of the answer must be held (at least from the biocentric perspective defended in chapter 2) to concern the preservation of intrinsically valuable natural creatures, and thus of as many species and habitats (some of them as wilderness) as possible; this interpretation of sustainability would normally cohere with the others, but would cast doubt on the sustainability of many current practices where species extinctions and habitat loss are among the side-effects. (While biological diversity is neither intrinsically valuable nor necessarily related to sustainability, there remain strong enough contingent connections between this kind of diversity and both natural value and sustainability for it to form a valuable indicator of values beyond itself.) These various ways of conceptualizing sustainability would avoid some of the shortcomings of standard approaches.

Since, however, current senses of 'sustainability' in terms of capital may by now be too entrenched to be revised, it may be better to regard these answers as contributions to the specification of environmentally and socially sustainable development. This concept is usually understood more broadly than that of sustainability, as being relevant to concerns about distribution (both inter-generational and intra-generational) as well as to concerns about environmental protection. (Without entailing that these kinds of equity are delivered, sustainable development involves attempts to provide for the basic needs of each relevant society and generation.)

One problem confronting advocates of sustainable development arises from Wilfred Beckerman's understandable resistance to any suggestion that there are obligations (whether of benevolence or of justice) to produce an ever-increasing quality of life across the future, something that the *Caring for the Earth* definition of 'sustainable development' in terms of 'improving the quality of life' might be taken to imply.[35] However, neither a perennially rising quality of life seems to have been intended in the various definitive reports (nor at Rio), nor for that matter a perennially equal quality of life across the generations, let alone perennial economic growth. Hence, sustainable development should be taken to involve raising the quality of life to one where needs (and particularly basic needs) cease to be unsatisfied and facilitating practices likely to sustain the satisfaction of needs indefinitely (as was suggested above), without perpetual increments to quality of life being envisaged. As Alan Carter has pointed out, 'sustainable development' need not be construed as processes of development that 'proceed forever', and could instead be used to refer to 'the attainment of a certain level that is viewed as a precondition for sustainable lifestyles',[36] or (to formulate the same thought more explicitly) as the participatory attainment of a developed condition of society involving ecologically and socially sustainable practices.

Another problem is Andrew Dobson's criticism that sustainable development essentially involves an anthropocentric theory of environmental sustainability, which values nature merely as **critical natural capital**, or as a stock of resources that happen to be indispensable for human survival and development.[37] While this classification has apparent analytic advantages, seemingly allowing sustainable development to be related to some forms of strong sustainability theory and contrasted with others, it unnecessarily renders sustainable development incompatible with any recognition of inter-species equity, overlooking explicit recognition of the intrinsic value of nature in the Brundtland Report.[38] In fact concern for sustainable development, even when given the radical interpretation suggested by Jacobs above, need not be anthropocentric; environmentally sustainable development can be harnessed to a non-anthropocentric conception of environmental sustainability which recognizes both human needs and the independent value of non-human nature.

So the ethical and environmental inadequacies of economic theories of sustainability redirect us to issues of whether sustainable development offers a framework within which these inadequacies can be made good. Sustainable development may not imply the full range of future-related responsibilities identified in chapter 4, but is almost certainly compatible with those that it does not directly embody. Much the same applies to its relation to intragenerational equity. Since sustainable development seeks to remedy the causes of poverty, to make provision for enhanced qualities of life, and (at least on the radical interpretation) to secure the participation of everyone affected, it encapsulates some central requirements of social justice, and is arguably reconcilable with others. With regard to environmental protection, the non-anthropocentric interpretation commended here supplements the undoubted provision for environmental resources that is implicit in all interpretations, and requires its adherents to recognize and protect natural values.[39]

Sustainable development is not a ready-made panacea for the solution of all the problems; nor can it be expected to guarantee that long-term responsibilities with regard to distant generations which happen to have no positive impact on nearer generations are met. But it would be mistaken to reject it on grounds of inadequate environmental sensitivity, just as it should not be rejected because some of its adherents pay insufficient regard to social justice. On the contrary, the concept of sustainable development has sufficient promise to be embraced rather than rejected, and to be developed in accordance with the radical and non-anthropocentric versions that (subject to the support of the precautionary approach, which, as will be seen on pp. 145–6, it certainly receives) are emerging as preferable. In this form it offers probably the most promising route towards the combined destinations of social justice, environmental sensitivity and the discharge of future-related responsibilities, without itself being definitionally committed or essentially (rather than contingently) conducive to those values.

Issues to ponder before population issues are introduced include whether the concept of sustainable development is capable of objective application, the relation of economic sustainability to sustainable development, how far non-anthropocentric and bottom-up interpretations of sustainable development diverge from interpretations accepted by governments, and whether environmentalists and developmentalists can make common cause under the banner of sustainable development.

Population policies and sustainable development

We should now consider the bearing of sustainable development on population issues and policies, and thus on **population ethics**, and relate these questions to the conclusions of previous chapters. The human population of the planet has grown to just over 6 billion, and its continuing growth compromises the ability of governments to deliver acceptable levels of health care, education, fresh water and other services,[40] although rates of population increase have recently been declining. There is also a potential problem regarding food-supply. While 11 billion people could be supported by the current cultivated acreage at current levels of consumption if rates of food production increase by 150 per cent, far fewer (the figure supplied by Brundtland is 7.5 billion) could even so be fed at a more adequate level of consumption, suited to supporting a less marginal and more decent quality of life, such as 9,000 calories per day. Increases in acreage or further increases in productivity on a sustainable basis could raise this figure,[41] but could well be hard to sustain in view of global warming and other environmental problems such as the salination of cultivable land and the growth of deserts.

All this already supplies strong grounds for the total of the human population to be stabilized (as argued in chapter 1), and at a potentially sustainable level such as 8 billion (the level suggested on a similar basis in chapter 3), at which the evils of environmental degradation and recurrent famine could (with goodwill, effort and good planning) be avoided. Higher, unsustainable levels of population would be likely (as was mentioned there) either to undermine the quality of life of many people through overcrowding, or to consume resources in ways that could not be made good through inter-communal exchanges such as trade, or seriously to disrupt the environment. (The outlook might change if the colonization of other planets were in prospect, but we cannot afford to rely on such developments.) Yet sudden or large reductions in population would produce other evils such as reduced morale and an ageing population; such problems suggest that any reductions of the global total should either be gradual or be avoided altogether. Granted the foreseeable population increase of the next two decades, stabilization at a sustainable level is thus preferable both to overpopulation and to significant population decline.

As was added in chapter 4, there would be dire consequences if the human population increases to a level at which it cannot be recurrently sustained by the life-support systems of the planet. Such a level would involve fluctuations of the human population on a scale so severe that they should not be risked. Even before that point, population increases are likely to conflict with biodiversity preservation, as was also mentioned there. While current rates of species loss may not be due so much to population growth as to economics-driven deforestation, further rapid population growth is likely to make the destruction of wildlife habitats inevitable. Accordingly, as was argued in that chapter, non-human interests (in combination with human interests) support a somewhat lower target for stabilization than human interests alone suggest. This consideration suggests that the target for stabilization should be somewhat lower than 8 billion, even if a level of 8 billion could have proved to be sustainable.

Let us suppose that the target for stabilization should be 7.5 billion. Does that mean that we should plan for this level of population, when planning energy supplies and (relatedly) when calculating the carbon emissions of the middle and later decades of this century? To plan on the assumption that the target will be met could be highly irresponsible. While rates of population increase are recognized to be diminishing, there is a significant likelihood that a somewhat higher level than 7.5 billion will be reached before population stabilizes. This being so, we should plan for the level that is probable, even if it is undesirable. Even if we believe that 7.5 billion is a sustainable total and that the likely higher total is unsustainable, we should still plan for the foreseeable needs of the likely larger total. Otherwise we are likely to be responsible for the basic needs of very large numbers of people not being satisfied, and for the climatic side-effects of their lives and activities not being foreseen or mitigated. This would in turn make it harder for them to plan to reduce their numbers to a sustainable level, and to implement such a plan.

These considerations further illustrate why we should be reluctant to endorse Holland's view (mentioned in chapter 4) that the uncertainty of future outcomes means that there are no responsibilities to generate or facilitate such outcomes, as opposed to unspecified 'procedural' (deontological) responsibilities to treat future generations fairly.[42] Certainly, plans need to be flexible and revisable precisely because future outcomes are less than certain and prospects are continually changing. Yet planning for future decades and generations is likely to remain a key responsibility of every generation from the present onwards, since each future generation is likely to need to inherit a strategy to cope with the interrelated problems of food supply, energy supply, access to fresh water, environmental quality and human numbers, if disastrous outcomes are to be avoided and quality of life upheld. It can take decades to secure international agreement even on a single global problem, such as global warming. So problems may become insoluble for a given generation, and disasters inevitable, unless their predecessors have laid plans to make tolerable outcomes possible once the given generation itself arrives.

Such plans can justifiably include policies encouraging people to limit the size of their families, as long as their doing so is voluntary, minorities are not discriminated against, people's vulnerability is not manipulated to induce them to comply with national objectives, and the people concerned are encouraged to participate freely and democratically in elaborating and implementing the policy. Population policies fostering education, particularly the education of girls and women, have the merit of combining the intrinsic value of education itself with prospects of reduced fertility (that is, reduced rates of births per woman of childbearing age). Yet such policies are most likely to be effective where healthcare provision and other social services mean that parents no longer need a large family to ensure that they will have surviving children to care for them in their old age (see **the child-survival hypothesis** and **the demographic transition theory**, presented in chapter 3); and people can fairly be expected to participate in such policies only in this kind of social environment.[43]

Population policies, therefore, should not be adopted in isolation, but should be components in integrated policies of development, as was maintained in Principle 5 of the Cairo Conference on Population and Development Program of Action.[44] Improved provision for education in developing countries at the same time provides opportunities for environmental education, itself vital if environmental sustainability (including protection of wild species and their habitats) is to be attainable. **Integrated policies of sustainable development** would therefore include provision for environmental education as well as for education in literacy, healthcare and family planning. Such policies are equally applicable to countries of the North as well as of the South.

Some further links between stabilizing the human population at a sustainable level and environmental sustainability should be underlined. This process is most likely to take place if the current trend for rates of population growth to diminish and fall away continues worldwide until the populations of most countries have ceased to grow, as has happened already in several countries in Europe. In this kind of scenario, some of the pressures to build houses on yet more green fields or countryside and to colonize yet further wild places can be expected to abate as population stability is reached. Not all such pressures are likely to abate unless the commercial rewards for the kinds of so-called 'development' just mentioned are counteracted by governmental regulation. But the justification currently available that rural space is needed to house a growing population would no longer be available.

Nor would poor people in Third World countries be under pressure to bring more and more marginal land under cultivation to anything like the current extent, at least if systems of land tenure allow them to take over unused land that has already been culti-vated in the past. Failing that, current incentives to cultivate marginal land will remain in place. This suggests that in the Third World policies of land reform have an indispensable role in environmental sustainability as well as in social justice, and should receive a high priority even where they are not expected to transform agricultural production.[45] Land security is often a condi-tion of falling birth rates, and is likely to be required by the goal of stabilizing population levels as well as by these other goals.

Population, neo-Malthusianism, justice and sustainability

However, in periods of population increase, environmentalists are sometimes tempted to treat population as the main source of environmental problems, and to speak and write as if the growth of human numbers were a cancerous growth on the face of the planetary biosphere. Besides inclining towards the theory that the growth of human numbers is the cause of these problems (a theory already discussed in chapter 1), such **neo-Malthusians** (latter-day followers of the eighteenth-century economist Thomas Robert Malthus) are prone to regard this growth as itself an evil, though usually without endorsing the view of the historical Malthus that nothing can be done to tackle it. Such was the stance, for example, of the neo-Malthusian Paul Ehrlich in *The Population Bomb*,[46] for whom 'overpopulation' was the key global problem.

Recently a much more sophisticated version has been adopted by Holmes Rolston, when writing about habitat loss in the Third World and the impact of population growth, and in the course of arguing that feeding starving people is not always the first prior-ity. 'For a couple to have two children', he recognizes, 'may be a blessing', but the tenth child is 'a tragedy'.[47] In this context, much of the current human population of the world is said to resemble a cancer (glossed here as 'an explosion of unregulated growth') and many of its individuals as 'another cell of cancerous growth'.[48] Such tragic growth, he suggests, amounts to overpopulation, and leads to a deteriorating quality of life for humanity, to deterior-ating natural resources, and to declining ecosystem health and integrity.[49]

But can population growth be regarded as a cancer? The answer has to be in the negative. A cancer is not just 'an explosion of unregulated growth'. If it were, then species such as mushrooms, rabbits and locusts would often be cancerous too. A cancer is also a growth bearing no positive intrinsic value, that is potentially fatal to a living creature capable of health, a creature which is thus a potential bearer of intrinsic value itself (as I have argued more fully in chapter 2 and elsewhere).[50]

Yet the suggestion that the current human population of the Earth is a cancer is deeply at variance with all this. On the one hand, unlike a cancer, this population consists of potential bearers of intrinsic value; and to represent such individuals (when numerous) as cancerous is to disregard this value, and to think of them instrumentally, as means only, and as nothing but dysfunctional ones too. On the other hand, what the collection of these intrinsically valuable individuals is supposed to be fatal to is the biosphere, which (I have argued in chapter 2) is highly valuable not in itself but because it generates bearers of intrinsic value such as individual humans and other creatures. But if the underlying suggestion is that human beings might be a cancer because they could threaten fellow creatures and each other, it is an exaggeration which distracts attention from ways in which these same human beings, in the same numbers, could (if better and more fairly organized) avoid posing any such threats either to humanity or to other species.

The discourse of human population as cancer is also dangerous. If, beyond certain numbers, humans comprise a cancer, then the motivations to save human life, to heal injury and to cure illness are likely to wither away. For if each individual existence beyond a certain numerical level is an evil, then (whatever humanitarianism may dictate) there must be virtue in letting such individuals die, if not in speeding the process. This discourse thus generates a reluctance to show solidarity with vulnerable humans, and can predispose those who endorse it to misanthropy, and to the kind of holistic ethic that is committed to **ecosystem** health and **integrity** but not so clearly to the health and integrity of individuals. Yet it is from the health and integrity of individuals that the analogy of ecosystem health and integrity was derived in the first place. Thus the purportedly factual claim that population growth is cancerous turns out to carry unacceptable conceptual and normative implications. As such, it should be firmly rejected.[51]

The suggestion that a choice has to be made between feeding people and saving nature is also misleading, since (as Rolston recognizes) other strategies for feeding people are usually available, not involving destruction of remaining areas of natural habitat. (As David Schmidtz has shown, strategies have often been found in the Third World that combine environmental protection with the participation of and benefits for local people.)[52] However, while this misleading antithesis appears central in the later stages of Rolston's text, the question mark in his title 'Feeding People Versus Saving Nature?' hints that these courses of action are not after all exclusive alternatives. So also do his passages about poverty having a range of causes including unjust distribution, and including the refusal to redistribute resources needed by the poor, both within societies and internationally. Here the suggestion is that solutions to poverty involve rectifying past or present injustices rather than releasing areas of natural habitat for cultivation, which, he adds, is in any case unlikely to produce sustainable benefits.[53]

The rectification of injustices is thus part of Rolston's account of sustainable development, alongside environmental protection. Rolston quotes with approval Principle 4 of the Rio Declaration, which declares environmental protection a constitutive part of the development process, and vital for achieving sustainable development.[54] Sustainable development, in other words, besides requiring greater social justice to meet the needs of the poor, and structural change (both at national and international levels) to entrench such an improved distribution of resources, also involves environmental protection, without which it is not environmentally sustainable, and without which the poor will be among the sufferers.[55]

Yet these important conclusions need to be supplemented where problems of famine and of population are concerned. As Onora O'Neill and David Crocker have remarked, the problem underlying famine is liable to be persistent malnutrition and, if this is tackled soon enough, famines can be averted. Tackling it involves a combination of a population policy to minimize population growth and of a resources policy to ensure that the poor have access to the food that they need.[56] Crocker goes on to cite evidence from Jean Drèze and Amartya Sen that famines are preventable by human action, and argues that this is usually the case with regard to malnutrition too.[57] However, these same policies cohere best and have lasting value only within integrated policies of development (see p. 140), of the kind alluded to in the UN Declaration on the Right to Development. Within such policies, women as well as men would have the opportunity not only to plan their families but also to share in democratic decision-making.[58]

Thus, before we reach for neo-Malthusian diagnoses (whether of famine, of malnutrition, or of environmental degradation) in terms of 'overpopulation', we need to think through the full implications of social and economic development. For the ultimate goal of development is, as Crocker says, *human* development.[59] We also need to ponder the full implications of its effective frustration in many exploitative societies, and not to forget the capabilities of human beings to solve their own problems, including problems of population growth, as long as they are given the opportunities to do so.

Sustainable development should, then, be conceptualized not only in terms of social development and environmental protection but also in terms of the capacities of human beings to develop themselves and their societies autonomously. Without this basis, programmes and policies of environmental protection are likely to founder, something which applies to population policies too. Given this basis, and given an awareness of nature's multiple value, development has good prospects of becoming and remaining sustainable, environmentally as well as socially.

The Precautionary Principle

Sustainable development, as has been mentioned, for good reasons seeks to respect environmental limits. But it is not easy to reach scientific consensus about where these limits lie. By the time they have been identified it would often be too late to take preventive action, and serious or irreversible damage would have been done. To resolve this problem, **the Precautionary Principle** has been devised, first in German and European legislation, and later in legislation in Britain and internationally. In general terms, this principle declares that where there is reason to regard a substance or process as environmentally damaging, preventive action or regulation should be undertaken despite the absence of scientific certainty. While this is not a basic principle, it gives valuable guidance and valuably supplements other principles when decisions have to be taken against a background of qualified uncertainty.

This principle takes stronger and weaker forms. An example of a stronger form is the London Declaration (1987) on the Protection of the North Sea. This Declaration authorizes the regulation of substances 'when there is reason to assume that certain damage or harmful effects on the living resources of the sea are likely to be caused by such substances, even where there is no scientific evidence to prove a causal link between emissions and effects'.[60] If such a strong principle were generalized, a very great deal of regulation of potentially dangerous substances and processes would be authorized. An example of a weaker form is found in the Rio Declaration (1992), which states that 'where there are threats of serious or irreversible damage lack of full scientific certainty shall not be used as a reason for postponing cost-effective measures to prevent environmental degradation'.[61] This is weaker because a smaller range of potential damage is recognized and because other reasons than the lack of scientific certainty might be found against regulatory action.

The reference in the Rio Declaration to serious or irreversible damage was probably intended to be construed as concerning damage to human interests, present or future. But since ecosystems that make little difference to human interests could also be damaged, and there are (as was seen in chapter 4) non-anthropocentric reasons to protect such systems as well as the others, the principle could readily be reinterpreted as concerning damage to all the ecosystems of the planet.

The restriction to damage that is 'serious or irreversible' appears wise, since otherwise too much regulation and too much caution would have become mandatory. There are certainly problems for the interpretation of both these terms. (Is damage that replaces one species of butterfly in an ecosystem with another serious or not? Does the loss of a subspecies of invertebrate that is a variant of a populous and widely distributed species count as irreversible damage?) Yet the problems encountered over borderline cases do not show that there are no clear cases, nor that phrases such as 'serious or irreversible damage' cannot be interpreted in practice. Thus where there is a risk of human action crossing some ecological threshold or destabilizing something as crucial to terrestrial life forms as the ozone layer, the principle is clearly brought into play, even in its weaker versions. Accordingly the precautionary approach already clearly supports a strong or radical rather than a weak interpretation of sustainable development.

Weaker versions of the principle, however, are themselves at risk of excessive attenuation when preventive measures are required to be 'cost-effective'. This requirement could easily be interpreted by a corporation or agency liable to pay such costs either as justifying less expensive kinds of preventive action only or as precluding such action altogether (on grounds such as that costs per life saved would be greater than the rate currently recognized in economists' costings). But interpretations like these would undermine the rationale of the principle, which is to prohibit potentially disastrous undertakings. So requirements of cost-effectiveness should not be included in the principle.[62] The alternative requirement that the best available technology be employed is intrinsically more promising,[63] but would need to be interpreted so as not to stop preventive action being initiated; in many countries the latest technology could not be afforded, and 'best available' would have to be interpreted as 'best among technologies accessible at the relevant time and place'.

The phrase from the Rio Declaration 'lack of full scientific certainty' may appear too inclusive, since scientific certainty (let alone full scientific certainty) is seldom if ever attained. What is in fact appealed to, for example by those who question the justification of the Kyoto process and its attempts to mitigate global warming, is lack of complete scientific consensus on the part of all reputable scientists in the relevant field. But this is just the kind of case where a principle of precaution is needed, for in the absence of a long-term international agreement on actions and policies the probable large-scale environmental damage (for example, from global warming) is likely to become irremediable. Since uncertainty is perennially likely to be the background of much environmental decision-making, no requirement that it be replaced either by scientific certainty or even by scientific consensus before action is taken can be either prudent or acceptable. In these circumstances, the emphatic wording of the Rio Declaration can also be regarded as acceptable.

These interpretations allow the Precautionary Principle to be used as guidance in a wide range of issues relating to environmental limits, and thus allow the first two words of the key phrase 'environmentally sustainable development' to be readily understood as indicating preventive action. The principle does not provide for the full range of the goal of environmentally sustainable development, since it gives no relevant guidance on how to initiate programmes of (for example) sustainable agriculture, forestry or fisheries. Nor can it invariably be given the last word in decision-making, since preventive action could in theory conflict with requirements of (say) social justice, which might supply a strong reason against such action. Yet for all that, the principle is proving indispensable in a wide range of cases of uncertainty (as the global problems of the ozone layer and of global warming have made clear).[64] It can be defended by reference to the likely favourable balance of the consequences of its habitual observance, and particularly by the evils likely to be prevented, and is likely to be needed by every legislature and in all international environmental decision-making. (One example of what is needed is the Biosafety Protocol, for which G77 and African countries in particular have been pressing, giving such countries entitlements to regulate trade in genetically engineered products in their territories, and enshrining the Precautionary Principle accordingly. The ratification of this protocol by European powers is currently awaited.)[65]

Sustainable development and liberal democracy

Despite the endorsement of environmental sustainability at Rio by most of the world's liberal democracies, there are genuine problems about whether liberal democracy and environmental sustainability are even compatible. Writers such as Andrew Vincent argue that there are deep tensions between liberalism (with its stress on freedom) and environmental sensitivity (with its support for regulation of production and consumption), and that in its stronger versions liberalism rejects any curtailment of the powers of the individual agent, and acknowledges no value not dependent on human agency or choice.[66] Similarly Marius de Geus maintains that the individualism inherited from John Locke and favoured within liberal democracy, together with the close links between liberal democracies and market interests, make liberal democracy unlikely to endorse any 'hard' or substantial concept of sustainability.[67] Both Vincent and de Geus recognize alternative versions of liberalism, such as that of John Stuart Mill, as less intransigent and more promising, but have reservations about their adequacy where either environmentalism or the advocacy of sustainability are in question.

In addition, it is widely held that in a liberal democracy the state is and must remain neutral between conceptions of the good life,[68] and that advocates of environmental sustainability implicitly favour the adoption by the state of such a conception. Liberal democracies provide a neutral, politically pluralistic forum in which different conceptions of the good can compete and be freely debated, and as such cannot endorse any of them; yet advocates of environmentally sensitive lifestyles, compatible with environmentally sustainable practices, the abatement of pollution and the greening of production and consumption, are committed to seeking just such an endorsement of a conception of the good.

Andrew Dobson, however, brings in some important qualifications. Even if the liberal state has to be neutral, citizens are entitled to argue for an environmentalist ethic and for corresponding policies. Besides, the liberal discourse of individual rights can itself be extended in environmentally sensitive directions, for example to non-human animals.[69] Indeed, as Tim Hayward has observed, constitutions have recently been drafted to include among human rights the right to sustainable environment, and there is scope (and a strong case) for this tendency to be taken further.[70] Dobson has also argued that there is no serious incompatibility between the kind of environmental sustainability that seeks to preserve critical natural capital for the sake of present and future human interests and liberal notions of justice involving impartial respect for different theories of the good for human beings, although he anticipates greater problems with regard to non-anthropocentric versions of sustainability.[71] This view still allows for tensions between advocates of regulation to preserve critical natural capital in the form (for example) of clean air, and people who emit fumes from their property (whether homes, gardens, cars or factories). But appeal (whether by legislators or in public enquiries) to the common good is capable of resolving such tensions without liberal traditions being superseded. (This already suggests that liberal traditions may not be neutral in all respects with regard to conceptions of the good.)

Another basis for liberalism to cope with environmental sustainability and the constraints that it calls for consists in resort to Mill's **Harm Principle**, and the kind of social liberalism flowing from it. This principle authorizes coercion (and a fortiori regulation) to prevent the harming of parties other than the agent of the harm. The recognition of future interests broadens the scope of this principle, since the preservation of many ecosystems and the absence of long-lasting pollution are required if such harm is to be prevented. Besides, since harm can be done through inaction, the principle can call for proactive policies, as well as just for restrictions. While de Geus is right that such policies and restrictions are likely to be resisted by vested interests, and that appeals are likely to be made to other liberal values, the significant point is that appeal to the Harm Principle opens the door to considerable provision for sustainability without transgressing liberal traditions.

There are conceptual issues, arising from the work of Derek Parfit, about whether future people can actually be harmed by present action if in the absence of that action they would not have existed. But Parfit reasonably maintains that causing the quality of life of future people to be avoidably lower than that of alternative future people would have been is just as bad as reducing the quality of life of identifiable people.[72] Followers of Mill could therefore reasonably extend the Harm Principle to reductions of the quality of life of future people, whether they take the view that this literally counts as harm[73] or not.

Since the Precautionary Principle seeks to prevent serious or irreversible environmental damage, and this includes both harm and reductions of the quality of life of future generations, this widely recognized principle is available to liberal democracies whenever the Harm Principle becomes applicable to environmental issues in circumstances of uncertainty. This principle, as John

Barry points out in the same connection, is by now entrenched within liberal societies; indeed Barry holds that it can actually be derived from the Harm Principle,[74] and that the Harm Principle can be 'ecologized' by being interpreted in terms of the Precautionary Principle.[75] While additional premises would be required to carry through this derivation to the satisfaction of logicians, adherents of the Harm Principle have considerable difficulty in resisting the Precautionary Principle, and, to secure a hearing in opposition to it, have to resort to caricatures of what it says (for example, claiming that it bans adventurousness).

If, further, the principle is given a non-anthropocentric interpretation, as suggested in the previous section, then harms to ecosystems and wild habitats (as well as to individual animals) fall more clearly within its scope. While this interpretation would not be as widely recognized to be an implication of the Harm Principle, there is a growing number of precedents for applying the Precautionary Principle to the defence of vulnerable ecosystems, and the logic of applying it to potential harm that could affect systems of non-human creatures is difficult to contest.

Since unsustainable practices will often be potentially harmful, appeals to the Precautionary Principle may seem to establish that sustainability is compatible with liberal democracy after all. But the problem of the neutrality of liberal democracy remains to be confronted. Granted that liberal democracies can accommodate both the advocacy and also the implementation of policies of sustainability, it must also accommodate at least the advocacy of unsustainable policies and practices. If so, must it not uphold its neutrality by allowing for their acceptance through the ballot-box and their enactment through legislation? To this question, the answer could be in the negative in a state with constitutional rights to a sustainable environment, as these policies would breach those rights. (Much the same applies to a state like Britain which lacks a written constitution, but which might entrench such rights by subscribing to international treaties guaranteeing rights of this kind.) But would not the establishment of such rights be an infringement of the state's indispensable neutrality?

Not necessarily. For all states, liberal democracies included, depend on a sustainable local environment, and in some measure on a sustainable global environment. Thus practices liable to subvert the safety of the water supply or the wholesomeness of the air are intolerable on grounds of environmental health, and have to be prohibited, and much the same applies to toxic emissions, whether into rivers, the sea or the atmosphere. Since other states have parallel interests, the exporting of unsustainability also has to be debarred in its more clear-cut forms. There are also cases where states need to act together for the sake of global sustainability; ratification of the Kyoto Protocol (in the version elaborated at Bonn and at Marrakesh in 2001) is arguably a good example (see chapter 6), and would oblige the legislatures of countries thus committed to implement cuts of greenhouse gas emissions, and to refrain from adopting legislation likely to generate environmentally unsustainable outcomes (such as increasing or non-declining carbon emissions).

Then again, future international agreements might easily require national regulations limiting petrol and diesel emissions from lorries and other automobiles. While this might seem to conflict with traditional freedoms, such regulations could readily be justified as necessary for a particular country to play its part in making global sustainability possible in the matter of global warming. (In view of the gains to individuals, they could also be represented as increasing rather than reducing individual freedoms.) Further, if the objection were raised that introducing such regulations involved state endorsement of a conception of the good (a 'green' or pro-sustainability conception, maybe), it could be replied that this kind of endorsement of such a conception has become indispensable for the sake of national and of global survival.[76] Thus the constitutional entrenching of policies of sustainability would at least in some cases be justified. Similarly, if in these circumstances an elected government attempted to introduce legislation subversive of international environmental commitments, the country's constitutional courts would be justified in declaring it null and void. Yet its liberal democracy could remain intact.

Whether this constitutional approach could be extended to full endorsement of sustainability must be a matter of debate. The case is strong where tracts or processes of nature can be regarded as critical natural capital, since by definition these form a stock of resources indispensable for human survival and development. Environmentally sustainable development (in this important but limited sense) could justifiably be entrenched in a state's constitution on this basis, and this would give substance to Dobson's claim that this kind of sustainability is substantially compatible with liberal notions of justice. However, where environmentally sustainable development involves conserving nature's intrinsic value, some distinctions are needed. Policies which put this conception of sustainability into practice can, I have suggested, consistently be adopted in a liberal democracy, and such adoption would sometimes involve legislation, for example to protect particular rare or endangered species. But the constitutional entrenchment of such policies might be unwise, except where international treaties required it, since this might make the repeal of these constitutional provisions and withdrawal from related treaties and international groupings the goals of a perennial campaign on the part of anthropocentric and/or nationalist political groups, and thus commit non-anthropocentric and internationalist groups to an avoidable perennial rearguard action.

However, even if there are limits to the wisdom of the constitutional entrenchment of environmentally sustainable development, the practical possibility of liberal democratic legislatures and systems adopting related policies without undermining themselves underlines the contention that liberal democracy is not fundamentally incompatible even with quite strong conceptions of environmental sustainability. Nor, come to that, is it incompatible with commitment to certain related conceptions of the good involving (for example) a positive quality of environmental health (and acceptance of the constraints necessary to achieve this), and positive valuations of recycling and of access to tracts of non-human nature. While these valuations might in turn be related to environmental virtues, the state would not need to go so far as to endorse (let alone require) such virtues when adopting environmental and developmental policies.

Julie Davidson has suggested that the radical interpretation of sustainable development commended by Michael Jacobs involves a distinctive conception of the good life (and 'a New Way of Living') emphasizing human embeddedness in nature, community management of human activities, and an understanding of nature's intrinsic value as constitutive of human flourishing.[77] Certainly, acceptance of the Precautionary Principle is already tantamount to recognition of the need for some amount of regulation of production and consumption, partly on the basis of human embeddedness in nature. But (as I have argued above in chapter 3) neither awareness of nor caring about the intrinsic value to be found in nature need be regarded as constitutive of human flourishing. Hence this particular understanding of human flourishing cannot be regarded as essential to the introduction of environmentally sustainable development, even though both an awareness of the intrinsic value of flourishing natural creatures and an enlarged, multidimensional Aristotelian conception of human flourishing (as commended in chapter 3) would be desirable within such a society, as in any and every society.

Where Davidson is right, as over human embeddedness in nature and over the need for an increased sense of community, this conception of the good remains compatible with a liberal society, just as the Precautionary Principle itself is. But attempts to go beyond this and privilege or even require a particular conception of human flourishing could constrict political freedoms and unduly narrow the state's impartiality. This much must be allowed to stand of the widely accepted belief in the neutrality of the liberal democratic state.

What goes for policies of environmentally sustainable development goes also for integrated development policies, which would often include non-coercive population policies. Population policies are acceptable, I have suggested, as long as participation is voluntary, minorities are not discriminated against, people's vulnerability is not manipulated to induce them to comply with national objectives, and the people concerned are encouraged to participate freely and democratically in elaborating and implementing the policy. Many developing states should adopt such policies, in the interests of stabilizing their own numbers, for the sake of the members of their own future population, for the sake of the non-human species that would otherwise be put at risk, and also to play their part in stabilizing the global population.

Equally, developed countries too should adopt such policies, since increases of their populations exercise much greater environmental impact than increases in developing countries, and also because they cannot expect the South to adopt such policies unless they are willing to play their own part. Developed countries should further consider subsidizing integrated policies of development in developing countries, including population policies, on the consequentialist basis presented by Jesper Ryberg[78] (see chapter 3). Indeed, global sustainability is likely to depend on such policies being adopted in most if not all countries. Since these are non-coercive policies, dependent on voluntary participation and respect for people's rights, they overcome the objections to coercive population policies, and are consistent with liberal democratic systems of government and social life.

While global sustainability is as yet an unrealized goal, considerable strides towards both sustainable development and the stabilization of population have been taken at subnational level within a democratic state since the 1960s in the Indian state of Kerala, through policies of redistributive development. Thus Govindan Parayil relates that:

> In less than thirty years, Kerala, with a population of nearly 30 million (larger than Canada's), has made remarkable progress in lowering infant mortality, decreasing population growth, increasing life expectancy at birth, achieving full literacy, and eliminating extreme poverty and deprivation, all despite very low per capita income.[79]

Land-reform programmes have been introduced, primary and preventive health care promoted, economic inequality reduced, while at the same time strong democratic institutions have taken root. At the same time population growth has been reduced to replacement level, and forest cover, which had previously decreased, is now increasing again, as also is environmental awareness.[80]

Parayil recognizes that Kerala has a long way to go before becoming an exemplar of sustainable development.[81] However, William Alexander is cited as regarding Kerala as a 'prototype' of such development,[82] a reasonable interpretation in the circumstances, while Samir Amin has concluded that the achievements of Kerala show the incorrectness of the view that 'nothing can be done until revolution',[83] and Arran Gare has hailed the success of Kerala in creating autonomous methods of self-liberation from misery, inequity and dependency in all forms.[84] If so much can be achieved in Kerala with such scant resources, the possibilities for the introduction of environmentally sustainable development elsewhere cannot be negligible.

In general, **integrated policies** of development and population can and should thus be welcomed by supporters of sustainable development, or at any rate of its radical interpretation. Thus interpreted, environmentally sustainable development remains at least as promising a route as any other towards the combined goals of social and international justice, sustainable practices and societies, environmental sensitivity and also the discharge of intergenerational responsibilities.

Issues for reflection include how far liberal democracy can accommodate sustainable development, how far the implications of the Precautionary Principle extend, whether voluntary population policies are necessary constituents of policies of sustainable development, whether sustainable development promotes intergenerational equity, and whether sustainable development and biodiversity preservation can always be reconciled.

Summary

The concept of sustainable development combines an internationally agreed concept of development with sustainability and implicit recognition of environmental limits. The strong, egalitarian, bottom-up and broad interpretations of sustainable development supply a coherent radical platform, consistent with biocentrism. The un-acceptability of the assumption of the debate about economic sustainability that nature is simply capital suggests a broader understanding of sustainability in terms of a non-anthropocentric, radical version of sustainable development. Population policies should be integrated with policies of sustainable development and, in the Third World, of land reform. While population growth should not be considered cancerous, Rolston is right to make the rectifica-tion of injustices a condition of sustainable development, which should be understood in terms of the capacities of human beings to develop their societies autonomously. The Precautionary Principle clearly supports a radical rather than a weak interpretation of sus-tainable development, which also proves compatible with liberal-democratic systems of government.

Notes

1 World Commission on Environment and Development, *Our Common Future*.
2 For the Rio Declaration, see Louis P. Pojman (ed.), *Environmental Ethics*, pp. 501–3. One dilution of the message of *Our Common Future* concerns the explicitly anthropocentric posture of the Rio Declara-tion, contrasting with one or two non-anthropocentric passages in *Our Common Future* (see pp. 45 and 57).
3 United Nations, *Declaration on the Right to Development*, preamble, paragraph 2. The apparent circularity of this definition can be rem-edied if we substitute for the word 'development' near the end of this passage the words 'this process', understood in the sense of the open-ing phrase of the definition.
4 Dennis Clark Pirages (ed.), *The Sustainable Society: Implications for Limited Growth*.
5 World Commission on Environment and Development, *Our Common Future*, p. 8.
6 World Commission on Environment and Development, ibid., p. 8.
7 World Commission on Environment and Development, ibid., p. 75.
8 World Commission on Environment and Development, ibid., p. 57.
9 United Nations Environment Programme/World-Wide Fund for Nature/World Conservation Union, *Caring for the Earth*.
10 Michael Jacobs, 'Sustainable Development: A Contested Concept', in Andrew Dobson (ed.), *Fairness and Futurity: Essays on Environmental Sustainability and Social Justice*, at p. 23.
11 World Commission on Environment and Development, *Our Common Future*, p. 75.
12 Jacobs, 'Sustainable Development: A Contested Concept', p. 24.
13 Jacobs, ibid., pp. 25–6.

14   Jacobs, ibid., pp. 31–2.
15   Julie Davidson, 'Sustainable Development: Business as Usual or a New Way of Living?', p. 29.
16   Felix Dodds, 'Reviewing the Achievements Since Rio', p. 5.
17   Johan Hattingh, 'Sustainability in a Developing Country such as South Africa: A Philosophical Analysis'.
18   UNCED, *Agenda 21*.
19   Jacobs, 'Sustainable Development: A Contested Concept', p. 27.
20   Jacobs, ibid., p. 281, n. 19.
21   Jacobs, ibid., pp. 35–8.
22   Jacobs, ibid., pp. 38–9. See also Jacobs, *Reflections on the Discourse and Politics of Sustainable Development, Part 1: Faultlines of Contestation and the Radical Model*.
23   Jacobs, 'Sustainable Development: A Contested Concept', p. 45.
24   Davidson, 'Sustainable Development'; see her subtitle, 'Business as Usual or a New Way of Living?'
25   Jacobs, 'Sustainable Development', p. 39.
26   Michael Jacobs, 'Sustainable Development, Capital Substitution and Economic Humility: A Reply to Beckerman'.
27   Jacobs, 'Sustainable Development: A Contested Concept', p. 32.
28   Alan Holland, 'Sustainability: Should We Start from Here?', pp. 57–62.
29   Herman Daly, 'On Wilfred Beckerman's Critique of Sustainable Development'.
30   Wilfred Beckerman, 'Sustainable Development: Is it a Useful Concept?', at pp. 194–5.
31   Holland, 'Sustainability: Should We Start from Here?', p. 68.
32   Christopher Belshaw, *Environmental Philosophy: Reason, Nature and Human Concern*, pp. 250–1.
33   Holland, 'Sustainability: Should We Start from Here?', pp. 63–5.
34   Holland, ibid., p. 65.
35   Wilfred Beckerman, 'Sustainable Development and our Obligations to Future Generations'.
36   Alan Carter, 'Distributive Justice and Environmental Sustainability', pp. 450–1.
37   Andrew Dobson, *Justice and the Environment: Conceptions of Environmental Sustainability and Theories of Distributive Justice*, ch. 2.
38   World Commission on Environment and Development, *Our Common Future*, p. 57. Dobson's assumption that sustainable development has to be understood as anthropocentric has also been criticized in Carter, 'Distributive Justice and Environmental Sustainability', at p. 448.
39   Such is J. Baird Callicott's understanding of sustainable development (as involving indigenous peoples living sustainably alongside and protecting the wildlife of their environment); see Callicott, 'The Wilderness Idea Revisited: The Sustainable Development Alternative'.
40   World Commission on Environment and Development, *Our Common Future*, p. 95.

41 World Commission on Environment and Development, ibid., pp. 98–9.
42 Holland, 'Sustainability: Should We Start from Here?', p. 67.
43 Frances Moore Lappé and Rachel Shurman, 'Taking People Seriously'.
44 Program of Action, 1994 International Conference on Population and Development, ch. II: Principle 5, p. 190.
45 Martin Adams, *Breaking Ground: Development Aid for Land Reform*, pp. 36–58, 120.
46 Paul R. Ehrlich, *The Population Bomb*.
47 Holmes Rolston III, 'Feeding People Versus Saving Nature', p. 259.
48 Rolston, 'Feeding People', p. 259.
49 Rolston, 'Feeding People', p. 259.
50 Robin Attfield, 'Preferences, Health, Interests and Value', *Electronic Journal of Applied Philosophy*, 3, 2 (1995), 7–15.
51 This and the two previous paragraphs are based on Attfield, 'Saving Nature, Feeding People and Ethics'.
52 David Schmidtz, 'Why Preservationism Doesn't Preserve'. As W. M. Adams and D. Hulme attest, in 'If Community Conservation is the Answer in Africa, What is the Question?', these strategies do not always work.
53 Rolston, 'Feeding People', pp. 253–8 and 265.
54 Rolston, 'Feeding People', p. 249.
55 Rolston, 'Feeding People', p. 249.
56 Onora O'Neill, 'Ending World Hunger'; David A. Crocker, 'Hunger, Capability, and Development', pp. 214–16.
57 Crocker, 'Hunger, Capability, and Development', p. 216; Jean Drèze and Amartya Sen, *Hunger and Public Action*, p. 47 and ch. 8.
58 Frances Moore Lappé and Rachel Shurman, 'Taking People Seriously'.
59 Crocker, 'Hunger, Capability, and Development', p. 222.
60 Jenneth Parker, 'Precautionary Principle', p. 634.
61 Parker, 'Precautionary Principle', p. 634; Parker ascribes the identification of these examples to Barnabas Dickson.
62 Robin Attfield, 'The Precautionary Principle and Moral Values'; also Attfield, 'To Do No Harm: The Precautionary Principle and Moral Values', *Reason in Practice* (2001), 11–20.
63 Michael D. Young, *For Our Children's Children: Some Practical Implications of Inter-Generational Equity and the Precautionary Principle*.
64 See Robin Attfield, *The Ethics of the Global Environment*, p. 186.
65 Joyce Hambling, 'Three Steps Forward, Two Steps Back'.
66 Andrew Vincent, 'Liberalism and the Environment'.
67 Marius de Geus, 'Sustainability, Liberal Democracy, Liberalism'.
68 Thus, for example, Andrew Dobson, 'Foreword' to Barry and Wissenburg, p. vii; also John Rawls, *A Theory of Justice*.
69 Dobson, 'Foreword', pp. vii–viii.
70 Tim Hayward, 'Constitutional Environmental Rights and Liberal Democracy'.
71 Andrew Dobson, *Justice and the Environment*, pp. 245–6.

72   Derek Parfit, 'Comments', pp. 854–62. Alan Carter argues well for a similar conclusion in 'Can We Harm Future People?' at pp. 447–9.
73   This view is taken in Alan Holland, 'Genetically Based Handicap', at p. 127, and in Carter, 'Can We Harm Future People?', at pp. 441–4.
74   John Barry, 'Greening Liberal Democracy', pp. 67–8.
75   John Barry, Marcel Wissenburg and Marius de Geus, 'Conclusion', in Barry and Wissenburg, at p. 208.
76   Robin Attfield, 'Sustainability, Global Warming, Population Policies and Liberal Democracy', p. 152.
77   Davidson, 'Sustainable Development', pp. 34, 37, and 41.
78   Jesper Ryberg, 'Population and Third World Assistance'.
79   Govindan Parayil, 'Sustainable Development: The Fallacy of a Normatively Neutral Development Paradigm', p. 190. Without endorsing all Parayil's views on normativity, I can endorse his critique of the superficial nature of conservative conceptions of sustainable development.
80   Parayil, 'Sustainable Development', pp. 190–1; see also Parayil, 'The "Kerala Model" of Development: Development and Sustainability in the Third World'.
81   Parayil, 'Sustainable Development', p. 191.
82   William Alexander, 'Prototype for Sustainable Development: Kerala', unpublished paper.
83   Samir Amin, 'Four Comments on Kerala', p. 28.
84   Arran E. Gare, *Postmodernism and the Environmental Crisis*, p. 146.

Further Reading

Barry, John and Wissenburg, Marcel (eds), *Sustaining Liberal Democracy: Ecological Challenges and Opportunities* (Palgrave, Basingstoke and New York, 2001); presents contrasting views on the possibility of making liberal democracy sustainable.

Jacobs, Michael, 'Sustainable Development: A Contested Concept', in Andrew Dobson (ed.), *Fairness and Futurity: Essays on Environmental Sustainability and Social Justice* (Oxford University Press, Oxford, 1999), pp. 21–45; a stimulating essay, criticized over concepts and applauded over interpretations above.

Davidson, Julie, 'Sustainable Development: Business as Usual or a New Way of Living?', *Environmental Ethics*, 22 (2000), 25–42. Develops Jacobs' ideas in communitarian and non-anthropocentric directions.

Attfield, Robin, 'To Do No Harm?: The Precautionary Principle and Moral Values', *Reason in Practice*, 1.3 (2001), 11–20; the implications of the precautionary principle are revisited, in a new journal of philosophy of management.

Ekins, Paul, 'Making Development Sustainable', in Wolfgang Sachs (ed.), *Global Ecology* (Zed Books, London and Atlantic Highlands, NJ, 1993), pp. 91–103; sustainable development is possible – if we restructure the world.

Some Useful Websites

www.id21.org Website of Insights: Development Research, supported by the British government's Department of International Development (DfID), and hosted by the Institute of Development Studies, University of Sussex: brings together international development research.

www.sustdev.org Website of Sustainable Development International.

www.undp.org.in Website of Human Development Report, 2002, with regard to India.

hppt://iisd1.iisd.ca/ Website of International Institute for Sustainable Development.

www.oneworld.org Website of One World, a community of over 1,000 organizations working for social justice.

www.wdm.org.uk Website of the World Development Movement, a pressure group campaigning on behalf of the Third World and for international justice.

www.ukabc.org Website of the UK Agricultural Biodiversity Coalition; explains the Biosafety Protocol.

6 The Global Community and Global Citizenship

The global nature of many environmental problems calls for a global, cosmopolitan ethic, and for its recognition on the part of agents who thereby accept the role of **global citizens** (see below) and membership of an embryonic global community. Problems such as global warming affect global systems, and can only be tackled if many individuals and most countries agree to cooperate in resolving or mitigating them; without such a sense of participation in a developing global community jointly confronting shared challenges, the problems are unlikely to be addressed with sufficient conviction. In this chapter, the relevant concepts are clarified, the shape of a **global ethic** and the concept of **the common heritage of humankind** are discussed, some conclusions are drawn about common ground between the adherents of different stances in normative ethics, and about principles needed for international agreements, and the issue of **global warming** is used to illustrate these themes and conclusions. Finally the conclusions of the book as a whole are presented.

Global citizenship and a cosmopolitan ethic

The notion of **global citizenship** is likely to be criticized from two different directions. The most obvious critique maintains that citizenship presupposes a sovereign state, and that as there is no such global state, the very concept of global citizenship is an absurdity, short of the establishment of a world government. But this critique assumes a narrow and strictly political conception of 'citizenship',[1] for the loyalties of citizens can be focused not only on states but (at a lower level) on cities (for example, St Paul was a citizen of Tarsus, 'no mean city',[2] as well as of the Roman state),[3] and (at a more inclusive level) of one or another international community, such as the commonwealth of learning, or the universal church.[4] In this broader sense, ancient Stoics such as Epictetus (c. 55–135 AD) commended people regarding themselves as world citizens, alongside their other roles.[5] Global citizens recognize ties of loyalty and obligation not only to fellow citizens of their political state but also to those of the world; and people who recognize such ties are well on the way to becoming global citizens.

The recent growth of international societies and bodies, and of an international culture, has made this ancient notion increasingly accessible and applicable. Users of electronic mail and of the internet often have as many contacts outside the state of their political citizenship as within it, plus a matching awareness of belonging to an international culture as well as the local one. In any case, global citizenship essentially involves commitment (whether implicit or explicit) to one or another form of **global ethic**, for which obligations do not stop short at national boundaries and are not grounded solely in any less-than-universal interest. Far from being absurd, such global citizenship is morally as important as it has always been, and for practical purposes increasingly urgent too.

The other criticism regards belief in the potential global citizenship of the whole of humanity as excessively narrow. Thus when Aldo Leopold wrote of the role of *Homo sapiens* changing 'from conqueror of the land community to plain member and citizen of it', he immediately went on to say that the related ethic (which he called 'the land ethic') 'implies respect for his fellow-members, and also for the community as such'.[6] According to Leopold, then, the members and citizens of the land community include not only humanity but also fellow creatures, and also the soils and waters that, together with plants and animals, make up 'the land'.[7] On this basis it could be suggested that global citizenship is not restricted to human beings, but belongs also to everything that moral agents should respect or treat as morally considerable. While moral considerability has been argued above not to attach to inanimate entities (see chapter 2), it was recognized there as a characteristic of living creatures such as animals and plants. Cannot these fellow creatures be understood (such critics might ask) as fellow citizens of the planetary biosphere?

The problem with this suggestion is that in standard political and cultural senses citizens have loyalties and responsibilities, and it does not make sense to ascribe these characteristics to plants or (with a few possible exceptions) to non-human animals. The main point of talk of global citizenship is that global citizens would show awareness of such loyalties and responsibilities, and this again disqualifies non-human creatures. So if we were to accept that they are global citizens on the basis that they have moral considerability and should be respected as such, and that humans are included among global citizens on the same basis, we would need to distinguish this relatively undemanding sense of 'global citizen' from a more demanding sense requiring awareness of loyalties and responsibilities. Almost certainly, in this more demanding sense, none but human beings are global citizens.

The same distinction can be made between senses of 'community'. There is a broader biological sense, that used by Leopold when he writes of 'the land community',[8] which concerns sets of interacting, interdependent and more-or-less contiguous natural entities, whether animate or inanimate (such as the creatures, the air, the soils and the rainfall of a forest), and a more demanding political or cultural sense, which refers to interactions on the part of conscious participants, capable of shared traditions, standards and/or aspirations (such as the community of Friends of the Earth, or of Nottingham Forest Association Football Club).[9] In the more demanding sense of 'citizen' and of 'community', the notions of global citizen and global community belong together, since responsible global citizens are (at least potentially) members of a global community, and bearers of shared concerns.

As long as the more and the less demanding senses of 'global citizen' are clearly distinguished, there is no harm in using both of them, not least of human beings. J. Baird Callicott rightly points out that ampler forms of citizenship do not preclude citizenship of smaller communities; awareness of patriotic duties is compatible with local loyalties (not least as a local citizen), and similarly recognition of the biotic community is compatible with membership of the human community or 'the family of man', and with responsibilities 'to respect human rights and uphold principles of human worth and dignity'.[10] Callicott seems not to recognize that different senses of 'citizen' and of 'community' are here in play, and his conflation of these senses is one of the obstacles to acceptance of the 'land ethic' of Leopold (see above) that he advocates. Yet the valuable recognition emerges from his remarks that global citizenship at the level of membership of the human community need not stop short at loyalty to that community or at inter-human responsibilities, but can include, as an aspect of global citizenship, responsibilities with regard to the non-human members of the biotic community that are global citizens (if at all) in a very different sense. (Adherents of biocentric consequentialism can readily share in this recognition, despite their different understanding of the range of non-human members of the biotic community.)

Consequentialism is also an example of the kind of normative ethic consistent with global citizenship. Other widespread examples are Kantianism (for example, as interpreted by Onora O'Neill),[11] contractarianism (such as the position of John Rawls),[12] and theories for which universal rights are regarded as the non-derivative basis (such as the position of Alan Gewirth).[13] While certain problems for these other normative theories have been presented above (in chapters 2 and 4), they resemble consequentialism in being kinds or species of cosmopolitan ethic.

Cosmopolitan ethicists maintain that ethical responsibilities apply everywhere and to all moral agents capable of shouldering them, and not only to members of one or another tradition or community, and that factors which provide reasons for action for any agent, whether individual or corporate, provide reasons for like action for any other agent who is similarly placed, whatever their community may be or believe.[14] They also deny limits such as community boundaries to the scope of responsibilities; responsibilities (they hold) do not dwindle because of spatial or temporal distance, or in the absence of reasons transcending particular facts or identities. They do not deny responsibilities to family, friends, colleagues or country, but regard such special obligations as derivative from universal considerations such as the general good, respect for persons, universal rights, or what agents would consent to in a fair bargaining situation. Hence they are sometimes called 'universalists'.

Cosmopolitanism is often contrasted with **communitarianism**. Actually, there is no conflict between ethical cosmopolitanism and the kind of communitarianism which stresses the value of community and deplores its decline in the world in the twentieth and twenty-first centuries, since this kind of view suggests that community is desirable anywhere and everywhere.[15] The contrast is rather with the kind of communitarianism (briefly mentioned in chapter 4) that maintains that all ethical obligations derive from and depend upon relationships, and that where there are no ties of community and no relationships there are no such obligations, nor motivations to behave as if there were.

In its narrower forms, communitarianism holds (with Martin Golding) that we have obligations only to those who share our values, and that this probably excludes most future people.[16] In its broader forms, it maintains (with John O'Neill) that we have responsibilities to make it possible for future people to belong to a community with ourselves and to share in our own valuable activities,[17] or with Avner de-Shalit that ties of community and related obligations extend into the future as long as either cultural interaction of moral similarity remain,[18] but decline in strength over time and 'fade away' as ties weaken.[19] All these varieties, however, allow of the possibility of there being people of the distant future (and current strangers too) whose values are so different from ours that no ties exist between us and them, and no responsibilities in their regard exist on our part. Hence those who accept responsibilities with regard to the entire foreseeable future need at this point either to move beyond communitarianism, to revert to being communitarians simply in the unproblematic sense of advocating the value of community, or to reject communitarianism (in the other sense) in favour of one or another form of cosmopolitanism.

Perhaps communitarianism can be reinterpreted. Thus Alan Carter, who refers to it as 'particularism', observes that it is not clear that 'cultural and moral similarity' must decline over time.[20] (Carter is probably not to be taken as actually supporting communitarianism here, but rather as resisting too ready a rejection of it.) Even if moral similarity is supposed to involve holding a similar range of values, it is certainly possible that no such decline may take place, and, this being so, communitarianism can recognize responsibilities to people of the distant future – as long as they will belong to our community.

The problem remains, though, that communitarianism seems not to provide for responsibilities with regard to current strangers, people, that is, who do not belong to our community, let alone making room for their successors, whether of the near or the distant future. (An example of such problems surfaced in chapter 4 in connection with the trade in nuclear wastes; as Andrew Dobson warns, if policies are determined by communitarian rather than universalist principles, there is a danger that the environmental health of economically vulnerable countries of the Third World, and of coming generations in those countries, will continue to be endangered.)[21] For reasons such as this, global citizens will be reluctant to be confined within communitarianism. As for responsibilities with regard to non-human creatures, communitarianism would seem at best to make provision where such creatures are regarded as adoptive members of our community, but not where they are spatially or temporally distant, let alone undiscovered and unidentified. This being so, non-anthropocentrist ethicists will also find communitarianism too restrictive.

Cosmopolitanism is also contrasted (where international relations are concerned) with **realism**, which usually bases obligations on self-interest (whether individual or national).[22] Realism (in this sense) makes provision for responsibilities, whether with regard to the future or to non-humans, only where benefits (direct or indirect) are in prospect for the agent (whether an individual, a corporation or a government). While this is manifestly a defective basis, which would fail to recognize or uphold many responsibilities discussed in previous chapters, this kind of basis probably underlies and explains a great many international transactions. Hence it often proves valuable to work with this basis and thus discover what parties could be expected to agree to in so far as they take an enlightened view of their own interest. (The limits of the implications of enlightened self-interest are prone to depend on different understandings of identity, and whether the self whose interest is to be interpreted lapses with individual death or, as is plausible with corporations and states, extends into at least the next few generations.)

Indeed some of the policies required to tackle global environmental problems (such as global warming) can be supported on a realist basis of national self-interest, or again on a communitarian basis, as well as on the basis of a cosmopolitan ethic. Even if such support is contingent and vulnerable, its availability can sometimes make a great difference to the prospects of global cooperation. Common ground between different ethical stances is thus to be found at the level of policies, at least in matters such as cooperation over global warming, and comparably over acid rain and ozone depletion.

Now that these contrasting normative approaches have been noted and contrasted, it is time to turn to the different varieties of cosmopolitan ethic, and to the different forms of global citizenship.

Varieties of global citizenship and cosmopolitan ethic

International non-governmental organizations (NGOs) and their worldwide membership supply a good example of global citizenship. Examples mentioned in previous chapters include the World Wide Fund for Nature, Friends of the Earth, and the World Development Movement, plus its counterparts outside the United Kingdom; another is the United Nations Association. Their role is partly to lobby national and international agencies, and partly to educate the public of the countries where they are based, in support of goals and policies such as environmental protection, sustainability and development.

Such bodies are manifestly appealing, explicitly or implicitly, to some form of normative ethic, which (if the argument of the previous section is a sound one) would have to comprise one or another form of cosmopolitanism. For the links between realism (in the sense used in this book) and these goals and policies are little more than coincidental, and the links between communitarianism and these goals and policies are (as has been argued in the previous section) contingent to the point of vulnerability. Since NGOs are eager to mobilize as wide a range of support as their goals allow (commonplace ethical standards permitting), they are unlikely to specify any such allegiances, or to criticize (for example) arguments from self-interest, except where their opponents resort to these arguments and recognize no others. Yet their concern for living nature and for sustainable development everywhere and in all foreseeable generations inclines these bodies perforce towards a universalist ethical stance.

We should also bear in mind another type of global citizenship, that of the staff of official international organizations, such as the United Nations Organization (UNO) and its affiliates the World Health Organization, the Food and Agriculture Organization, and other specialist bodies like UNESCO (the United Nations Economic, Social and Cultural Organization). Having the support of member governments of UNO (at least in theory), these bodies seek to contribute to global governance by fostering cooperation in relevant areas, including the areas of environment and development. The related international bodies concerned with finance and trade should also be mentioned here: the World Bank, the International Monetary Fund and the World Trade Organization, whose staff purport to foster economic cooperation. While it was suggested in chapter 4 that government circles tend to favour a top-down, conservative model of sustainable development, and this tendency is often borne out in practice, it is not inevitable, and the possibility exists of these bodies becoming much more accountable and much more committed to the full range of interests affected by their decisions.

Among the commitments of the staff of these bodies, secondary values such as compromise between clashing interest groups will often predominate, and the decisions taken will often reflect the self-interest of particular states, or the values of the more influential communities and alliances. The current system of **global governance** is manifestly in need of revision and improvement, and specific criticisms and suggestions for improvement will be offered below. Yet personal experience suggests that in tackling global problems many of the staff of these organizations contrive to show adherence to universal values, and attempt to apply to such problems the kind of cosmopolitan principles implicit in the United Nations Charter (1946) and the Universal Declaration of

Human Rights (1948), which in one way or another authorize their existence.

A third kind of global citizenship is found in the news and information media, which report on international conferences and happenings to a variety of audiences, expose shortcomings, and (like the international NGOs) monitor achievements, drawing attention to gaps between promises and delivery. These media (again like the NGOs) also seek to influence decision-making, sometimes from the self-interested perspective of one state or another, sometimes from a sectional or confessional perspective, but often on a recognizably universalist basis. Typically they are committed to freedom of speech and expression, and frequently they defend the cause of exploited groups (of the present or the future), which may have been neglected in official, inter-governmental dealings, not from self-interest or partiality but from a sense of justice.

In most countries, NGOs and the media form a key part of **civil society**, that network of voluntary bodies independent of the direct authority of the state which often serves as the public conscience,[23] and which is widely considered crucial for the maintenance of democracy.[24] Other branches of civil society are trade unions, churches and other religious bodies, and sporting and cultural bodies too. At international level the corresponding bodies (from the International Federation of Philosophical Societies to Médecins sans Frontières) may be said to form global civil society,[25] whose participants (not only those in NGOs or the media) may be considered global citizens. Their characteristic concerns are toleration, impartiality, civil and political freedoms and human rights. Another is environmental sustainability, conceptualized in the World Council of Churches as 'the integrity of creation', a conception recognized to indicate (at the very least) efforts to mitigate global warming and other kinds of climate change.

Appeals to human rights are rightly prominent in the armoury of global citizens, for example when seeking to prevent the abuse of women, of minorities or of prisoners, the maltreatment of refugees or of immigrants, or the exploitation of workers. Often, however, appeal has to be made beyond rights, not least in environmental contexts, since there are limits to the applicability of rights to non-human creatures (whose moral standing has been argued, in chapter 2, not to depend on their bearing rights), and because future-related responsibilities often turn on the quality of life of whoever there will be in a certain stretch of the future, rather than on the rights of one or another set of possible people which might be alive at that time (see chapter 4).[26] Nevertheless the rights of existing people (including children) support strenuous efforts being made to attain international cooperation over a range of issues including global warming.

Kantian approaches also have been put to good use where respect for persons is at risk and needs to be asserted, as where force or fraud are used to the disadvantage of minorities. Onora O'Neill has well deployed a Kantian ethic in drawing to attention these kinds of oppression of Third World women.[27] Once again, however, there are limits to such approaches in environmental contexts. The Kantian emphasis on duties is not itself a problem, but rather the view that duties are invariably owed to actual identifiable beings or sets of such beings (which seems to be involved in treating beings as ends: see chapter 4), or even (in the views of Kant himself) to actual identifiable rational beings. These approaches need to be supplemented by a direct appeal to valuable, non-disastrous outcomes, and thus to consequentialism, if the full range of environmental problems is to be tackled. Yet once again, Kantians can consistently support attempts to negotiate (for example) a global warming agreement.

So can contractarians, whose ethical theory of itself suggests that free and open negotiations have the potential to arrive at a just agreement. For the theory implicitly claims that just arrangements simply are whatever people in a fair bargaining position (or, as the expression goes, 'on a level playing field') would agree to, and implicitly commends bargaining which approximates as closely as possible to such a situation. But this theory has difficulty in representing and coping with future interests, as Carter has recently underlined.[28] Besides, short of being restructured so as to bring non-humans into the contract,[29] it can only cover non-human interests in so far as human interests coincide with them. In the matter of global warming they probably do, at least where the near future is concerned, although stronger policies for that period are probably indicated as soon as non-human interests are considered for their own sake.

Biocentric consequentialism (as I have attempted to argue above) overcomes these problems, while at the same time being applicable to those issues where rights-based approaches, Kantianism and contractualism are at their strongest (issues such as global warming). However, biocentric consequentialism is a controversial view, and it is not for a moment suggested here that global citizens are committed as such to this normative stance, or even that they can only be consistent through commitment to it. For one thing, not all the issues are among the concerns of each and every global citizen or NGO. However, I am maintaining that global citizens will need a cosmopolitan stance of some kind or other if they are consistently to be concerned with the broad range of global issues (and with a biocentric position at that if they are to avoid the limitations of anthropocentrism). For realism and communitarianism are liable to de-select large subsets of that range as either not in the interests, or not consonant with the community values, of many of the parties represented in international fora.

This can be illustrated from an issue discussed at a recent UNESCO Conference on the ethics of science and technology, held at Beirut in October 2001.[30] Topics discussed at this Conference ranged from medical ethics and information ethics to environmental ethics, including the ethics of the use of outer space. Issues in medical ethics and information ethics can be handled from any of the cosmopolitan stances reviewed above (with the possible exception of choices in genetic ethics between the generation of one possible person and another), but not as well by realism (liable not to recognize obligations to assist health-care provision in foreign countries), nor invariably by communitarianism (liable to assist only those countries that share its adherents' values). Urgent action on some environmental issues, such as global warming, can be supported from all these stances, although some forms of environmental protection are (I have argued in chapters 3 and 4) less well tackled by anthropocentric theories (including, as can now be added, cosmopolitan anthropocentric ones).

But where the issue of uses of the stratosphere and outer space are concerned, cosmopolitan theories cope far better than others. A system of protection of the Earth from collisions with asteroids, for example, is much easier to justify if one is concerned with the entire foreseeable future of humanity rather than just with the interests of the current generation, or just with national self-interest, or just with the future of one or another community, but only for the duration of its present values. So, for the same reasons, is a system of global insurance against falling anthropogenic debris from previous space missions, or a system to remove such debris from the stratosphere. Further, what applies to outer space applies to many other issues where future interests are at stake. To be consistent, a global citizen needs to endorse cosmopolitanism in one form or another.

Issues to think about at this stage include whether both the broader and narrower senses of global citizenship are needed, whether you agree that global citizenship requires a cosmopolitan rather than a communitarian or a 'realist' ethic, and to what extent either a communitarian or a 'realist' ethic can underpin solutions to global environmental problems.

The common heritage of humankind

The argument that natural features should be preserved because of their historic cultural significance is an important one in certain times and places. Where a particular rock has served as a landmark throughout the history of a settlement, or a particular tree has provided a meeting-place for as long as anyone can remember, there is a case for preserving them because of their historical significance and because the identity of many current people has been moulded around their presence.[31] Admittedly, inanimate nature is as likely as living creatures to have such heritage value, and many thriving creatures and pristine habitats will lack such value, if only because this kind of value depends on continuous human habitation. Yet the fact that the spread of heritage value is scattered, and (unlike certain other kinds of value) corresponds to sites of long-standing human settlement, makes this kind of value an important supplement to other preservationist arguments. While heritage value will not always serve as a knock-down argument for preservation, particularly when a conflict arises with satisfying basic needs, possibilities often exist for respecting such value and meeting basic needs simultaneously,[32] and in these circumstances arguments from heritage value are capable of carrying weight. This much can be accepted by (at least) communitarians and consequentialists alike.

However, a case has also been presented for regarding much wider tracts of nature as heritage, in the sense of common resources, rather than cultural heritage, and as the inheritance not of single communities but of humanity as a whole: as, that is, **the common heritage of humankind**. Tracts of nature thus characterized (and later internationally recognized as such) include the seas and oceans beyond territorial limits. Such recognition was proposed in 1967 by the Maltese delegate to the United Nations, Ambassador A. Pardo, who ascribed to 'the common heritage of mankind' the following central characteristics. These resources are not property, not being owned either by a sovereign state or by humanity itself (a recognizable echo of a central tenet of the stewardship tradition), but are resources to which all present and future human beings have or will have a right of access. Every generation has obligations to humanity to conserve and transmit this heritage. The heritage should thus be managed internationally on behalf of humanity, and for the shared benefit of humanity (present and future).[33]

An amended version of this proposal came to fruition subsequently in the Law of the Sea Treaty, together with international endorsement of such rights and obligations. (Here we can set aside conceptual scruples about the rights of future people, having discussed this subject in chapter 4, and interpret this talk as concerning the rights that actual future people will have once they have come into being.) The case for incorporating proposals of this kind into international law can readily be accepted, given the overall desirability of access to unowned seas remaining open to the shipping of all nations and of their being managed for the common good in perpetuity.

Although the original intention behind the proposal of this Treaty was that the mineral resources of the seabed should be deployed in a particular way (to promote the development of inland countries), its emphasis on future people having equal access to communal resources as their predecessors of the present discloses that common heritage resources are generally ones not to be consumed but to be preserved for access or use of a non-consumptive kind. This being so, other unowned tracts of nature seem equally suited to a common heritage approach as the oceans, such as Antarctica (recognized as such in a subsequent treaty), the absorptive capacities of the atmosphere (the subject of the Kyoto Protocol), and also the stratosphere and outer space (on which, see the previous section).

Emmanuel Agius has further suggested that the genetic system (comprising the genes of all existing species, and not only of humanity) should be thus recognized, and made subject to a World Patent Convention on Biotechnological Inventions. Ownership of genes, as in the current patent system, would be rejected, and genetic diversity would be managed by an international body in such a manner as to benefit both present and future people.[34] Agius also suggests that a Guardian of future interests be appointed (compare the discussion of related provision for representing the future in chapter 4) and empowered to review all forms of genetic engineering which may affect the welfare of posterity.[35] In view of the shortcomings of the currently recognized trade-related intellectual property system (TRIPS),[36] there is much to commend Agius' proposal on biotechnological inventions; however, his proposals cannot be debated in detail here. For common heritage proposals are subject to a large apparent objection.

It should first be explained that Agius advocates a large change in human attitudes both to genes and to nature in general. Humanity needs to abandon the still prevalent spirit of ruthless domination of nature, and to replace this he commends adoption of 'the philosophy of the common heritage of mankind', with its associated themes of protection and conservation (both of nature in general and of the Earth's genetic heritage in particular). A sustained educational effort is required, so that awareness of nature (and of genes) as a heritage becomes more prevalent; this would be the backdrop of the proposed new system to regulate biotechnology.[37]

Once again, these ideas commendably reflect the superiority of the stewardship approach over the attitude of domination (although they probably exaggerate the historical predominance of the latter, and underestimate the long-standing and widespread influence of the former approach). They are also commendably expressed in a secular mode liable to be or become acceptable internationally, and not only in a largely Catholic country such as Malta. On the other hand, this is an entirely human-centred version of the stewardship tradition, the goal being to benefit human beings alone, whether of the present or of the future; other creatures are to be preserved only in so far as this promotes human purposes. If the criticisms of anthropocentrism in previous chapters are accepted, this is a serious defect. So the proposed change is open to the criticism of being insufficiently radical, and not moving far enough from the spirit of human domination to which Agius urges us to be opposed.

Can advocacy of 'the common heritage of humankind' be rescued from these shortcomings? It has been seen not, in general, to advocate the consumption of resources but their conservation for non-consumptive access or use, which could include enjoyment, study, recreation or refuge. Yet nature is still regarded as nothing but resources, albeit ones to be carefully protected to prevent future sufferings or harms. Perhaps this is a proper approach to genetic resources. But if, as has been argued in previous chapters, non-human creatures are not just resources but have an independent value of their own, and if their welfare and future have ethical importance alongside human welfare and the human future, then regarding them as a common human heritage begins to seem misplaced, at least if this heritage is to be administered for human benefit.

Yet human beings are the only responsible agents capable of planning for the future (whether human or non-human), and the responsibilities of preserving the planetary biosphere and providing for foreseeable future needs are theirs. As such, the natural environment of the planet really is our heritage, but not in the sense of inherited assets, to be spent for our own benefit either now or later. Instead it is best understood as a trust, of which the beneficiaries are not only those currently alive but future generations, and not only future human generations but other species as well, including those yet to evolve. The heritage is common to humanity not only because no one should be denied their share of the benefits, but also because universal or at least near-universal human cooperation is going to be needed if our responsibilities are to be successfully discharged. (Thus in matters of abandoning the use of CFCs and of reducing global warming, non-compliance by significant minorities can undermine the cooperative efforts of the majority of humanity.) Agius' emphasis on the unity of humanity is thus crucial, as long as the correctives just mentioned are recognized.

The **global commons** then (as unowned aspects and tracts of the planetary biosphere are prone to be called) should be regarded as the common heritage of humankind, because nothing less than humanity as a whole inherits them as a trust, which can and should be managed for universal (and not only for human) benefit. This heritage doubtless includes the genetic diversity of life on Earth. It also includes (at least) the oceans, the atmosphere and the stratosphere. (Despite problems of ownership and of selection, it may also include places or items significant as cultural heritage, like the temple at Abu Simbel in Egypt, rescued and preserved as one of a number of World Heritage Sites.)

Fred Steward represents participation in the common human inheritance as a right, at least of global citizens: 'Global citizenship expresses the right to a common human inheritance regardless of nation',[38] and in so far as this is a right it will also belong to those yet to recognize their global citizenship. Yet since the common human heritage can be understood in terms of global citizenship, the introduction of the language of rights here should not be regarded as making talk of this heritage open to criticisms of **Eurocentrism** or of dependence on Enlightenment values. For what is at stake is the heritage of common goods inherited in every society from previous generations, capable of being transmitted to coming generations, and capable of being valued as such in all societies.[39]

As argued above, some form of cosmopolitan normative ethic is likely to be needed for global citizens and global agencies to shoulder responsibilities of this kind, and in the light of the argument of the previous paragraphs a biocentric form is clearly preferable to one that is anthropocentric. Yet cooperation can begin simply with awareness of the vital importance for the common good of such cooperation, and in advance of acceptance of the principles on which it should proceed.[40] These matters all need to be borne in mind when issues of global governance are brought under consideration.

Issues of global governance

Global cooperation is needed in a wide range of fields. Global warming is a prominent example, on which more will be said below. Other environmental issues include biodiversity **preservation** (and funding to make it possible), the regulation of various kinds of **pollution**, including that from radioactive sources, and the facilitation of environmentally **sustainable development**. Further related issues include international trade and its regulation, the promotion of health and of health-care facilities, the enhancement of world food production, provision for supplies of energy and of fresh water, and the provision of loans for development. Many of these issues were themes of the recent Johannesburg Summit on sustainable development, and remain subjects of ongoing international negotiations.

The phenomenon of **globalization** (the process of worldwide economic and cultural integration), while making international communication much easier, has increased the urgency and intensity of many of these problems. While the governments of the developed world seek to further this process through liberalization of trade, it is less than clear that the international bodies whose brief is to foster this process are sufficiently democratic or accountable to allow developing countries to benefit, or that the economic erosion of national boundaries is overall beneficial to the nations concerned. Thus Herman Daly has recently argued, in 'Globalization and Its Discontents', that a system that preserves national integrity while strengthening international agreements ('internationalization') is preferable to the globalization of trade, finance and services.[41]

Nor should we assume that international trade is invariably more beneficial than resilient local production, which is often a mainstay of Third World economies and a precondition of development, in extreme circumstances forming a bulwark against famine. As John Maynard Keynes once maintained, 'Ideas, knowledge, science, hospitality, travel – these are the things which should of their nature be international. But let goods be homespun whenever it is reasonably and conveniently possible, and above all, let finance be primarily national.'[42] States should not in any case be pressurized into acceptance of trade liberalization involving renunciation of their powers to regulate imports (including genetically modified products and including pollutant substances), to control the provision of services in their territories, or to safeguard environmental standards.

However, the antithetical proposition that states (and inter-state authorities) should be disowned and discarded is unlikely to supply a solution to any of these problems. The state, Alan Carter suggests, is a source of militarism, injustice and environmental degradation, and should be replaced by community decisions taken on a voluntary basis, and by voluntary agreements between communities.[43] But a world of communities would need to tackle all the inter-societal and global issues mentioned at the start of this section (and many more), as well as local decisions, and would need to establish coordinating agencies at multiple levels, regional, continental and global among them, plus probably an agency to coordinate these agencies (what Robert Goodin, an advocate of such coordination, has called 'a central agency').[44] Further, decision-making powers in most areas of activity would have to be delegated to the various coordinating bodies, on pain of their inability to function, at least if the technology of recent decades is to remain in use (which would surely be necessary in order to tackle the problems).[45]

The only alternative is a world of small, largely self-sufficient communities functioning without high technology and without the large organizations and networks that it requires. But the transition to such a system would be likely to involve massive suffering and starvation. It seems better to retain states and international authorities, to monitor them, to institute checks and balances to provide against injustices and related dangers, and to seek to make them accountable and, as far as possible, democratic.

As Goodin has more recently written, ecological issues may after all best be tackled in a decentralized manner involving local 'small-scale participatory democracies'.[46] Indeed this may often be necessary for people to feel responsible for tackling them. Besides, there is a widespread feeling that decision-making at governmental and inter-governmental levels removes from people control over their lives, their cultures and their environments.[47] The risk of this kind of alienation strengthens the case for decisions being taken at the lowest feasible level. Yet the delegation of selected decision-making to localities (now apparently favoured by Goodin) is compatible with the coordination of policies at national and international levels in issues (of which there are many) which will be tackled either at these levels or not at all, and thus with the existence of states and of international authorities. Global governance in its current form has serious defects, but the defects do not warrant its abandonment.

The trouble with many international agencies is their lack of accountability. Thus the World Trade Organization, despite superficially democratic decision-making procedures (each state having an equal vote), embodies substantive inequalities of power. At the ministerial meeting in Seattle in 1999, the forty-nine Least Developed Countries brought a total of 210 technical advisers, who only narrowly outnumbered the United States advisory team of 182 such advisers. In such ways, developed countries are able to monopolize decision-making at the expense of poor countries.[48] This is further borne out by the character of the subsequent meeting at Doha (Qatar) of November 2001, where the European Union had 502 delegates, St Vincent just one, and Haiti none, as it could not afford to send a delegate; where developed countries held meetings from which Third World delegates were excluded; and where developing countries were subsequently persuaded to accept the resulting packages by such means as threats to remove trade preferences or to reduce aid.[49] Such procedures are just neither on a Rawlsian nor a Kantian, nor a rights-based footing, nor, come to that, on a consequentialist one either. They are also subject to the critiques of Marxists, ecofeminists, and social ecologists alike against discrimination and domination, if anything ever is.

To remedy this state of affairs, global organizations and their decision-making need to be made far more accountable and transparent through a range of structural changes. Thus governing bodies need to be brought within the control of their members (which would require rectification of the inequalities of representation and the procedural inequities just mentioned), and to adopt equitable procedures for taking into account impacts on external stakeholders. They also need to adopt compliance mechanisms and complaint mechanisms, to adopt fair and open recruitment procedures for senior staff positions, to make relevant information freely available, and to undergo evaluation (not least of their own social and environmental footprints) by an independent body, whose findings would be published.[50] In the absence of such changes, people are likely to continue to be alienated not only from the process of globalization and the economic forces that drive it, but also from the agencies devised to tackle and alleviate global problems. While the changes just presented are not a panacea, they could facilitate agencies of global governance achieving much wider acceptance within civil society (at both national and global levels), enhance the cogency of the widespread view that such global governance is often preferable to abandonment of efforts towards global cooperation, and foster positive willingness to participate in internationally approved policies (such as sustainable development) at local level.

Corresponding changes to make the government of states more accountable and more democratic are also in place. Democratic participation is much more feasible at this level, and probably comprises the best antidote to the widespread tendencies towards militarism and oppression which Carter correctly notes. (But Carter also overplays these tendencies, representing them as endemic and inescapable while states remain.) Yet democratic participation remains a comparative rarity within systems of national government (only a minority of which are remotely democratic), and there is enormous scope for its introduction.

If environmental problems were confined within state frontiers or even within local authority boundaries, the need would be greatly reduced to address these problems at inter-locality and international levels, and thus for national and international authorities to tackle them. It might then be argued that they were superfluous, at least where environmental considerations are concerned. That this is not the case is well illustrated by the pervasive global problem of greenhouse gas emissions, considered in the coming section.

Global warming: principles for a possible agreement

Global warming is the foremost environmental problem confronting the twenty-first century. Successive findings of the Inter-Governmental Panel on Climate Change attest a worldwide near-consensus among scientists that atmospheric concentrations of gases, including carbon dioxide, which have the effect of raising temperatures through the 'greenhouse effect' ('greenhouse gases') are rising, and that these increases are anthropogenic, or due to human-generated emissions of these gases. Sea and ocean levels have risen, according to this same scientific consensus, will continue to rise as a result of past and present emissions, and will rise yet faster unless coordinated action is taken to reduce significantly the rate of emissions in future.[51]

Certainly there are scientists who offer rival explanations of global warming, but their theories remain highly speculative, and are supported by far weaker evidence than the standard anthropogenic theory. Although it is theoretically conceivable that this standard theory might be overthrown, the prospect of severe and irreversible environmental damage makes this a clear case for application of the Precautionary Principle (see chapter 5) and the planning of preventive action without delay. While the Kyoto Protocol (1997) involved cuts to carbon emissions of developed countries averaging 5.2 per cent of 1990 levels, it is widely held (not least by the Royal Commission on Environmental Pollution, an official think-tank of the British authorities) that cuts on the part of these countries rising to 60 per cent of 1997 levels are necessary by 2050 and to almost 80 per cent by 2100.[52]

As was argued above, there is good reason to regard the absorptive and recycling capacities of the planetary atmosphere as the common heritage of humankind, goods inherited from the past and worth preserving for our successors. Non-human species too are legatees and beneficiaries, but to humanity belongs a heritage of responsibilities to preserve these goods for future generations, both of humanity and of other species. In view of the conclusions of previous chapters about future-related responsibilities and sustainable development, there is an overwhelmingly strong ethical case for recognizing obligations in this matter on the part of all individuals, corporations, authorities and governments capable of making a difference.

Historically, the Alliance of Small Island States (AOSIS, comprising states at risk of inundation from rising seas) secured during the early 1990s the support of most developing countries, including the larger ones (China, India and Brazil), for 'a proposal for a protocol that would require industrialized countries to meet the Toronto target of 20% reductions in greenhouse gas emissions by 2005', without developing countries being expected to accept reductions in the first instance. This proposal secured first the support of the EU countries including the UK, and eventually that of the G-7 countries as a whole, at the Conference of the Parties to the Rio Convention, held in Berlin in 1995.[53] With difficulty, and despite intermittent demands from the USA and certain other developed countries for commitments from the outset on the part of developing countries, this tentative agreement was translated into targets and timetables at Kyoto in 1997.[54]

Subsequently, in the spring of 2001, President George W. Bush renounced the entire agreement, probably expecting it to collapse in consequence. But a few months later (in July 2001) 178 countries, recognizing that global sustainability was at stake, achieved in Bonn an agreement based on the Kyoto Protocol, further details of which were resolved that autumn in Marrakesh. These agreements involved Southern participation on monitoring bodies, and in energy-related aid arrangements. Developing countries are not expected to make cuts at this stage, but are to receive aid to assist such participation at a later date.[55] While the targets of these agreements are modest, what is important is that multilateral agreements exist which can be revised and developed in the coming years.

Further, as Arran Gare (writing from a postmodernist perspective) remarks, the struggle for global sustainability requires each nation to devise its own distinctive pathway or 'narrative', and thus its own contribution to agreements about the global environment. Despite the repudiation of universal principles and systems that is characteristic of postmodernism, environmental problems are, for Gare, so acute and pervasive that the various local 'narratives' have to be capable of contributing to 'a new grand narrative, the global struggle for environmentally sustainable civilisation' (however defective the various 'grand narratives' of the past may have been).[56] In this struggle, the roles of different nations and regions will differ 'according to their situations within the global economy'.[57] Contrary to Gare's stance, they will not invariably comprise 'a nationalist struggle',[58] and many of the links between developed and developing countries will need to be maintained, rather than severed,[59] if sustainable development is to be attained. But it is vital (and here his stance can be applauded) that every nation and region plays its distinctive part.[60]

Good reasons why countries of the South should not be expected to reduce emissions at present are readily available. While all countries emit carbon dioxide and other greenhouse gases, developing countries can reasonably claim that the problem arises largely from the emissions of developed countries (although the percentages are likely to change with time), and also that as long as energy generation depends for practical purposes on carbon sources, the Third World cannot limit its carbon emissions, as it actually needs to increase them to meet the basic needs of its citizens. In developing countries, the basic needs of many people remain unsatisfied, and their satisfaction is not feasible without the generation of more electricity.[61] Hence developed countries are morally obliged to accept quotas and limit their emissions, without expecting quotas to be accepted in the first instance by developing countries. It would be inequitable and counterproductive to expect their acceptance of such quotas, and therewith the frustration of many of their development goals. Taking steps to equip developing countries to enter the Kyoto regimen is a different matter, and the agreements at Bonn and Marrakesh have begun taking just such steps.

In any case, the basis of the Kyoto agreement is entirely inapplicable to developing countries. Countries whose levels of carbon emissions were comparatively high in 1990 might reasonably be expected to be content with quotas only slightly less high, particularly in view of new opportunities for introducing new, less pollutant technology. But countries whose emissions were much lower cannot be expected to accept similar quotas or cuts. The historical basis accepted at Kyoto just happens to be the basis on which agreement could be negotiated between the developed countries represented there at the time, but has no other justification. It could even be accused of rewarding the big polluters, except that most of the relevant countries agreed to (slight) reductions below their 1990 emission levels. It is not a basis with which Southern countries could reasonably be expected to concur or comply. (Why should the least developed countries be expected to accept emission limits corresponding to any envisageable proportion, however high, of their very low historical emission rates?) Some other basis is clearly going to be needed.

A principled replacement for the historical basis of the Kyoto regimen has been suggested by Michael Grubb, who has proposed recognition of the principle of the equal entitlement of all current human beings to access to the absorptive capacities of the planet. This approach has received the endorsement of the Royal Commission on Environmental Pollution.[62] It is certainly difficult to justify unequal entitlements, granted that everyone needs access to these capacities, and granted that in practice nearly everyone needs to have electricity generated on their behalf. (It might even be argued that recognition of the absorptive capacities of the atmosphere as an element of the common heritage of humankind supports equal per capita entitlements. But this argument would depend on the common heritage being regarded as divisible into shares, and the shares belonging to human beings only, two implausible premises which are in any case superfluous, granted the reasoning just supplied.)

If we can grant the proposition that individuals' quotas should be credited to the governments of their state (a rather fragile proposition which, granted the prevailing system of national sovereignty, must perforce be granted in the absence of feasible alternatives), what follows is the principle that the emission quotas of the various states should be proportioned to population (let us call this **the Population Principle**). Countries seeking to exceed their quota would then need to purchase some of the unused quotas of countries with large populations not requiring the full use of their own quota. Such a system would grant the Third World financial resources for development and environmental conservation, and simultaneously promote energy efficiency in developed countries.[63] This proposal might be thought to reward population growth,[64] but could readily be adapted to avoid this possible implication; for example, a cut-off date could be agreed for national populations after which population changes would cease to affect quotas.[65] This whole approach, since it involves reductions in emissions and converging emissions rates, has become known as Contraction and Convergence, and, like the principle of equal entitlements and the

Population Principle, is supported by the Royal Commission just mentioned.[66]

While it might be objected that **the Contraction and Convergence approach** involves a large sacrifice on the part of countries with above-average emission rates, it is difficult to justify their being entitled to continue to degrade the global systems in this disproportionate manner without even paying compensation. (This being so, their foregoing current expectations of emitting greenhouse gases at an above-average level would not be a sacrifice, since no sacrifice is involved in losing what was never a rightful entitlement.) If, perhaps for the sake of global economic stability, Contraction and Convergence were to be phased in gradually over a number of years, this would allow of the gradual entry of developing countries into the global emissions regimen. It would also allow the big polluters time to invest in the kind of cleaner technology and of energy generation from renewable sources that should be introduced in any case.

Another objection concerns the possible impact of this proposed system on the poorest citizens of the least developed countries. Thus Fidel Castro, who recognizes the good intentions of the proposal, nevertheless warns that the financial resources thus generated could be largely swallowed up in the servicing of existing debt, or even in the imaginable payment of existing debt in the form of debt-for-emission-quota exchanges, deals potentially leaving Third World countries without emission quotas, with unaltered structures and still beset by their current difficulties.[67] This problem, however, could be averted if quotas for emissions required to satisfy basic needs were made untradeable, as Shue advocates,[68] and perhaps through an embargo on trading emissions quotas geared to a quality of life slightly higher than this (pegged, possibly, to provide for secondary as well as primary education). It could alternatively be averted if unpayable debts of Third World countries were first written off, for which there is in any case an overwhelmingly strong ethical case.[69]

Whether the eventual international regimen follows Contraction and Convergence in whole or in part, or adopts a quite different basis, some inclusive global agreement is imperative. The total emissions of countries such as China and India could well come to bear comparison in a few decades with those of the USA, even though China has substantially reduced its emissions in recent years. If Chinese or Indian emissions were to rise enough to approach current per capita USA emissions, then because of the size of the populations of these countries global warming would be hopelessly beyond control. Due allowance needs to be made for China and other developing countries to satisfy the needs of their citizens, but before that is achieved a ceiling will need to be agreed (something which is also in the interest of China and most other Third World countries, granted the threat posed by global warming to their coastlines and their large coastal populations).

But crucially, American governments (who also have a long and flood-prone coastline to consider) cannot expect such a ceiling to be agreed if they continue to reject proposals agreed by the rest of the world involving concessions on all sides in this matter, nor if they continue to resist or disown international agreements in general (such as the Convention on Biological Weapons and the Nuclear Test Ban Treaty). Whatever motives may be in play, the full and willing participation of every government in agreements that are necessary for global sustainability is indispensable. Indeed this principle outweighs all comparable principles of international politics.

> Readers are encouraged to reflect in what form, if any, belief in nature as the common heritage of humanity is acceptable, what forms of global governance and of international relations are best suited to tackling global environmental problems, and whether the equal entitlements approach and the Population Principle, and thus the Contraction and Convergence approach, comprise an appropriate basis for international agreements on global warming.

Global problems, global ethics and global decision-making

Environmental problems, as we have seen, are increasingly global problems, either because they are repeated from country to country with matching problems (of which traffic congestion and the related pollution are good examples) or because they involve disruption to global systems (like the disruption brought by global warming). In chapter 1 these types of problems were characterized as 'repetitive' and 'systemic' respectively. Many of these problems are also global in the sense of impacting on most if not all of the planet's species, which, if we are to avoid arbitrary preference in favour of our own species (speciesism), should themselves be taken into account (chapters 1 and 2). They also put at risk future generations, both of humanity and of other species (chapter 4), the interests of which need to be considered if they are adequately to be tackled.

The possibilities of tackling them by applying ethical judgements, standards and principles should not be underestimated, whether through actions on the part of individuals as consumers, or on the part of investors, corporations or governments (chapter 3). A universal or cosmopolitan normative ethic is needed (chapter 6), of which I have argued biocentric consequentialism to be the most acceptable form (chapters 2 and 3). Environmental concerns need to be interwoven with the needs of the poor and of developing countries for economic and social development. Thus, as long as pitfalls are avoided, policies of environmentally sustainable development are likely to be needed to put such an ethic into effect (chapter 5). These policies can consistently include biodiversity preservation (chapter 5), justified by the long-term good of non-human species as well as of humanity (chapter 4).

Global citizens are people who recognize the global responsibilities involved, and are also concerned with enhancing global governance with a view to the problems being tackled through international cooperation. Every bearer (present or future) of moral standing, or considerability (a notion introduced in chapter 1) is thereby a global citizen (in a broader sense), but where citizenship implies responsibility it is restricted (short of the arrival of intelligent extraterrestrials) to human beings and (derivatively) their institutions (chapter 6). This is why the resources of the planet may be regarded as the common heritage of humankind. While the biosphere is more than resources, and humanity is not justified in deploying its resources for human good alone, the current generation inherits the responsibility to protect natural goods for the benefit of present and future generations of all species (chapter 6). For these purposes, both national governments and institutions of global governance are needed, but they need to become much more accountable and democratic than is often currently the case (chapter 6). They should also make some express provision for unrepresented interests, such as those of future generations (chapters 4 and 6).

Global warming well illustrates both environmental problems and the difficulties involved in tackling them. Self-interested and communitarian approaches in their different ways give (at best) vulnerable and insecure support to tackling this long-term, universal problem. However, cosmopolitan systems of ethics require plans to be laid and sacrifices to be made for the long-term common good, and biocentric ones insist on this not being restricted to human good. Biocentric consequentialism in particular urges integrated solutions to be found for the sake of the future of humanity and other species, solutions that also respond to the needs for development and for environmental sustainability. Since such solutions depend on co-operation and on planning at national and international levels, the problem of global warming (like several other global problems) involves national governments and international agencies each making its own distinctive contribution to the mitigation or alle-viation of this common problem, not least through reaching and implementing global agreements based on defensible universal prin-ciples (chapter 6).

Global governance and decision-making, however, is beset by the traditional problem of securing the consent of the governed, and twice over at that. For, as well as the consent of nations, states and governments being needed, so is that of their citizens and other subjects. This is a practical as well as a moral imperative; even the wisest of international agreements becomes futile if those concerned cannot be persuaded to participate and comply. Top-down governance and imposed decisions are no more acceptable at the global level than at national levels; hence the importance of global institutions and of national authorities being or becoming as accountable and as democratic as possible, of environmental education being promoted at all levels, and of opportunities for participation in policy-making being fostered both nationally and locally. Networks of global citizens also have a role to play; civil society (including NGOs and religious and cultural bodies), both at national level and at global level, can make a significant differ-ence in proposing and generating agreements and in fostering public participation in the implementation of what is agreed, as well as in pressing for its enhancement and revision.

These will be among the central issues confronting humanity throughout the twenty-first century. Nothing less than a global ethic, such as that presented here, will be needed to address them. Because of the nature and scope of environmental problems, environmental ethics has made and is likely to continue to make an important contribution in both disentangling and confronting such issues.

Summary

Environmental problems call for a global ethic and for global citizenship, which requires a normative ethic of the cosmopolitan variety. While Kantianism, rights-theories and contractarianism can cope with many of the problems, consequentialism (particularly in its biocentric form) has fewer limitations. The global commons should be considered the common heritage of humankind, since humanity as a whole inherits them as a trust, subject to their being managed for universal (and not only human) benefit. International cooperation is vital, but international organizations such as WTO need to become far more accountable and transparent, while national governments need to become more democratic. To tackle global warming, the paradigmatic global environmental problem, the principles of proportioning emission quotas to national population and of Contraction and Convergence are needed, as is that of the willing participation of all governments in international agreements. The conclusions of the book are restated in this context; in particular, widespread commitment to a global ethic such as that defended here will be needed on the part of individuals, corporations, governments and global agencies alike, together with structures to make it effective.

Notes

1   This is, in fact, just one of five conceptions of global citizenship presented in Richard Falk, 'The Making of Global Citizenship', in Bart van Steenbergen (ed.), *The Condition of Citizenship*. These five conceptions are discussed in Robin Attfield, *The Ethics of the Global Environment*, pp. 197–201.
2   Acts, 21: 39.
3   Acts, 22: 26–8.
4   Ephesians 2: 19.
5   Epictetus, 'Discourses', 2.10ff., in A. A. Long and D. Sedley (eds), *The Hellenistic Philosophers*, vol. I, p. 364.
6   Aldo Leopold, 'The Land Ethic', in Donald VanDeVeer and Christine Pierce (eds), *People, Penguins and Plastic Trees*, p. 74b.
7   Aldo Leopold, ibid., p. 74a.
8   Aldo Leopold, ibid., p. 74b.
9   This distinction was first drawn, in criticism of Leopold, by John Passmore, in *Man's Responsibility for Nature*, p. 116, and qualified by Robin Attfield in *The Ethics of Environmental Concern*, p. 157.
10   J. Baird Callicott, *In Defense of the Land Ethic*, p. 93.
11   Onora O'Neill, *Faces of Hunger: An Essay on Poverty, Justice and Development*.
12   John Rawls, *A Theory of Justice*.
13   Alan Gewirth, *Reason and Morality*.
14   This definition is borrowed from Attfield, *The Ethics of the Global Environment*, p. 29.
15   Thus Herman E. Daly and John B. Cobb Jr, *For the Common Good: Redirecting the Economy towards Community, the Environment and a Sustainable Future*, ch. 9.
16   Martin Golding, 'Obligations to Future Generations'.
17   John O'Neill, *Ecology, Policy and Politics*, p. 34.

18   Avner de-Shalit, *Why Posterity Matters: Environmental Policies and Future Generations.*
19   de-Shalit, *Why Posterity Matters*, p. 13.
20   Alan Carter, 'Distributive Justice and Environmental Sustainability', p. 453.
21   Andrew Dobson, *Justice and the Environment*, p. 106.
22   Nigel Dower, *World Ethics: The New Agenda*, chs 2 and 3.
23   O'Neill, *Ecology, Policy and Politics*, pp. 177f.
24   Michael Walzer, 'The Civil Society Argument', in Ronald Beiner (ed.), *Theorizing Citizenship*, p. 170.
25   A Millennium Assembly of Global Civil Society has recently taken place (2002). See Richard Falk, 'Reviving the 1990s Trend toward Transnational Justice: Innovations and Institutions', at p. 187.
26   See also Derek Parfit, 'Comments', pp. 854–62, and Alan Carter, 'Can We Harm Future People?', p. 436.
27   Onora O'Neill, 'Justice, Gender and International Boundaries', in Robin Attfield and Barry Wilkins (eds), *International Justice and the Third World.*
28   Carter, 'Can We Harm Future People?', pp. 437–41.
29   As is suggested in Mark Rowlands, *Animal Rights: A Philosophical Defence.*
30   UNESCO International Symposium on the Ethics of Science and Technology, Beirut, Lebanon, 8–10 October 2001.
31   Janna Thompson, 'Environment as Cultural Heritage', pp. 241–2, 247 and 255.
32   Thompson, 'Environment as Cultural Heritage', p. 258.
33   A. Pardo, 'First Statement to the First Committee of the General Assembly, November 1, 1967', in A. Pardo, *The Common Heritage: Selected Papers on Ocean and World Order: 1967–74*, cited in Emmanuel Agius, 'Patenting Life: Our Responsibilities to Present and Future Generations', p. 75.
34   Agius, 'Patenting Life', pp. 72–4; see also pp. 75–81.
35   Agius, ibid., p. 79.
36   See Vandana Shiva, *Protect or Plunder: Understanding Intellectual Property Rights* (Zed Books, London, 2001).
37   Agius, 'Patenting Life', p. 82.
38   Fred Steward, 'Citizens of Planet Earth', p. 74.
39   Janna Thompson, 'Planetary Citizenship: The Definition and Defence of an Ideal' (closing passage).
40   As Carter remarks, communitarians could recognize good reason to cooperate not on grounds of distributive justice, but for the sake of the survival of their community. See Carter, 'Distributive Justice and Environmental Sustainability', p. 452.
41   Herman Daly, 'Globalization and Its Discontents'.
42   John Maynard Keynes, 'National Self-sufficiency', p. 236.
43   Alan Carter, 'A Radical Environmentalist Political Theory: Part Three of "Foundations for Developing a Green Political Theory"'.

44 Robert E. Goodin, *Green Political Theory*, p. 167.
45 Tackling ozone depletion and global warming requires more than refraining from certain activities (Carter's suggestion, in 'A Radical Environmentalist Political Theory', p. 215a; see also Alan Carter, *A Radical Green Political Theory*, p. 241); they require the coordinated introduction of alternative systems and practices.
46 Robert E. Goodin, 'Introduction', in Robert E. Goodin, *The Politics of the Environment*, p. xvii.
47 Janna Thompson, 'Planetary Citizenship' (opening passage).
48 Hetty Kovach and Simon Burall, *Charter 99 Global Accountability Project*, p. 6.
49 Letter of Barry Coates, Director of the World Development Movement, to members, of 23 November 2001.
50 Kovach and Burall, *Charter 99 Global Accountability Project*, pp. 6–14. See also the website of Charter 99, listed below.
51 See, for example, J. T. Houghton et al., *Climate Change 1995: The Science of Climate Change*, pp. 3–7.
52 Royal Commission on Environmental Pollution, Twenty-second Report, *Energy – The Changing Climate*, 4.51.
53 Michael Grubb, 'From Rio to Kyoto via Berlin: climate change and the prospects for international action'.
54 Michael Grubb, presentation on Kyoto, Royal Institute of International Affairs, London, 17 December 1997.
55 This information was supplied by a Finnish participant in an NGO delegation present at the Bonn conference of 2001.
56 Arran E. Gare, *Postmodernism and the Environmental Crisis*, p. 160.
57 Gare, *Postmodernism*, p. 161.
58 Gare, ibid., p. 162.
59 Gare, ibid., p. 161.
60 Attfield, 'Differentiated Responsibilities', forthcoming in Markku Oksanen and Juhani Pietarinen (eds), *Philosophy and Biodiversity*.
61 Henry Shue, 'Equity in an International Agreement on Climate Change' in *Proceedings of IPCC Workshop, Nairobi, July 1994*.
62 Royal Commission, *Energy – The Changing Climate*, 4.47–4.70.
63 Michael Grubb, *The Greenhouse Effect: Negotiating Targets; Energy Policies and the Greenhouse Effect*.
64 Finn Arler, 'Justice in the Air: Energy Policy, Greenhouse Effect, and the Question of Global Justice', p. 56b.
65 Royal Commission, *Energy – The Changing Climate*, 4.50.
66 Royal Commission, *Energy – The Changing Climate*, 4.47–4.70.
67 Fidel Castro, *Tomorrow is Too Late: Development and the Environmental Crisis in the Third World*, p. 29. The current passage is based on Robin Attfield, *The Ethics of the Global Environment*, pp. 93–4.
68 Shue, 'Equity in an International Agreement'.
69 Robin Attfield, 'Are Promises to Repay International Debt Binding?'.

Further Reading

Attfield, Robin, *The Ethics of the Global Environment* (Edinburgh University Press, Edinburgh, and Purdue University Press, West Lafayette, IN, 1999), ch. 11, 'World Citizenship in a Precarious World', pp. 191–208. Discusses global citizenship, civil society and global ethics.

Shue, Henry, 'Ethics, the Environment and the Changing International Order', *International Affairs*, 71 (1995), 453–61. Leading article from veteran applied ethicist.

Thompson, Janna, 'Planetary Citizenship: The Definition and Defence of an Ideal', in Brendan Gleeson and Nicholas Low (eds), *Governing for the Environment: Global Problems, Ethics and Democracy* (Palgrave, Basingstoke, 2001), pp. 135–46. Insightful cosmopolitan contribution to environmental ethics.

Royal Commission on Environmental Pollution, Twenty-second Report, *Energy – The Changing Climate*, Cm. 4749 (Her Majesty's Stationery Office, London, 2000); for once a Royal Commission illuminates the way ahead (on tackling global warming).

Kovach, Hetty and Burall, Simon, *Charter 99 Global Accountability Project* (One World Trust, London, 2001). Salutary prescription for making global institutions accountable.

Some Useful Websites

http://fsw.kub.nl/globus Website of Globus, Institute for Globalization and Sustainable Development, University of Tilburg, Netherlands.

www.medact.org Website of Medact, an organization of health professionals challenging social and environmental barriers to health worldwide: see speech of Medact's Director, Mike Rowson, on globalization.

www.rcep.org.uk/newenergy.html Website of Royal Commission on Environmental Pollution, with recent report on energy; see fourth chapter.

www.ifrc.org Website of International Federation of Red Cross and Red Crescent; see World Disasters Report, Box 7.2, on Contraction and Convergence.

www.newint.org Website of *The New Internationalist* magazine.

www.unedforum.org/2002/uk2002.htm Website of UNED Forum, the United Nations Environment and Development Forum, presenting UK preparations for Summit 2002, the Rio + 10 Summit of Johannesburg, September 2002.

www.charter99.org Website of Charter 99, The Charter for Global Democracy.

Glossary of Key Terms

Acts and Omissions Doctrine	The normative theory according to which agents are less responsible for their omissions than for their actions, or alternatively less responsible for the foreseeable consequences of their omissions than for exactly similar foreseeable consequences of their actions.
animal-welfarism	The approach to agricultural, environmental, veterinary and other issues that focuses on animal welfare, emphasizing either sentience or consciousness, and the related animal interests.
anthropocentrism, normative	A stance that limits moral standing to human beings, confines the scope of morality and moral concern to human interests, and regards nothing but human well-being as valuable intrinsically. (Literally, anthropocentrism of values, norms and principles.)
anthropocentrism, teleological	The metaphysical belief that the whole of creation exists for the sake of humanity. (Literally, anthropocentrism of goals or purposes.)
anthropogenic	Generated by humanity. Global warming is probably anthropogenic. The anthropogenic theory of value claims that all value and disvalue are dependent on human valuations.

a priori grounds	Grounds of a non-empirical character; grounds not based, that is, on observation and experience.
Aristotelian account of human flourishing	An account for which human good involves the development of characteristic human faculties and capacities, as held by Aristotle.
Average View or Theory, the	The normative consequentialist theory holding that agents should maximize the average per person of whatever makes life worthwhile (rather than the total). Has some strongly counterintuitive implications.
axiology	The philosophical study of values and of theories of value.
biocentric consequentialism	*See* consequentialism *and* biocentrism.
biocentrism	A normative stance that holds that all living creatures have a good of their own, and have moral standing accordingly, and that their flourishing or attaining their good is intrinsically valuable.
biodiversity	Biological diversity among species, sub-species and their habitats. An international Convention on Biodiversity was agreed at the Rio Summit in 1992.
capitalism	The global economic system of production and exchange whereby prices and wages are determined by the interplay of forces of supply and demand, with or without governmental regulation.
carrying capacity	The capacity of a particular territory to support no more than a certain fixed number of a given non-human species. This biological concept has sometimes been applied tendentiously to human populations, as if such populations were unaffected by trade and by social and international decisions.
CFCs	Chloro-fluoro-carbons (gases found to be depleting the ozone layer).
child-survival hypothesis, the	The theory holding that when the chances of child-survival in a community are increased through improved nutrition and

medical facilities, the average number of pregnancies and births tends to decrease.

civil society

The network of voluntary bodies and news media independent of the direct authority of the state, which often serve as the public conscience. Corresponding international bodies and news media comprise global civil society.

climate change

Changes, typically anthropogenic, to the climate of the planet, such as global warming, acid precipitation and ozone depletion. Another example is the Asian Brown Cloud, discovered in 2002 to stretch from Pakistan to Indonesia. A Climate Change Convention was initiated at the Rio Summit in 1992 and developed in the Kyoto Protocol of 1997.

cognitivism

The meta-ethical stance that holds that knowledge of value, rightness and obligation is possible, and can sometimes be expressed as statements.

common heritage of humankind, the

Common resources, regarded as the inheritance not of single communities but of humanity as a whole, and as suited to conservation rather than consumption. Includes at least the global commons such as the oceans, Antarctica, the atmosphere and outer space.

communitarianism

The meta-ethical stance that holds that obligations necessarily arise from loyalties and ties within communities, and are constrained by community boundaries. Contrasts with cosmopolitanism or universalism, which rejects such limits to obligations.

consequentialism

The normative theory that holds that the morality of actions and policies depends on foreseeable outcomes (*see also* practice-consequentialism, below); can be combined with either anthropocentrism, sentientism, biocentrism, or ecocentrism.

constitutiveness theory, the

The theory holding that care for natural goods is constitutive of, or essential to, a flourishing human life.

Contraction and Convergence approach, the

A widely supported approach to negotiations on greenhouse gas emissions, involving international reductions in emissions and converging emissions rates, partly through adoption of the Population Principle.

contract-theorists (or contractarians)

Theorists who hold the normative stance that ethical rules and practices are ones that individuals who were ignorant of their own prospects would freely choose if they were bargaining on an utterly equal basis (or on 'a level playing-field'). John Rawls adopts such a stance in *A Theory of Justice*.

convergence claim, Bryan Norton's

The claim that policies serving the interests of humanity as a whole and in the long run will also serve the interests of non-human nature. This would make separate appeals to non-human interests redundant.

convergence theory, John Passmore's

The theory holding that obligations are to immediate posterity only, supposedly (but not historically) supported by a convergence of several theories, including Rawlsian contractarianism and the consequentialism of the nineteenth-century philosophers Jeremy Bentham and Henry Sidgwick.

cosmopolitanism

The meta-ethical stance that holds that ethical responsibilities apply everywhere and to all moral agents capable of shouldering them, and not only to members of one or another tradition or community. Contrasts with meta-ethical communitarianism, which relates responsibilities to community membership.

critical natural capital

The stock of those natural resources that are indispensable for human survival and development.

Deep Ecology Movement, the

Movement initiated by Arne Naess that supports the holistic Deep Ecology Platform, aiming at the flourishing or self-realization of all Earth's species, and advocating the identification of the self with the biosphere.

demographic transition theory, the	The theory holding that when standards of living in poor countries improve, these countries tend (like developed countries before them) to undergo a transition from high death rates and fertility rates to low ones.
deontological theories	The kind of normative theories that reject consequentialism and work from some other basis.
development	An economic, social, cultural and political process, which aims at the constant enhancement of the well-being of all the inhabitants of a territory on the basis of their active, free and meaningful participation in this process and in the distribution of the resulting benefits to satisfy their basic needs, and/or the state of society that results from this process.
discounting	The practice whereby future benefits and costs are discounted (that is, counted for less) at an agreed social discount rate (e.g. of 5 per cent per annum).
domination	The kind of control exhibited when humans treat the non-human world as they please, with little or no respect, and often other humans as well. Domination needs to be contrasted with dominion (see below).
dominion over nature	The Jewish and Christian belief that humanity has been granted an authority to manage the living world of nature that makes responsibility possible; usually interpreted as stewardship (see below). Interpretations involving despotism, however, are inappropriate, as they suggest human domineering or domination (see above).
dualistic conception of nature and humanity	A metaphysical understanding of nature and humanity as two sharply discontinuous, contrasting entities. (But not all dualisms can be misguided: for example, the dualism that contrasts books and their readers.)
ecocentrism	The normative stance that holds that ecosystems have a good independent of that of their component individuals, and as such

have their own moral standing; and that their attaining or sustaining their good has intrinsic value.

ecofeminism

Relates feminist critiques of gender relations to the relations between humanity and nature, regarding these sets of relations as involving connected kinds of oppression, and/or as turning on distorted conceptions of rationality and the self, and disparagement of nature, the body, emotion and human relations.

ecological problems

See environmental problems.

ecophilosophy

The philosophical study of the environment and of ecology.

ecosystem

Interacting natural system comprising living organisms and non-living entities such as soils and rocks. Examples of ecosystems include forests and estuaries.

ecosystemic integrity

The continuing integrity of ecosystems.

ecosystem services

Services to humanity performed by ecosystems, such as the purification of air and water, and the retention of potential floodwaters by forests

environment

The objective encompassing system of nature, whether encompassing ourselves or members of other species (*see* pp. 1–3).

environmental ethics

The study of the ethics of human interactions with and impacts upon the natural world and natural systems; the branch of ethics concerned with practical issues (such as pollution and biodiversity preservation) and matters of principle arising from such interactions.

environmental footprint

The full environmental impact across the full territorial swathe of space as well as of future time affected by a city or country and its decisions.

environmental injustices

Instances of environmental rights being overridden or of central environment-related interests being overridden.

Environmental Justice Movement, the

A movement based in USA, that campaigns for recognition and redress for environmentally disadvantaged communities.

environmental pollution   Processes, usually anthropogenic, that discharge toxic or other harmful substances or phenomena (such as noise or radiation) in ways liable to damage the health or well-being of human beings, non-human creatures or ecosystems.

environmental (or ecological) problems   Those problems that arise from human dealings with the natural world and its systems. (These are not so much scientific or technological problems as normative ones, problems concerning what ought to be done to avert avoidable harms or dangers.)

environmental racism   Discriminatory practices that impose unfair environmental risks to health and well-being upon people of a different ethnic origin from those in power in society.

equity between generations   Ethically acceptable relations or relations of fairness between the current generation and other generations such as generations of the past and those of the foreseeable future.

essential human capacities   Capacities which, if absent from most members of a species, mean that species would not be a human species.

ethical consumerism   The practice of consumers putting pressure on corporations and other organizations to adopt environmentalist or other ethical policies or practices.

Eurocentrism   Understandings of the world that are too heavily dependent on European or Western values and perspectives, or on Enlightenment values such as human rights.

extrinsic value   Derivative value, for example the instrumental value that things have because of their actual or potential usefulness, or the value that works of art have because people are benefited through appreciating them. Contrasts with intrinsic value.

fair trade commodities   Commodities produced in cooperatives whose workers receive a fair reward for their work, funded by consumers in developed countries who purchase such commodities at above-market prices.

feminism

A type of philosophical approach critical of patriarchal and gender-biased understandings of humanity and human society as objectionably dualistic and unduly preoccupied with rationality. Seeks to develop integrated understandings compatible with the natural and social setting in which human beings are born, and develop their full range of powers and relations.

future interests

The interests of whichever human beings and non-human creatures will live in the future, or of future generations (currently unidentifiable ones included). These interests should, it is argued here, be represented in legislatures.

future-related responsibilities

Obligations (that is, actions that it would be wrong not to perform and/or omissions to do what it would be wrong to do) with regard to whichever human beings and non-human creatures will live in the future, including those currently unidentifiable, and those that would or could live if current decisions facilitate their lives.

Gaia hypothesis, the

The theory that the Earth is a self-regulating system, maintaining the conditions that support life, and that it is thus a 'superorganism' (*see* Excursus in chapter 1).

global citizen

Member of the global community, with awareness of worldwide loyalties and responsibilities (and thus implicit recognition of a global ethic), and with concerns for issues such as the global environment and enhanced global governance.

global commons

Unowned areas of the planet such as the oceans, Antarctica, the atmosphere and outer space.

global environment

The actual natural systems of planet Earth. (Contrasts with the Earth's environs, with local, national and regional environments, and with environments as fields of significance.)

global ethic

A normative ethic of the kind in which obligations do not stop short at national boundaries and are not grounded solely in any particular interest. Examples include Kantianism, rights-theories, contractarianism and consequentialism.

global governance

Systems of international cooperation and agreement, involving international agencies in matters including biodiversity preservation and the promotion of environmentally sustainable development. Need not involve world government; but United Nations agencies play a crucial and growing role.

global warming

The phenomenon in which atmospheric concentrations of gases that have the effect of raising temperatures through the 'greenhouse effect' ('greenhouse gases') are rising. The scientific consensus is that these increases are anthropogenic.

globalization

The process of worldwide economic and cultural integration. Promotes global access to ideas, but embodies the threat of the global growth of the power of transnational corporations and of international agencies that serve their interests.

Harm Principle, the

The liberal principle holding that coercion is justified only to prevent the harming of parties other than the agent of the harm.

holistic value-theories

Theories of value that locate independent value in wholes (such as species or ecosystems or society as a whole) rather than in individual organisms or members of society.

independent value

Value that is not dependent on any other kind of value such as that attaching to human interests.

inherent value

The kind of extrinsic value that works of art or other objects of appreciation such as natural objects have because people are benefited through appreciating them.

instrumental value

The value that things have because of their actual or potential usefulness.

instrumentalist view of nature

The value-theory that treats nature as exclusively a means to human ends, and as lacking intrinsic value.

integrated policies of sustainable development	*See* sustainable development, integrated policies of.
intrinsic value	The kind of value that a thing has when it is valuable because of its very nature. Things are intrinsically valuable when there is reason to promote, cherish or protect them because of their own nature, even in the absence of other grounds.
Kantianism (in ethics)	The normative deontological theory that (in line with Immanuel Kant's Categorical Imperative) makes those actions permissible which a rational agent could consistently will to be universally performed, and that requires agents to treat persons as ends, and never as means alone.
Last Man	A thought-experiment devised by Richard Routley. The Last Man, who is the last human survivor of a global catastrophe, needlessly and aimlessly destroys the living animals and plants around him. Most people who consider this scenario condemn what the Last Man does. Their judgement is difficult to reconcile with anthropocentric value-theories.
mediated consequences	Consequences of, for example, consumer decisions that are mediated (indirect or in some other way distanced from those decisions).
meta-ethics	The study of issues concerning the status of normative discourse, issues such as whether judgements of value can be objective, and whether or not values always depend on the judgements of human valuers.
modernist assumptions	Assumptions ascribed to philosophical systems of the period since Descartes, such as the distinction between primary qualities and secondary qualities.
moral standing/ considerability	The status of entities that ought to be taken into consideration when decisions are being made. In the terminology of Kenneth Goodpaster, these entities are 'morally considerable'.
motivation theory, the	The theory holding that we should care for and promote natural goods simply because

such care is constitutive of a flourishing human life.

neo-Malthusians

Contemporary followers of the eighteenth-century economist and population theorist Thomas Robert Malthus. Prone to ascribe problems to 'overpopulation'.

NGOs

Non-governmental organizations.

non-cognitivism

The kind of meta-ethical theory that holds that claims about value or obligation can never be known to be true or false, as opposed to being e.g. expressions of emotion or prescriptions. Characteristically, non-cognitivists also hold that such claims are neither true nor false.

normative ethics

The study of what ought to be the case: of principles of value and of obligation, of virtues and other traits of character, and of their bearing on action and policy.

objectivism

The meta-ethical theory that holds that judgements of value and obligation are capable of being true or false, and capable of justification on an unrestricted interpersonal basis.

patriarchy

The oppression of women by men. Suggested by some ecofeminists as underpinning the oppression of nature.

phenomenology

The study of feelings and perceptions. Thus 'the phenomenology of action' concerns the study of people's feelings about their actions (and thus their sense of responsibility, or lack of such a sense).

population ethics

The study of ethical issues relating to the human population, such as those of whether the planetary population or the population of a particular country should be stabilized, and of the means by which any such goal may be achieved.

Population Principle, the

The principle advocating that the emission quotas for greenhouse gases of the various states should be proportioned to their population.

postmodernism

The kind of perspective that seeks to avoid the 'grand narratives' and other characteristics associated with the systems of modernism, and emphasizes local struggles and related, fragmentary narratives.

practice-consequentialism   The kind of consequentialism (*see above*) according to which actions and omissions are right not only if they optimize the foreseeable balance of good over bad directly, but also if they comply with practices general compliance with which would optimize the foreseeable balance of good over bad at least as well as alternative practices (or states of society lacking such practices); and actions and omissions are obligatory if the difference to this balance made by the action or omission or the relevant practice is significant and greater than that of alternatives. Can be combined with diverse value-theories including biocentrism.

Precautionary Principle, the   The principle that (in one of its weaker versions) holds that where there are risks of serious or irreversible damage, lack of full scientific certainty should not be used as a reason against taking measures to prevent environmental or other degradation.

preservation, environmental   The preservation of non-human species, subspecies and their habitats. Often contrasted with the conservation of resources, a practice usually undertaken for the sake of eventual human consumption.

Prior Existence View, the   The normative theory that confines moral standing to people and other creatures which either exist already or are going to exist whatever current agents may do, and disregards the interests of possible people and creatures.

psychological egoism   The belief that all human motivations reduce to self-interest. Implications include that we are incapable of caring about the distant future, and that therefore we can have no obligation to care about it.

realism, normative and meta-ethical   The normative and meta-ethical theory that bases obligations on self-interest, whether individual or national. (I do not use in this book the other meta-ethical sense of 'realism', concerning the theory that moral claims are capable of truth and falsity.)

reductionism

The analytical theory that discourse of one kind, e.g. value-talk, can be translated without remainder into discourse of another kind, e.g. that of perspectives.

relativist analysis

The analytic theory that a property such as rightness or value must be regarded as dependent upon the judgements of one or another human group.

Repugnant Conclusion, the

The implication ascribed to consequentialism by Derek Parfit that a very large population of uniformly but barely happy people (happy enough for life to be worth living, but by a narrow margin only) has to be regarded as preferable to a smaller population of very happy people.

rights-theorists

Theorists who hold the normative stance that having a point of view betokens having irreducible rights such as the rights not to be made to suffer, not to be confined and not to be killed by human agents. Unlike other believers in rights, these theorists believe that rights are fundamental rather than derivative.

self-transcendence

Commitment to concerns and causes that transcend one's own interests.

sentientism

The normative stance that holds that all sentient creatures should be given moral consideration, but that creatures lacking sentience have no good of their own and thus lack moral standing as well.

Socially Responsible Investment

The practice, urged by campaigning bodies and individuals on corporations such as banks and pension funds, to employ ethical and environmental selectivity when making decisions about investment.

stewardship of nature, the human

The belief (which can assume religious or secular forms) that human beings hold the planetary biosphere as a trust, and are both responsible and answerable for its care, whether to God or to the community of moral agents.

substitutability

The possibility of substituting or replacing natural resources (or 'natural capital') with human-made capital (machines and technological know-how). While 'weak sustainability' sets few limits to such substitution, 'strong sustainability' recognizes ecological limits thereto.

sustainability

A practice or social system is sustainable if it is capable of being practised or maintained indefinitely, regard being had to ecological limits. Sustainable practices and systems must also be possible parts of a sustainable world system; hence, as well as not undermining themselves, they will not undermine other practices or systems that would otherwise be sustainable.

sustainable development

See the above definitions of 'development' and of 'sustainability', and the discussion of this concept and related debates in the first half of chapter 5.

sustainable development, integrated policies of

Policies of development and of sustainability (see above) involving improved provision for health care, for education in literacy, health care and family planning, for environmental protection and for land security.

systemic value

The value present in systems such as ecosystems and the entire evolutionary process that facilitate the existence of living creatures in all their diversity.

total-use scenario

A scenario that envisages the whole surface of the planet being used or manipulated to serve human purposes.

Total View or Theory, the

The normative consequentialist theory holding that agents should optimize the total (rather than the average) balance of whatever makes life worthwhile over whatever detracts from it, in terms of the full range of foreseeable consequences of action and inaction. Can be combined with a variety of value-theories including biocentrism, and also with practice-consequentialism.

UNCED

United Nations Conference on Environment and Development.

vertebragenic

Generated by vertebrates.

virtue ethics

The normative theory that represents as right those actions that a virtuous person would perform, and virtue as a more basic concept than rightness.

Bibliography

Adams, Martin, *Breaking Ground: Development Aid for Land Reform* (Overseas Development Institute, London, 2000).

Adams, W. M. and Hulme, D., 'If Community Conservation is the Answer in Africa, What is the Question?', *Oryx*, 35 (2001), 193–200.

Agius, Emmanuel, 'Patenting Life: Our Responsibilities to Present and Future Generations', *Philosophy and Medicine*, 55 (1998), 67–83.

Aiken, William, 'The "Carrying Capacity" Equivocation', in William Aiken and Hugh LaFollette (eds), *World Hunger and Morality*, 2nd edn (1996, see below), pp. 16–25.

Aiken, William and LaFollette, Hugh (eds), *World Hunger and Moral Obligation* (Prentice-Hall, Englewood Cliffs, NJ, 1977).

Aiken, William and LaFollette, Hugh (eds), *World Hunger and Morality*, 2nd edn (Prentice-Hall, Upper Saddle River, NJ, 1996).

Alexander, William, 'Prototype for Sustainable Development: Kerala' (unpublished paper).

Allaby, Michael, *Basics of Environmental Science* (Routledge, London and New York, 1996).

Amin, Samir, 'Four Comments on Kerala', *Monthly Review*, 42 (1991), 28–33.

Anderson, Terry L., 'Free Market Environmentalism', in Richard G. Botzler and Susan J. Armstrong (eds), *Environmental Ethics: Divergence and Convergence*, 2nd edn (1998, see below), pp. 527–39.

Anderson, Terry L. and Leal, Donald R., *Free Market Environmentalism* (Westview Press, Oxford, 1991).

Andrews, Geoff (ed.), *Citizenship* (Lawrence & Wishart, London, 1991).

Aquinas, Thomas, *Summa Contra Gentiles*, trans. Anton Pegis et al. (5 vols, Image Books, Garden City, NY, 1955–7).

Arler, Finn, 'Justice in the Air: Energy Policy, Greenhouse Effect, and the Question of Global Justice', *Human Ecology Review*, 2 (1995), 40–61.

Attfield, Robin, 'Supererogation and Double Standards', *Mind*, 88 (1979), 481–99.

Attfield, Robin, 'The Good of Trees', *Journal of Value Inquiry*, 15 (1981), 35–54.

Attfield, Robin, *The Ethics of Environmental Concern* (Basil Blackwell, Oxford and Columbia University Press, New York, 1983).

Attfield, Robin, 'Christian Attitudes to Nature', *Journal of the History of Ideas*, 44 (1983), 369–86.

Attfield, Robin, 'Western Traditions and Environmental Ethics', in Robert Elliot and Arran Gare (eds), *Environmental Philosophy: A Collection of Readings* (1983, see below), pp. 201–30.

Attfield, Robin, *A Theory of Value and Obligation* (Croom Helm, London, New York and Sydney, 1987).

Attfield, Robin, *The Ethics of Environmental Concern*, 2nd edn (University of Georgia Press, Athens, GA and London, 1991).

Attfield, Robin, 'Development and Environmentalism', in Robin Attfield and Barry Wilkins (eds), *International Justice and the Third World: Essays in the Philosophy of Development* (1992, see below), pp. 151–68.

Attfield, Robin, *God and the Secular*, 2nd edn (Gregg Revivals, Aldershot, 1993).

Attfield, Robin, 'Rehabilitating Nature and Making Nature Habitable', in Robin Attfield and Andrew Belsey (eds), *Philosophy and the Natural Environment* (1994, see below), pp. 45–57.

Attfield, Robin, 'Has the History of Philosophy Ruined the Environment?', in Robin Attfield, *Environmental Philosophy: Principles and Prospects* (1994, see below), pp. 77–87.

Attfield, Robin, 'Biocentrism, Moral Standing and Moral Significance', reprinted in Attfield, *Environmental Philosophy: Principles and Prospects* (1994, see below), pp. 173–82.

Attfield, Robin, 'Development and Environmentalism', reprinted in Robin Attfield, *Environmental Philosophy: Principles and Prospects* (1994, see below), pp. 221–35.

Attfield, Robin, *Environmental Philosophy: Principles and Prospects* (Ashgate, Aldershot and Brookfield, VT, 1994).

Attfield, Robin, 'The Precautionary Principle and Moral Values', in Tim O'Riordan and James Cameron (eds), *Interpreting the Precautionary Principle* (1994, see below), pp. 152–64.

Attfield, Robin, *Value, Obligation and Meta-Ethics* (Éditions Rodopi, Amsterdam and Atlanta, GA, 1995).

Attfield, Robin, 'Preferences, Health, Interests and Value', *Electronic Journal of Applied Philosophy*, 3, 2 (1995), 7–15.

Attfield, Robin, 'Discounting, Jamieson's Trilemma and Representing the Future', in Tim Hayward and John O'Neill (eds), *Justice, Property and the Environment* (1997, see below), pp. 85–96.

Attfield, Robin, 'Environmental Ethics and Intergenerational Equity', *Inquiry*, 41 (1998), 207–22.

Attfield, Robin, 'Saving Nature, Feeding People and Ethics', *Environmental Values*, 7 (1998), 291–304.

Attfield, Robin, 'Environmental Ethics, Overview', in Ruth Chadwick (ed.), *Encyclopedia of Applied Ethics* (1998, see below), vol. 2, pp. 73–81.

Attfield, Robin, *The Ethics of the Global Environment* (Edinburgh University Press, Edinburgh, and Purdue University Press, West Lafayette, IN, 1999).

Attfield, Robin, 'Depth, Trusteeship and Redistribution', in Klaus Brinkmann (ed.), *Proceedings of the Twentieth World Congress of Philosophy* (1999, see below), vol. 1, 'Ethics', pp. 159–68.

Attfield, Robin, 'Christianity' in Dale Jamieson (ed.), *A Companion to Environmental Philosophy* (2000, see below), pp. 96–110.

Attfield, Robin, 'Evolution, Theodicy and Value', *Heythrop Journal*, 41 (2000), 281–96.

Attfield, Robin, 'Postmodernism, Value and Objectivity', *Environmental Values*, 10 (2001), 145–62.

Attfield, Robin, 'Meaningful Work and Full Employment', *Reason in Practice*, 1.1 (2001), 41–8.

Attfield, Robin, 'Sustainability, Global Warming, Population Policies and Liberal Democracy', in John Barry and Marcel Wissenburg (eds), *Sustaining Liberal Democracy: Ecological Challenges and Opportunities* (2001, see below), pp. 149–60.

Attfield, Robin, 'Are Promises to Repay International Debt Binding?', *Journal of Social Philosophy*, 32 (2001), 505–11.

Attfield, Robin, 'To Do No Harm?: The Precautionary Principle and Moral Values', *Reason in Practice*, 1.3 (2001), 11–20.

Attfield, Robin, 'Ecological Policies and Ecological Values', trans. K. Boudouris as 'Oikologikes politikes kai oikologikes axies', in Konstantine Boudouris (ed.), *Oikologikes Axies* (2002, see below), pp. 9–26.

Attfield, Robin, 'Differentiated Responsibilities', forthcoming in Markku Oksanen and Juhani Pietarinen (eds), *Philosophy and Biodiversity* (see below).

Attfield, Robin, 'Biocentric Consequentialism, Pluralism and "The Minimax Implication": A Reply to Alan Carter', forthcoming in *Utilitas*, 15 (2003).

Attfield, Robin and Belsey, Andrew (eds), *Philosophy and the Natural Environment* (Cambridge University Press, Cambridge, 1994).

Attfield, Robin and Wilkins, Barry (eds), *International Justice and the Third World: Essays in the Philosophy of Development* (Routledge, London and New York, 1992).

Ball, J., Goodall, M., Palmer, C. and Reader, J. (eds), *The Earth Beneath* (SPCK, London, 1992).

Bambrough, Renford, *Moral Scepticism and Moral Knowledge* (Routledge & Kegan Paul, London and Henley, 1979).

Barr, John (ed.), *The Environmental Handbook: Action Guide for the UK* (Ballantine/Friends of the Earth, London, 1971).

Barry, Brian, 'The Ethics of Resource Depletion', in Brian Barry, *Liberty and Justice: Essays in Political Theory, 2* (1991, see below), pp. 259–73.

Barry, Brian, *Liberty and Justice: Essays in Political Theory, 2* (Clarendon Press, Oxford, 1991).

Barry, John, 'Greening Liberal Democracy', in John Barry and Marcel Wissenburg (eds), *Sustaining Liberal Democracy: Ecological Challenges and Opportunities* (2001, see below), pp. 59–80.

Barry, John and Wissenburg, Marcel (eds), *Sustaining Liberal Democracy: Ecological Challenges and Opportunities* (Palgrave, Basingstoke and New York, 2001).

Barry, John, Wissenburg, Marcel and de Geus, Marius, 'Conclusion', in Barry and Wissenburg, *Sustaining Liberal Democracy: Ecological Challenges and Opportunities* (2001, see above), pp. 205–12.

Beauchamp, Tom L. and Childress, James F., *Principles of Biomedical Ethics* (4th edn, New York and Oxford: Oxford University Press, 1994).

Beckerman, Wilfred, 'Sustainable Development: Is it a Useful Concept?', *Environmental Values*, 3 (1994), 191–204.

Beckerman, Wilfred, 'Sustainable Development and our Obligations to Future Generations', in Andrew Dobson (ed.), *Fairness and Futurity* (1999, see below), pp. 71–117.

Beiner, Ronald (ed.), *Theorizing Citizenship* (Albany, State University of New York, 1995).

Belshaw, Christopher, *Environmental Philosophy: Reason, Nature and Human Concern* (Acumen, Chesham, Bucks, 2001).

Benson, John, *Environmental Ethics: An Introduction with Readings* (Routledge, London and New York, 2000).

Berry, Wendell, 'The Gift of Good Land', in Richard G. Botzler and Susan J. Armstrong (eds), *Environmental Ethics: Divergence and Convergence*, 2nd edn (1998, see below), pp. 221–8.

Blackstone, William T. (ed.), *Philosophy & Environmental Crisis* (University of Georgia Press, Athens, GA, 1974).

Bookchin, Murray, 'Thinking Ecologically: A Dialectical Approach', *Our Generation*, 18, 2 (1987), 3–40.

Botzler, Richard G. and Armstrong, Susan J. (eds), *Environmental Ethics: Divergence and Convergence* (2nd edn, McGraw-Hill, Boston, MA, 1998).

Boudouris, Konstantine (ed.) *Oikologikes Axies*, University of Athens Technology Institute of Applied and Ecological Philosophy, University of Athens, Athens, 2002.

Bratton, Susan Power, 'The Original Desert Solitaire: Early Christian Monasticism and Wilderness', *Environmental Ethics*, 10 (1988), 31–53.

Brennan, Andrew, *Thinking About Nature: An Investigation of Nature, Value and Ecology* (University of Georgia Press, Athens, GA, 1988).

Brinkmann, Klaus (ed.), *Proceedings of the Twentieth World Congress of Philosophy* (12 vols, Philosophy Documentation Center, Bowling Green State University, 1999), vol. 1, *Ethics*.

Broome, John, *Counting the Cost of Global Warming* (The White Horse Press, Cambridge, 1992).

Brown, Lester (ed.), *State of the World* (W. W. Norton, New York, 1987).

Brown, Lester R., 'Challenges of the New Century', in Lester R. Brown, Christopher Flavin and Hilary French, *State of the World 2000*, Linda Starke (ed.), (2000, see below), pp. 3–21.

Brown, Lester R., Flavin, Christopher and French, Hilary, *State of the World 2000*, Linda Starke (ed.), (Earthscan, London, 2000).

Brown, Lester R. and Postel, Sandra, 'Thresholds of Change', in Lester Brown (ed.), *State of the World* (1987, see above), pp. 1–4.

Bullard, Robert, 'Overcoming Racism in Environmental Decisionmaking', *Environment*, 36 (1994), 10–20, 39–44.

Callicott, J. Baird, 'Animal Liberation: A Triangular Affair', *Environmental Ethics*, 2 (1980), 311–38.

Callicott, J. Baird, 'Hume's *Is/Ought* Dichotomy and the Relation of Ecology to Leopold's Land Ethic', *Environmental Ethics*, 4 (1982), 163–74.

Callicott, J. Baird, 'Animal Liberation: A Triangular Affair', reprinted in J. Baird Callicott, *In Defense of the Land Ethic: Essays in Environmental Philosophy* (State University of New York Press, Albany, NY, 1989), pp. 15–38.

Callicott, J. Baird, 'Animal Liberation and Environmental Ethics: Back Together Again', in J. Baird Callicott, *In Defense of the Land Ethic: Essays in Environmental Philosophy* (1989, see below), pp. 49–59.

Callicott, J. Baird, *In Defense of the Land Ethic: Essays in Environmental Philosophy* (State University of New York Press, Albany, NY, 1989).

Callicott, J. Baird, 'The Wilderness Idea Revisited: The Sustainable Development Alternative', *The Environmental Professional*, 13 (1991), 235–47.

Callicott, J. Baird, 'Rolston on Intrinsic Value: A Deconstruction', *Environmental Ethics*, 14 (1992), 129–43.

Callicott, J. Baird, 'Environmental Philosophy is Environmental Activism: The Most Radical and Effective Kind', in Don Marietta Jr. and Lester Embree (eds), *Environmental Philosophy and Environmental Activism* (1995, see below), pp. 19–35.

Carlson, Allen, 'Nature and Positive Aesthetics', *Environmental Ethics*, 6 (1984), 5–34.

Carson, Rachel, *Silent Spring* (Hamish Hamilton, London, 1962).

Carter, Alan, 'A Radical Environmentalist Political Theory: Part Three of "Foundations for Developing a Green Political Theory"', *Cogito*, 10 (1996), 210–19.

Carter, Alan, *A Radical Green Political Theory* (Routledge, London and New York, 1999).

Carter, Alan, 'Humean Nature', *Environmental Values*, 9 (2000), pp. 3–37.

Carter, Alan, 'Distributive Justice and Environmental Sustainability', *The Heythrop Journal*, XLI (2000), 449–60.

Carter, Alan, Review of Robin Attfield, *The Ethics of the Global Environment*, in *Mind*, 110 (2001), 149–53.

Carter, Alan, 'Can We Harm Future People?', *Environmental Values*, 10 (2001), 429–54.

Castro, Fidel, *Tomorrow is Too Late: Development and the Environmental Crisis in the Third World* (Ocean Press, Melbourne, 1993).

Chadwick, Ruth (ed.), *Encyclopedia of Applied Ethics*, 4 vols (Academic Press, San Diego, 1998).

Chappell, Timothy, 'The Implications of Incommensurability', *Philosophy*, 76 (2001), 137–48.

Chappell, Timothy, 'Option Ranges', *Journal of Applied Philosophy*, 18 (2001), 107–18.

Chappell, Timothy, 'Two Distinctions that do make a Difference: The Action/Omission Distinction and the Principle of Double Effect', *Philosophy*, 77 (2002), 211–33.

Chase, Steve (ed.), *Defending the Earth: A Dialogue between Murray Bookchin and Dave Foreman* (South End Press, Boston, MA, 1991).

Clark, Stephen R. L., 'Gaia and the Forms of Life', in Robert Elliot and Arran Gare (eds), *Environmental Philosophy: A Collection of Readings* (1983, see below), pp. 182–97.

Cohen, M. F., 'The Practicality of Moral Reasoning', *Mind*, 78 (1969), 534–49.

Commoner, Barry, *The Closing Circle: Confronting the Environmental Crisis* (Jonathan Cape, London, 1972).

Cooper, David E., 'Other Species and Moral Reason', in David E. Cooper and Joy A. Palmer (eds), *Just Environments: Intergenerational, International and Interspecies Issues* (1995, see below), pp. 137–48.

Cooper, David E. and Palmer, Joy A. (eds), *Just Environments: Intergenerational, International and Interspecies Issues* (Routledge, London, 1995).

Crocker, David A., 'Hunger, Capability, and Development', in William Aiken and Hugh LaFollette (eds) *World Hunger and Morality*, 2nd edn (1996, see above), pp. 211–30.

Crocker, David A. and Linden, Toby (eds), *Ethics of Consumption: The Good Life, Justice, and Global Stewardship* (Rowman & Littlefield, Lanham, MD and Oxford, 1998).

Daly, Herman, 'On Wilfred Beckerman's Critique of Sustainable Development', *Environmental Values*, 4 (1995), 49–55.

Daly, Herman, 'Globalization and Its Discontents', *Philosophy & Public Policy Quarterly*, 21 (spring/summer 2001), 17–21.

Daly, Herman E. and Cobb, John B. Jr, *For the Common Good: Redirecting the Economy towards Community, the Environment and a Sustainable Future* (Beacon Press, Boston, 1989).

Dasgupta, Partha, *Human Well-Being and the Natural Environment* (Oxford University Press, Oxford, 2001).

Davidson, Julie, 'Sustainable Development: Business as Usual or a New Way of Living?', *Environmental Ethics*, 22 (2000), 25–42.

de Geus, Marius, 'Sustainability, Liberal Democracy, Liberalism', in John Barry and Marcel Wissenburg (eds), *Sustaining Liberal Democracy: Ecological Challenges and Opportunities* (2001, see above), pp. 19–36.

de-Shalit, Avner, *Why Posterity Matters: Environmental Policies and Future Generations* (Routledge, London, 1995).

Des Jardins, Joseph R., *Environmental Ethics: An Introduction to Environmental Philosophy*, 3rd edn (Wadsworth/Thomson Learning, Belmont, CA, 2001).

Dickson, Barnabas, 'The Ethicist Conception of Environmental Problems', *Environmental Values*, 9 (2000), 127–52 (also available online from Ingenta Journals and Bioline).

Dobson, Andrew, *Justice and the Environment: Conceptions of Environmental Sustainability and Theories of Distributive Justice* (Oxford University Press, Oxford, 1998).

Dobson, Andrew (ed.), *Fairness and Futurity: Essays on Environmental Sustainability and Social Justice* (Oxford University Press, Oxford, 1999).

Dobson, Andrew, 'Foreword' in John Barry and Marcel Wissenburg (eds), *Sustaining Liberal Democracy: Ecological Challenges and Opportunities* (2001, see above), pp. vii–ix.

Dodds, Felix, 'Reviewing the Achievements Since Rio', *Connections* (Special Conference Report, summer 2001), pp. 4–10.

Dower, Nigel, *World Ethics: The New Agenda* (Edinburgh University Press, Edinburgh, 1998).

Drèze, Jean and Sen, Amartya, *Hunger and Public Action* (Clarendon Press, Oxford, 1989).

Dubos, René, 'Franciscan Conservation versus Benedictine Stewardship', in David Spring and Eileen Spring (eds), *Ecology and Religion in History* (1974, see below), pp. 114–36.

Dubos, René and Ward, Barbara, *Only One Earth: The Care and Maintenance of a Small Planet* (Harmondsworth, Penguin, 1972).

Ehrenfeld, David and Bentley, Philip J., 'Judaism and the Practice of Stewardship', *Judaism*, 34 (1985), 301–11.

Ehrlich, Paul R., *The Population Bomb* (Pan Books/Ballantine, London, 1971).

Ekins, Paul, 'Making Development Sustainable', in Wolfgang Sachs (ed.), *Global Ecology*, (1993, see below), pp. 91–103.

Elliot, Robert, 'The Rights of Future People', *Journal of Applied Philosophy*, 6 (1989), 159–69.

Elliot, Robert, 'Intrinsic Value, Environmental Obligation, and Naturalness', *The Monist*, 75 (1992), 138–60.

Elliot, Robert (ed.), *Environmental Ethics* (Oxford University Press, Oxford, 1995).

Elliot, Robert, *Faking Nature: The Ethics of Environmental Restoration* (Routledge, London and New York, 1997).

Elliot, Robert and Gare, Arran (eds), *Environmental Philosophy: A Collection of Readings* (University of Queensland Press, St Lucia and Open University Press, Milton Keynes, 1983).

England, Paula, 'The Separative Self: Androcentric Bias in Neoclassical Assumptions', in Marianne A. Ferber and Julie A. Nelson (eds), *Beyond Economic Man: Feminist Theory and Economics* (1993, see below), pp. 37–53.

Falk, Richard, 'The Making of Global Citizenship', in Bart van Steenbergen (ed.), *The Condition of Citizenship* (1994, see below), pp. 127–40.

Falk, Richard, 'Reviving the 1990s Trend toward Transnational Justice: Innovations and Institutions', *Journal of Human Development: Alternative Economics in Action*, 3 (2002), 167–90.

Feinberg, Joel, 'The Rights of Animals and Unborn Generations', in Blackstone, William T. (ed.), *Philosophy & Environmental Crisis* (1974, see above), pp. 43–68.

Ferber, Marianne A. and Nelson, Julie A. (eds), *Beyond Economic Man: Feminist Theory and Economics* (University of Chicago Press, Chicago, 1993).

Feshbach, Murray and Friendly, Alfred, *Ecocide in the USSR* (Basic Books, New York, 1992).

Foltz, Bruce V., 'On Heidegger and the Interpretation of Environmental Crisis', *Environmental Ethics*, 6 (1984), 323–38.

Fox, Matthew, 'Creation Spirituality', in Richard G. Botzler and Susan J. Armstrong (eds), *Environmental Ethics: Divergence and Convergence*, 2nd edn (1998, see above), pp. 228–34.

Fox, Warwick, 'The Deep Ecology/Ecofeminism Debate and its Parallels', *Environmental Ethics*, 11 (1989), 5–25.

Gare, Arran E., *Postmodernism and the Environmental Crisis* (Routledge, London and New York, 1995).

George, Susan, *The Debt Boomerang: How Third World Debt Harms Us All* (Pluto Press, London, 1992).

Gewirth, Alan, *Reason and Morality* (University of Chicago Press, Chicago and London, 1978).

Glacken, Clarence J., *Traces on the Rhodian Shore: Nature and Culture in Western Thought from Ancient Times to the End of the Eighteenth Century* (University of California Press, Berkeley, CA and London, 1967).

Gleeson, Brendan and Low, Nicholas (eds), *Governing for the Environment: Global Problems, Ethics and Democracy* (Palgrave, Basingstoke, 2001).

Glover, Jonathan, *Causing Death and Saving Lives* (Penguin, Harmondsworth and New York, 1977).

Golding, Martin, 'Obligations to Future Generations', *The Monist*, 56 (1972), 25–36.

Golding, Martin, 'Obligations to Future Generations', reprinted in Ernest Partridge (ed.), *Responsibilities to Future Generations* (1981, see below), pp. 61–72.

Goodin, Robert E., *Green Political Theory* (Polity, Cambridge, 1992).

Goodin, Robert E., 'Introduction', in Robert E. Goodin, *The Politics of the Environment* (Edward Elgar, Aldershot, 1994), pp. ix–xx.

Goodpaster, Kenneth E., 'On Being Morally Considerable', *Journal of Philosophy*, 75 (1978), 308–25.

Goodpaster, Kenneth E., 'On Stopping at Everything: A Reply to W. M. Hunt', *Environmental Ethics*, 2 (1980), 21–35.

Gregorios, Paul, *The Human Presence* (World Council of Churches, Geneva, 1978).

Grubb, Michael, *The Greenhouse Effect: Negotiating Targets* (Royal Institute of International Affairs, London, 1989.

Grubb, Michael, *Energy Policies and the Greenhouse Effect* (Gower, Aldershot, 1990).

Grubb, Michael, 'From Rio to Kyoto via Berlin: climate change and the prospects for international action', in Michael Grubb and Dean Anderson (eds), *The Emerging International Regime for Climate Change: Structures and Options after Berlin* (1995, see below), pp. 79–96.

Grubb, Michael and Anderson, Dean (eds), *The Emerging International Regime for Climate Change: Structures and Options after Berlin* (Royal Institute of International Affairs, London, 1995).

Gruen, Lori and Jamieson, Dale (eds), *Reflecting on Nature: Readings in Environmental Philosophy* (Oxford University Press, New York, 1994).

Hale, Sir Matthew, *The Primitive Origination of Mankind* (London, 1677).

Hambling, Joyce, 'Three Steps Forward, Two Steps Back', *Splice: The Magazine of the Genetics Forum*, 6, 5 (July/August 2000), 10–11.

Hardin, Garrett, 'Lifeboat Ethics: The Case Against Helping the Poor', in William Aiken and Hugh LaFollette (eds), *World Hunger and Moral Obligation* (1977, see above), pp. 11–21.

Hardin, Garrett, *Living Within Limits* (Oxford University Press, Oxford, 1993).

Hare, R. M., *Moral Thinking: Its Levels, Method and Point* (Clarendon Press, Oxford, 1981).

Hare, R. M., 'Moral Reasoning About the Environment', in R. M. Hare, *Essays on Political Morality* (1989, see below), pp. 236–53.

Hare, R. M., *Essays on Political Morality* (Clarendon Press, Oxford, 1989).

Hargrove, Eugene C. (ed.), *Religion and Environmental Crisis* (University of Georgia Press, Athens, GA and London, 1986).

Hargrove, Eugene C., *Foundations of Environmental Ethics* (Prentice-Hall, Englewood Cliffs, NJ, 1989).

Harrison, Peter, 'Subduing the Earth: Genesis 1, Early Modern Science, and the Exploitation of Nature', *Journal of Religion*, 79 (1999), 86–109 (also available online from www.infotrac.london.galegroup.com).

Hattingh, Johan, 'Sustainability in a Developing Country such as South Africa: A Philosophical Analysis' (unpublished paper, 2001).

Hayward, Tim, *Ecological Thought: An Introduction with Readings* (Polity, Cambridge, 1994).

Hayward, Tim, 'Constitutional Environmental Rights and Liberal Democracy', in John Barry and Marcel Wissenburg (eds), *Sustaining Liberal Democracy: Ecological Challenges and Opportunities* (2001, see above), pp. 117–34.

Hayward, Tim and O'Neill, John (eds), *Justice, Property and the Environment* (Ashgate, Aldershot and Brookfield, VT, 1997).

Heidegger, Martin, 'The Question Concerning Technology', in David Farrell Krell (ed.), *Martin Heidegger: Basic Writings* (1978, see below), pp. 283–322.

Holland, Alan, 'Genetically Based Handicap', *Journal of Applied Philosophy*, 15 (1998), 119–32.

Holland, Alan, 'Sustainability: Should We Start from Here?', in Andrew Dobson (ed.), *Fairness and Futurity: Essays on Environmental Sustainability and Social Justice* (1999, see above), pp. 46–68.

Hooker, Brad, 'The Collapse of Virtue Ethics', *Utilitas*, 14. 1 (2002), 22–40.

Houghton, J. T., et al., *Climate Change 1995: The Science of Climate Change* (published for the Intergovernmental Panel on Climate Change by Cambridge University Press, Cambridge, 1996).

Hume, C. W., *The Status of Animals in the Christian Religion* (Universities Federation for Animal Welfare, London, 1957).

Hume, David, *A Treatise of Human Nature*, ed. Ernest C. Mossner (Penguin, Harmondsworth, 1969).

Hume, David, *An Enquiry Concerning the Principles of Morals*, in David Hume, *Enquiries Concerning Human Understanding and Concerning the*

Principles of Morals, ed. L. A. Selby Bigge, 3rd edn, revised P. H. Nidditch (Clarendon Press, Oxford, 1975).

Hursthouse, Rosalind, *On Virtue Ethics* (Oxford University Press, Oxford, 1999).

Hursthouse, Rosalind, 'Virtue Ethics vs. Rule-Consequentialism: A Reply to Brad Hooker', *Utilitas*, 14.1 (2002), 41–53.

Izzi Dean, M., *The Environmental Dimensions of Islam* (Lutterworth Press, Cambridge, 2000).

Jacobs, Michael, *Reflections on the Discourse and Politics of Sustainable Development, Part 1: Faultlines of Contestation and the Radical Model* (Centre for the Study of Environmental Change, Lancaster University, 1995).

Jacobs, Michael, 'Sustainable Development, Capital Substitution and Economic Humility: A Reply to Beckerman', *Environmental Values*, 4 (1995), 57–68.

Jacobs, Michael, 'Sustainable Development: A Contested Concept', in Andrew Dobson (ed.), *Fairness and Futurity: Essays on Environmental Sustainability and Social Justice* (1999, see above), pp. 21–45.

James, David N., 'Risking Extinction: An Axiological Analysis', *Research in Philosophy and Technology*, 11 (1991), 49–63.

Jamieson, Dale, 'Future Generations' (unpublished paper, presented to the Swedish Collegium for Advanced Study in the Social Sciences, Friiberghs Herrgård, Sweden, August 1995).

Jamieson, Dale (ed.), *A Companion to Environmental Philosophy* (Blackwell, Oxford and Malden, MA, 2000).

Karam, Khalil, 'Ethics of Sciences: Extra-Atmospheric Space', Chair's Remarks at International Colloquium on the Ethics of the Sciences and the Technologies', Beirut, October 2001 (unpublished text).

Katz, Eric, 'Judaism and the Ecological Crisis', in Mary Evelyn Tucker and John A. Grim (eds), *Worldviews and Ecology: Religion, Philosophy and Environment* (1993, see below), pp. 55–70.

Keynes, John Maynard, 'National Self-sufficiency', in Donald Moggridge (ed.), *The Collected Writings of John Maynard Keynes*, vol. 21, *Activities 1931–1939: World Crisis and Policies in Britain and America* (1982, see below), pp. 233–46.

Khalid, Fazlun and O'Brien, Joanne (eds), *Islam and Ecology* (Cassell, London and New York, 1992).

Kirchner, James W., 'The Gaia Hypotheses: Are They Testable? Are They Useful?', in P. Louis (ed.), *Environmental Ethics: Readings in Theory and Application* (1994, see below), pp. 146–54.

Kovach, Hetty and Burall, Simon, *Charter 99 Global Accountability Project* (One World Trust, London, 2001).

Kovesi, Julius, *Moral Notions* (Routledge & Kegan Paul, London, 1967).

Krell, David Farrell (ed.), *Martin Heidegger: Basic Writings* (Routledge and Kegan Paul, London and Henley, 1978).

Lappé, Frances Moore and Shurman, Rachel, 'Taking People Seriously', in Lori Gruen and Dale Jamieson (eds), *Reflecting on Nature: Readings in Environmental Philosophy* (1994, see above), pp. 328–32.

Laslett, Peter and Fishkin, James, 'Introduction: Processional Justice', in Peter Laslett and James Fishkin, *Justice Between Age Groups and Generations* (1992, see below), pp. 1–23.

Laslett, Peter and Fishkin, James, *Justice Between Age Groups and Generations* (Yale University Press, New Haven, CT, 1992).

Lee, Keekok, *The Natural and the Artefactual: The Implications of Deep Science and Deep Technology for Environmental Philosophy* (Lexington Books, Lanham, MD, 1999).

Lenman, James, 'Consequentialism and Cluelessness', *Philosophy & Public Affairs*, 29 (2000), 342–70.

Leopold, Aldo, *A Sand County Almanac and Sketches Here and There* (Oxford University Press, New York, 1949).

Leopold, Aldo, *A Sand County Almanac: With Other Essays on Conservation from 'Round River'*, Oxford University Press, New York, 1966.

Leopold, Aldo, 'The Land Ethic', in Donald VanDeVeer and Christine Pierce (eds), *People, Penguins and Plastic Trees* (Wadsworth, Belmont, CA, 1986), pp. 73–82.

Levin, Margarita Garcia, 'A Critique of Ecofeminism,' in Louis P. Pojman, *Environmental Ethics: Readings in Theory and Application* (1994, see below), pp. 134–40.

Lo, Y. S., in 'A Humean Argument for the Land Ethic?', *Environmental Values*, 10 (2001), 523–39.

Lomborg, Björn, *The Skeptical Environmentalist: Measuring the Real State of the World* (Cambridge University Press, Cambridge, 2001).

Long, A. A. and Sedley, D. (eds), *The Hellenistic Philosophers* (Cambridge University Press, Cambridge, 1987).

Louth, Andrew, *Maximus the Confessor* (Routledge, London and New York, 1996).

Lovelock, James, *Gaia: A New Look at the Earth* (Oxford University Press, Oxford, 1979).

Lovelock, James, *Gaia: The Practical Science of Planetary Medicine* (Gaia Books, London, 1991).

Lubchenko, Jane, 'Entering the Century of the Environment: A New Social Contract for Science', *Science*, 279 (23 January 1998), 491–7.

Lucas, Peter, 'Environmental Ethics: Between Inconsequential Philosophy and Unphilosophical Consequentialism', *Environmental Ethics*, 24 (2002), 353–69.

McDonagh, Sean, *To Care for the Earth, A Call for a New Theology* (Geoffrey Chapman, London, 1986).

MacLean, Douglas and Brown, Peter G. (eds), *Energy and the Future* (Rowman & Littlefield, Totowa, NJ, 1983).

Mannison, Don, McRobbie, Michael and Routley, Richard (eds), *Environmental Philosophy* (Australian National University, Canberra, 1980).

Marietta, Don Jr and Embree, Lester (eds), *Environmental Philosophy and Environmental Activism* (Rowman and Littlefield, Lanham, MD, 1995).

Marsh, George Perkins, *Man and Nature* (New York, 1864).

Marx, Karl, *Capital* (3 vols, International, New York, 1967).

Masri, Al-Hafiz B. A., 'Islam and Ecology', in Fazlun Khalid and Joanne O'Brien (eds), *Islam and Ecology* (1992, see above), pp. 1–23.

Meadows, Donella, Meadows, Dennis L., Randers, Jørgen and Behrens, William W., III, *The Limits to Growth*, a report for the Club of Rome's Project on the Predicament of Mankind (1972) (London and Sydney: Pan Books, 1974).

Meadows, Donella, Meadows, Dennis L. and Randers, Jørgen, *Beyond the Limits: Global Collapse or a Sustainable Future* (Earthscan Publications, London, 1992).

Mellor, Mary, *Breaking the Boundaries: Towards a Feminist Green Socialism* (Virago, London, 1992).

Midgley, Mary, 'Duties Concerning Islands', in Robert Elliot and Arran Gare (eds), *Environmental Philosophy: A Collection of Readings* (1983, see above), pp. 166–81.

Midgley, Mary, *Science and Poetry* (Routledge, London and New York, 2001).

Moggridge, Donald (ed.), *The Collected Writings of John Maynard Keynes*, vol. 21, *Activities 1931–1939: World Crisis and Policies in Britain and America* (Macmillan, London and Cambridge University Press, New York, 1982).

Moon, Peter and Thamotheram, Raj, 'Corporations Become Socially Responsible: Businesses around the World are Acting on the Growing Backlash against Global Capitalism', *The Independent* (12 December 2000).

Naess, Arne, 'The Shallow and the Deep, Long-Range Ecology Movement: A Summary', *Inquiry*, 16 (1973), 95–100.

Naess, Arne and Rothenberg, David, *Ecology, Community and Lifestyle* (Cambridge University Press, Cambridge, 1989).

Nash, Roderick Frazier, *The Rights of Nature: A History of Environmental Ethics* (University of Wisconsin Press, Madison, WI, 1989).

Norton, Bryan G., *Toward Unity among Environmentalists* (Oxford University Press, New York and Oxford, 1991).

Norton, Bryan G., 'Epistemology and Environmental Values', *The Monist*, 75 (1992), 208–26.

O'Connor, Martin (ed.), *Is Capitalism Sustainable? Political Economy and the Politics of Ecology* (The Guildford Press, New York, 1994).

Oksanen, Markku and Pietarinen, Juhani (eds), *Philosophy and Biodiversity* (Cambridge University Press, Cambridge, forthcoming).

O'Neill, John, *Ecology, Policy and Politics: Human Well-Being and the Natural World* (Routledge, London, 1993).

O'Neill, Onora, *Faces of Hunger: An Essay on Poverty, Justice and Development* (Allen & Unwin, London, 1986).

O'Neill, Onora, 'Justice, Gender and International Boundaries', in Robin Attfield and Barry Wilkins (eds), *International Justice and the Third World* (1992, see above), pp. 50–76.

O'Neill, Onora, 'Ending World Hunger', in William Aiken and Hugh LaFollette (eds), *World Hunger and Morality*, 2nd edn (1996, see above), pp. 85–112.

O'Riordan, Tim and Cameron, James (eds), *Interpreting the Precautionary Principle* (Cameron & May, London, 1994).

Osborn, Andrew, '50 Million Animals in Mass Test Plan', The *Guardian* (27 October 2001), p. 1.

Palmer, Clare, 'Stewardship: A Case Study in Environmental Ethics', in J. Ball, M. Goodall, C. Palmer and J. Reader (eds), *The Earth Beneath* (1992, see above), pp. 67–86.

Parayil, Govindan, 'The "Kerala Model" of Development: Development and Sustainability in the Third World', *Third World Quarterly*, 17 (1996), 941–57.

Parayil, Govindan, 'Sustainable Development: The Fallacy of a Normatively Neutral Development Paradigm', *Journal of Applied Philosophy*, 15 (1998), 179–94.

Pardo, A., *The Common Heritage: Selected Papers on Ocean and World Order: 1967–74* (University of Malta Press, Malta, 1975).

Parfit, Derek, 'Energy Policy and the Further Future: The Social Discount Rate', in Douglas MacLean and Peter G. Brown (eds), *Energy and the Future* (1983, see above), pp. 31–7.

Parfit, Derek, *Reasons and Persons* (Clarendon Press, Oxford, 1984).

Parfit, Derek, 'Comments', *Ethics*, 96 (1985–6), 832–72.

Parker, Jenneth, 'Precautionary Principle', in Ruth Chadwick (ed.), *Encyclopedia of Applied Ethics* (1998, see above), vol. 3, pp. 633–41.

Partridge, Ernest, 'Why Care about the Future?', in Ernest Partridge (ed.), *Responsibilities to Future Generations: Environmental Ethics* (1981, see below), pp. 195–202.

Partridge, Ernest (ed.), *Responsibilities to Future Generations: Environmental Ethics* (Prometheus, Buffalo, 1981).

Passmore, John, *Man's Responsibility for Nature* (Duckworth, London, 1974).

Passmore, John, 'The Treatment of Animals', *Journal of the History of Ideas*, 36 (1975), 195–218.

Piel, Gerard, (ed.), *The World of René Dubos* (Henry Holt, New York, 1990).

Pirages, Dennis Clark (ed.), *The Sustainable Society: Implications for Limited Growth* (Praeger, New York and London, 1977).

Plumwood (formerly Routley), Val, 'Nature, Self and Gender: Feminism, Environmental Philosophy, and the Critique of Rationalism', *Hypatia*, 6 (1991), 3–27.

Plumwood (formerly Routley), Val, 'Nature, Self and Gender: Feminism, Environmental Philosophy, and the Critique of Rationalism', reprinted in Robert Elliot (ed.), *Environmental Ethics* (1995, see above), pp. 155–64.

Pojman, Louis, P. (ed.), *Environmental Ethics: Readings in Theory and Application* (Jones & Bartlett, Boston, MA, and London, 1994).

Pompidou, Alain, 'La politique spatiale: quelle ethique pour un homme en mouvement?', International Colloquium on the Ethics of the Sciences and the Technologies', Beirut, October 2001, p. 4 (unpublished text).

Program of Action of the 1994 International Conference on Population and Development, *Population and Development Review*, 21 (1995), Part 1, pp. 187–213.

Rawls, John, *A Theory of Justice* (Harvard University Press, Cambridge, MA, 1971).

Regan, Tom, *The Case for Animal Rights* (Routledge & Kegan Paul, London, 1983).

Regan, Tom and Singer, Peter (eds), *Animal Rights and Human Obligations* (Prentice-Hall, Englewood Cliffs, NJ, 1976).

Rifkin, Jeremy, *The Biotech Century: Harnessing the Gene and Remaking the World* (Tarcher-Putnam, New York, 1998).

Rolston, Holmes III, 'Is There an Ecological Ethic?', *Ethics*, 85 (1975), 93–109.

Rolston, Holmes III, *Environmental Ethics: Duties to and Values in the Natural World* (Temple University Press, Philadelphia, 1983).

Rolston, Holmes III, 'Feeding People Versus Saving Nature', in William Aiken and Hugh LaFollette (eds), *World Hunger and Morality* (1996, see above), pp. 248–67.

Rolston, Holmes III, *Genes, Genesis and God* (Cambridge University Press, Cambridge and New York, 1999).

Ross, W. D., *The Right and the Good* (Clarendon Press, Oxford, 1930).

Routley (later Sylvan), Richard, 'Is There a Need for a New, an Environmental, Ethic?', *Proceedings of the World Congress of Philosophy* (Varna, Bulgaria, 1973), pp. 205–10.

Routley (later Plumwood), Val, Critical Notice of John Passmore, *Man's Responsibility for Nature*, *Australasian Journal of Philosophy*, 53 (1975), 171–85.

Routley (later Sylvan), Richard and Routley (later Plumwood), Val, 'Nuclear Energy and Obligations to the Future', *Inquiry*, 21 (1978), 133–79.

Routley (later Sylvan), Richard and Routley (later Plumwood), Val, 'Human Chauvinism and Environmental Ethics', in Don Mannison, Michael McRobbie and Richard Routley (eds), *Environmental Philosophy* (1980, see above), pp. 96–189.

Rowlands, Mark, *Animal Rights: A Philosophical Defence* (Macmillan, London, 1998).

Royal Commission on Environmental Pollution, Twenty-second Report, *Energy – The Changing Climate*, Cm. 4749 (Her Majesty's Stationery Office, London, 2000).

Ryberg, Jesper, 'Population and Third World Assistance', *Journal of Applied Philosophy*, 14 (1997), 207–19.

Sachs, Wolfgang (ed.), *Global Ecology* (Zed Books, London and Atlantic Highlands, NJ, 1993).

Scanlon, T. M., *What We Owe to Each Other* (Belknap Press of Harvard University Press, Cambridge, MA, and London, 2000).

Scherer, Donald, 'Anthropocentrism, Atomism, and Environmental Ethics', in Donald Scherer and Thomas Attig (eds), *Ethics and the Environment* (1983, see below), pp. 73–81.

Scherer, Donald and Attig, Thomas (eds), *Ethics and the Environment* (Prentice-Hall, Englewood Cliffs, NJ, 1983).

Schmidtz, David, 'Why Preservationism Doesn't Preserve', *Environmental Values*, 6 (1997), 327–39.

Schroeder, Doris, 'Homo Economicus on Trial: Plato, Schopenhauer and the Virtual Jury', *Reason in Practice*, 1.2 (2001), 65–74.

Schwartz, Thomas, 'Obligations to Posterity', in R. I. Sikora and Brian Barry (eds), *Obligations to Future Generations* (1978, see below), pp. 3–13.

Schwartz, Thomas, 'Welfare Judgments and Future Generations', *Theory and Decision*, 11 (1979), 181–94.

Searle, John, 'How to Derive "Ought" from "Is"'', *Philosophical Review*, 73 (1964), 43–58.

Shiva, Vandana, *Protect or Plunder: Understanding Intellectual Property Rights* (Zed Books, London, 2001).

Shue, Henry, 'Equity in an International Agreement on Climate Change', *Proceedings of IPCC Workshop, Nairobi, July 1994* (ICIPE Science Press, Nairobi, 1995), pp. 385–92.

Shue, Henry, 'Ethics, the Environment and the Changing International Order', *International Affairs*, 71 (1995), 453–61.

Sikora, Richard, 'Is it Wrong to Prevent the Existence of Future Generations?', in R. I. Sikora and Brian Barry (eds), *Obligations to Future Generations* (1978, see below), pp. 112–66.

Sikora, R. I. and Barry, Brian (eds), *Obligations to Future Generations* (Temple University Press, Philadelphia, 1978).

Singer, Peter, *Animal Liberation: A New Ethic for Our Treatment of Animals* (Jonathan Cape, London, 1976).

Singer, Peter, *Practical Ethics*, 2nd edn (Cambridge University Press, Cambridge, 1993).

Smith, Michael F., 'Letting in the Jungle', *Journal of Applied Philosophy*, 8 (1991), 145–54.

Spring, David and Spring, Eileen (eds), *Ecology and Religion in History* (Harper & Row, New York and London, 1974).

Sterba, James, 'From Biocentric Individualism to Biocentric Pluralism', *Environmental Ethics*, 17 (1995), 191–207.

Sterba, James, *Justice for Here and Now* (Cambridge University Press, Cambridge, New York and Melbourne, 1998).

Sterba, James, *Three Challenges to Ethics: Environmentalism, Feminism and Multiculturalism* (Oxford University Press, New York and Oxford, 2001).

Steward, Fred, 'Citizens of Planet Earth', in Geoff Andrews (ed.), *Citizenship* (Lawrence & Wishart, London, 1991), pp. 65–75.

Sylvan (formerly Routley), Richard, 'A Critique of Deep Ecology', *Radical Philosophy*, 40 (1985), 2–12 (Part I), and 41 (1985), 10–22 (Part II).

Talbot, Carl, 'Environmental Justice', in Ruth Chadwick (ed.), *Encyclopedia of Applied Ethics* (1998, see above), vol. 2, pp. 93–105.

Taylor, Paul, *Respect for Nature: A Theory of Environmental Ethics* (Princeton University Press, Princeton, 1986).

Thomas, Rosamund M. (ed.), *Teaching Ethics, Volume Three: Environmental Ethics* (HMSO and Ethics International Press, Cambridge, 1996).

Thompson, Janna, 'A Refutation of Environmental Ethics', *Environmental Ethics* 12 (1990), 147–60.

Thompson, Janna, 'Environment as Cultural Heritage', *Environmental Values*, 22 (2000), 241–58.

Thompson, Janna, 'Planetary Citizenship: The Definition and Defence of an Ideal', in Brendan Gleeson and Nicholas Low (eds), *Governing for the Environment: Global Problems, Ethics and Democracy* (2001, see above), pp. 135–46.

Thompson, Thomas H., 'Are We Obligated to Future Others?', in Ernest Partridge (ed.), *Responsibilities to Future Generations: Environmental Ethics* (1981, see above), pp. 195–202.

Tucker, Mary Evelyn and Grim, John A. (eds), *Worldviews and Ecology: Religion, Philosophy and Environment* (Bucknell University Press, Lewisburg, PA, 1993).

Turner, B. L., II, Kasperson, Roger E., and Meyer, William B., 'Two Types of Global Environmental Change', *Global Environmental Change*, 1, 1 (1990), 15–17.

United Nations, *Declaration on the Right to Development* (New York, United Nations, 1986).

United Nations Commission on Environment and Development, *Agenda 21* (UNCED, New York, 1992).

United Nations Environment Programme/World-Wide Fund for Nature/ World Conservation Union, *Caring for the Earth* (Earthscan, London, 1991).

VanDeVeer, Donald and Pierce, Christine (eds), *People, Penguins and Plastic Trees* (Wadsworth, Belmont, CA, 1986).

van Steenbergen, Bart, (ed.), *The Condition of Citizenship* (Sage, London, Thousand Oaks, CA and New Delhi, 1994).

Vincent, Andrew, 'Liberalism and the Environment', *Environmental Values*, 7 (1998), 443–59.

Walzer, Michael, 'The Civil Society Argument', in Ronald Beiner (ed.), *Theorizing Citizenship* (1995, see above), pp. 153–74.

Warren, Karen, 'The Power and Promise of Ecological Feminism', *Environmental Ethics*, 12 (1990), 121–46.

Wenz, Peter S., *Environmental Ethics Today* (Oxford University Press, New York and Oxford, 2001).

White, Lynn, Jr, 'The Historic Roots of Our Ecological Crisis', *Science*, 155, 37 (1967), 1203–7.

White, Lynn, Jr, 'The Historical Roots of Our Ecological Crisis', reprinted in John Barr (ed.), *The Environmental Handbook: Action Guide for the UK* (1971, see above), pp. 3–16.

Wilde, Lawrence, ' "The creatures, too, must become free": Marx and the Animal/Human Distinction', *Capital & Class*, 72 (2000), 37–53.

Woodward, James, 'The Non-Identity Problem', *Ethics*, 96 (1985–1986), 804–31.

Workineh, Kelbessa, *Indigenous and Modern Environmental Ethics: A Study of the Oromo Environmental Ethic and Oromo Environmental Ethics in the Light of Modern Issues of Environment and Development* (Ph.D. thesis, Cardiff, 2001).

World Commission on Environment and Development, *Our Common Future* (Oxford University Press, Oxford, 1987).

World Wide Fund for Nature, Scotland, *Stewardship of Natural Resources* (WWF Scotland, Aberfeldy, 2001).

Young, Michael D., *For Our Children's Children: Some Practical Implications of Inter-Generational Equity and the Precautionary Principle* (Resource Assessment Commission, Canberra, 1993).

Zimmerman, Michael E. (ed.), *Environmental Philosophy: From Animal Rights to Radical Ecology* (Prentice-Hall, Englewood Cliffs, NJ, 1993).

Index

*Index compiled by Meg Davies
(Registered Indexer, Society of
Indexers)*